GREENLAND

CANADA

1920

ATLANTIC
OCEAN

EEWATIN

HUDSON
BAY

LABRADOR
1949
(NEWFOUNDLAND)

St. John's

NEWFOUNDLAND

QUEBEC 1912

P.E.I.
1769   Charlottetown

ONTARIO 1912

1784

Port Arthur
Fort William

Quebec   St. John

NOVA SCOTIA
1784

LAKE
SUPERIOR

Montreal

NEW
BRUNSWICK

Halifax

Sudbury
L. HURON

Ottawa

ATLANTIC
OCEAN

Toronto

L. ONTARIO

UNITED
STATES

LAKE
MICHIGAN

L. ERIE

Scale of Miles
0   100   200   300   400

THE SEARCH FOR IDENTITY
Canada, 1945–1967

THE CANADIAN HISTORY SERIES

Edited by Thomas B. Costain

VOLUME I

THE WHITE AND THE GOLD: *The French Regime in Canada*

BY THOMAS B. COSTAIN

VOLUME II

CENTURY OF CONFLICT: *The Struggle Between the French and British in Colonial America*

BY JOSEPH LISTER RUTLEDGE

VOLUME III

THE PATH OF DESTINY: *Canada From the British Conquest to Home Rule, 1763–1850*

BY THOMAS H. RADDALL

VOLUME IV

FROM SEA UNTO SEA: *The Road to Nationhood, 1850–1910*

BY W. G. HARDY

VOLUME V

ORDEAL BY FIRE: *Canada, 1910–1945*

BY RALPH ALLEN

VOLUME VI

THE SEARCH FOR IDENTITY: *Canada, 1945–1967*

BY BLAIR FRASER

THE SEARCH
FOR IDENTITY

Canada, 1945-1967

BLAIR FRASER

Doubleday & Company, Inc., Garden City, New York
Doubleday Canada Limited, Toronto, Ontario
1967

Library of Congress Catalog Card Number 67–23823
Copyright © 1967 by Blair Fraser
All Rights Reserved
Printed in the United States of America
First Edition

To George Nelson
a man of saintly patience

Contents

THE SEARCH FOR IDENTITY

Canada, 1945–1967

Prologue

YESTERDAY'S NEWS is tomorrow's history. Meanwhile there is to-day, when it is deemed unfit for either category—for the one too old; for the other still unripe, still awaiting the nice blend of new knowledge and new ignorance that gives history an appearance of pattern and clears away the untidiness of reality.

Hence every man's acquaintance with affairs contains a time gap, the interval between the end of history and the beginning of his own direct awareness of contemporary events. This book is an attempt to close the gap, at least with a temporary filling, in the story of postwar Canada. Neither exhaustive nor definitive, it is the chronicle of an onlooker—occasionally an eyewitness, more often a gleaner of other men's observations, in both cases vulnerable to bias, to partial information, and to premature con-clusions. For all these defects the excuse is the same: this is how things looked, to people who were there at the time.

Such pattern as the tale may have is largely imposed by hind-sight. Events as they occur in the Eternal Now seem even more confused than they really are; the Moving Finger writes in char-acters too large to be deciphered from close up. Farce intrudes upon tragedy, melodrama on farce, and relevance is obscure and intermittent. But if any contemporary guess is worth making about the trend of the two decades just past, it must surely be that Canada was moving away from a new confidence, and to-ward new doubts, about her true identity as a nation.

Up to and during World War II, Canada was preoccupied with her emergence from the status of colony. This process, which

went on for two centuries, at no time got unanimous encourage-
ment from Canadians. Many preferred to be colonists, and apparently some still do. The Rebellion of 1837, for example, broke
out against a native-born Family Compact of colonial oligarchs,
described by Anna Jameson at the time as "a self-constituted
aristocracy based upon nothing real, nor even upon anything
imaginary." In far retrospect, interpreted by a century of Liberal
historians, the Rebellion may look like a success. In its own day
it was a failure, its leaders defeated not only in battle but in
prior and subsequent elections. The achievement a dozen years
later of responsible government is counted in history as a triumph,
yet its immediate effect was the burning of the Parliament Buildings in Montreal by an English-Canadian mob, outraged by the
British Governor-General's deference to French-Canadian rebels
and their sympathizers. Confederation itself was conceived as a
remedy for chronic deadlock between English and French in the
United Province of Canada, and was bitterly fought in both of
the other colonies it comprised. The fight for Canadian independence was never, on any significant scale, directed against the
British. It was always a running fight among Canadians.

By 1945 it did seem that the long struggle had ended in victory
for independence. A country violently, almost lethally split by
World War I had come through World War II apparently intact.
At home the wartime Government was re-elected, its strength reduced but still considerable in both English- and French-speaking
regions. Abroad Canada's right to membership in the new United
Nations was not even questioned, as it had been when the League
of Nations was formed a quarter century before. Those last survivors of the era of British imperialism, the professional armed
services in Whitehall, had grudgingly conceded the existence of a
Canadian army, navy, and air force. British emigrants learned
not to say, as they used to do, "That ain't the way we do it
back 'ome." Even Canadians themselves, perhaps last of all, began to take their national existence for granted.

No sooner had the sense of identity been attained than it began to be questioned on other grounds, and from new aspects.

Prologue 3

English Canadians had assumed for a century that French Canadians wanted no more than the independence of all Canada from any vestige of foreign rule, and to ultraloyalists this had seemed treason enough. Now even Liberals were astonished and dismayed to learn that French Canadians wanted more—wanted "equality," a sadly ambiguous word, throughout a nation of which they composed only a numerical thirty per cent. Equally startling, to those of British speech and tradition, was the discovery that they too had become a minority, still the largest of the many in Canada's mosaic but a minority nonetheless.

Most unsettling of all, though, was the new awareness of a tremendous gravitational force across the nation's southern border. While the British gave up one by one the constitutional instruments of imperial rule, Americans had been buying up one by one an impressive aggregate of Canadian industries and resources. No conspiracy for this purpose was required, not even a plan. By a kind of continental osmosis, the Canadian economy was at least half absorbed before anyone on either side of the border quite realized it.

Once realized, it became an internal controversy in Canada. Some viewed it with alarm as a threat to Canada's new-found identity. Some pointed with pride to its effect on Canada's newborn affluence. Most people, naturally, wanted the advantages without the penalties and were thus receptive to some of the arguments of either side.

Aside from the economic there was the cultural absorption to worry about. When some fifteen million people speak American, watch American TV, read American magazines, follow American fashions in everything from high style to low life, what, if anything, distinguishes them from Americans? The conventional wisdom, as expressed at international service club luncheons, was that Canada had a distinctive national character perceptible to the most myopic observer, but the distinction was embarrassingly difficult to describe, let alone define. Uncertainty thus eroded the very roots of the new self-assurance.

Yet the self-assurance was also there, to a degree never before attained in an insecure, introspective nation of defeated minorities. For a brief but glorious period after victory in Europe, Canadians enjoyed the feeling that they could do anything. Traces of this euphoria survive, along with a certain resentment that Canada's moral and material superiority is not more generally recognized (or, in some cases, the persistent illusion that it *is* recognized).

These are the complex and contradictory emotions that underlay the events of the postwar Canadian experience. To link all those events into a pattern, or relate them to any common theme, would be a distortion—many things happened, some of them important, that had nothing to do with Canada's search for identity. But insofar as a theme existed, this was it, and the first notes were sounded even before World War II began.

I

The Wound Beneath the Skin

EVEN IN MONTREAL, the English of Westmount couldn't quite understand why the Mackenzie King Government was so worried about a by-election in the slum district of St. Henri.

After all, the riding had never voted anything but Liberal since it was created. Paul Mercier, the former Member of Parliament who had just been made a judge, carried it in the 1935 general election by seventeen thousand. There had been some squabbling among the party faithful for the privilege of nomination to the safe seat Mercier had vacated, but this disappeared instantly when an external enemy appeared. Yet the Liberal Government, elected less than three years ago with the greatest majority in Canadian history (a record it was soon to break again), seemed to be in a panic.

Camillien Houde had entered the St. Henri by-election of January 1938, only a week before polling day, as an "independent anti-armament" candidate.

On his record Houde didn't look like much of a threat. He had been a political jack-in-the-box for years in local and provincial elections—returned and then defeated as member of the Quebec Legislative Assembly, as provincial chief of the Conservative Party (he was the predecessor of Maurice Duplessis in that office), but most notably and most notoriously as mayor of Montreal. Time after time he would run for mayor and win, only to lose again the next time around when the chaotic state of Montreal's finances, plus rumors of unsavory links between the Houde machine and the Montreal underworld, swept Houde's latest rival into temporary power. This year was one of his periods of retirement—he had been beaten in the biennial elections of 1936, and was not to win re-election as mayor until December 1938.

Personally, Houde didn't look very impressive either. He was physically grotesque—a short, squat, potbellied figure built on the general lines of Grandfather Frog, with a huge pocked nose, a purple complexion (though he had stopped drinking six years before) and a loose false tooth in front which fell out from time to time during Houde's more impassioned speeches, to be caught by its adroit owner and slipped into a side pocket without even a moment's pause in the flow of his rhetoric. True, even the starchy English actually voted for him more often than not, but theirs was a patronizing kind of support. They really couldn't imagine anyone taking old Camillien seriously.

Yet here was the Liberal Government at Ottawa taking him so seriously as to promise to the voters of St. Henri five million dollars or more of the taxpayers' money if a rabble of slum voters would defeat him. One after another the Liberal big guns trooped into St. Henri's dim little meeting halls to pledge colossal rewards for the election of their candidate (an inoffensive undertaker who, after this one brief moment of national fame, spent twenty peaceful and silent years on the back benches of the House of Commons). Public works of all kinds were to be showered upon the loyal voters, and all this without any reduction in the unemployment relief on which half the families of St. Henri were then living.

The "armament" program that was Houde's chief target was modest enough by the standards of a year or two later. A defense budget of $15 million had been raised to $35 million, of which only $32 million were actually spent. Houde's attacks had a ring of fantasy about them: "In Ottawa there is a secret document from British headquarters, saying we must launch an arms program that will enable us to send five divisions wherever they are needed for the defense of the British Empire."

Even in St. Henri they didn't believe that. Prime Minister King

declared it was "an entire fabrication," and Camillien himself
grew increasingly vague about what this secret document was
and what it said. But he did say, with more assurance: "I predict
that Liberals and Tories will again unite for the coming war, as
they did in 1914–18, and high finance will back them up, making
it impossible for anyone else to oppose them. This will mean
conscription for Quebec."

Nonsense, said Prime Minister King and all his spokesmen.
"Canada has made absolutely no commitments." The new, en-
larged defense budget was "solely for the defense of our own
shores." Indeed, he said in one speech to Parliament, "I may be
wrong but I doubt very much whether the British government
itself will ever again send an expeditionary force to Europe."

French Canadians were not alone in doubting his prediction,
or in voicing alarm about Canada's new "armament program."
The saintly J. S. Woodsworth, founder and leader of the socialist
Cooperative Commonwealth Federation, lost no opportunity to
voice his pacifist sentiments in the House of Commons, and to
smite hip and thigh those "merchants of death" who were plot-
ting wars in order to swell their profits. Even the Liberal Party's
own ranks were not solid. In addition to the restive members
from Quebec there was Joseph Thorson of Selkirk, Manitoba, a
veteran of World War I who had risen to the rank of captain in
the field, a former Rhodes Scholar, a future Cabinet minister and
judge of the Exchequer Court. Yet Joe Thorson had spoken
against the increase of the defense budget, a "preparation for
war" that would lead, he feared, to "participation in war."
(Within three years Thorson had become Minister of National
War Services in a war Cabinet, but these were the views he
sincerely held in 1938.)

Yet it wasn't the Thorsons or the Woodsworths of 1938 who
worried the Mackenzie King Government. King himself was a
self-styled "man of peace" to whom the very idea of war was
deeply repugnant. Moreover, in 1938 he really believed that the
danger of war was being vastly exaggerated. He had visited Adolf
Hitler in Berlin the previous summer, and had come away con-

vinced that this "rather simple, peasant type" wanted no more
than Germany's just rights, which could be got by peaceful
means. A political fight on the "anti-armament" issue had no
terrors for Mackenzie King, for he believed no one was more
anti-armament than he was himself. It was something quite different that made him and his ministers afraid of Houde.

In several speeches Houde had sounded a deeper, more ominous note: "If the federal Government continue their program
of armament they will drive Quebec into complete independence.
It cannot be otherwise."

This was not, of course, the first time separatism had been
proposed to *Québecois*. It has been cropping up from time to
time ever since 1763. Among contemporaries Canon Lionel
Groulx, the historian who (in the words of one critic) had
"given the French-Canadians a myth in which they could believe
and take pride," had long been trumpeting his belief in "a French
Catholic state on the banks of the St. Lawrence." He and his
followers even had a name for the new country—Laurentia. Only
a month before the St. Henri by-election Paul Bouchard, another French-Canadian nationalist, had fought another by-election in rural Quebec on a frankly separatist platform.

But these were spokesmen only for a handful of intellectuals.
Bouchard lost by fifty thousand votes to the Liberal old guardsman J. N. Francoeur. Canon Groulx's very name was hardly
known, then, to the rank and file of French-Canadian voters.

So long as they were its only spokesmen, separatism would be
what it had always been—an intellectual hobby for students,
young priests, and a fringe of right-wing radicals whom nobody
took very seriously. With Camillien Houde as its standard-bearer,
though, separatism took on a different aspect. Houde was no intellectual, but he was no fool either. He was a real, natural
demagogue who appealed to the working people of urban Quebec
because he was one of them, a son of the Montreal slums, half
orphaned at eight and sent to a *collège classique* by his widowed
mother only after he had already learned all the lessons of the
streets. As an orator for a big-city crowd he was without peer.

Never using a note, never retreating into pomposity or platitude, he gave the crowd what it wanted to hear—an endless outpouring of rather coarse wit, oversimplified common sense, verbal belligerence.

Also, Houde had plenty of courage. It took courage even in 1938 to stand up against the whole Canadian Establishment, French and English—stand up to them, fight them, and lose. The Liberal undertaker won St. Henri, though by no more than five thousand votes compared to Paul Mercier's seventeen thousand. Not for another eleven years, and then in the late twilight of his long political career, was Houde to win election to the Parliament of Canada.

But he did win another mayoralty election eleven months later, and he was Montreal's chief magistrate when King George VI and his Queen Elizabeth visited Canada in 1939. (Houde was charming to them. Unlike those of 1964, the separatists of 1939 were polite to royal guests.) However, though his role as host to royalty changed Camillien Houde's image somewhat in the eyes of English Canada, it didn't change Houde's political beliefs in the slightest. He remained an "anti-armament independent."

He proved this before another year was out. Canada went to war in September, its unity shored up by the promise of every federal minister from Quebec (all standing in their places in the House while Ernest Lapointe intoned the pledge) that "never, never, never" would they impose conscription. Quebec said nothing—did not even muster four members to stand up beside J. S. Woodsworth on the day war was declared and demand a recorded vote. After the fall of France and the catastrophe of Dunkirk, everyone's mood changed—the Government was able to bring in a law for compulsory mobilization in defense of Canada. (Most people on both sides of the argument accepted "conscription" as meaning "conscription for service overseas.")

Not Camillien Houde. "I declare myself unequivocally against national registration," he said in a formal statement as mayor of Montreal. "It is unequivocally a measure of conscription. Parliament, in my belief, has no mandate to vote conscription. I do not myself believe that I am obliged to conform to the said law, and I have no intention of doing so, and I ask the population not to conform, knowing full well what I am doing and to what I expose myself."

What he exposed himself to, for the time being, was merely censorship. Censors issued a stop order on Houde's statement; morning newspapers of the following day were commanded to kill the story. But English Canadians were no more willing than Houde himself to let the incident be suppressed. John Bassett, Sr., president of the Montreal *Gazette,* telephoned his friend R. B. Hanson, Leader of the Opposition, and dictated Houde's statement to Hanson's secretary. Hanson read it into Hansard, the record of Parliament, the Government not quite daring to suppress Hansard too. And with Houde's defiance thus made known to the public, the Government felt obliged (however reluctantly) to intern the mayor of Montreal under Defense of Canada Regulations.

For the time being, that act of suppression appeared to be wholly effective. Nothing more was heard from the anti-conscriptionists for some time. A few eccentric extremists had already been interned—such men as Adrien Arcand, the more or less self-appointed leader of Quebec Fascists, and others who'd been in the habit of wearing shirts of various colors with swastika badges, and giving the Hitler salute to various obscure fuehrers. But after the Houde incidents, no other French Canadians of any standing in the community were sent to internment camps.

Meanwhile the federal Government had fended off another flank attack in a provincial election on October 25, 1939. Maurice Duplessis, then only three years in power, thought he saw an easy way to win another five-year term. He called a snap election (as any Prime Minister in the Canadian system has a right to do at any time) on the issue of federal encroachment, a campaign that he directed quite clearly, though not quite explicitly, against Canada's participation in the war. Quebec's federal ministers took up the challenge. Intervening in a provincial election for the first time in memory, they told the people they would resign if Duplessis were re-elected—and thus, as they made quite plain, leave Quebec with no defenders in Ottawa against the menace of conscription. Duplessis was defeated. The compliant Liberal Government of Adelard Godbout took office and held it for the full five-year term. Five months later, with much greater ease, the Mackenzie King Government secured its own survival for the duration of the war by a federal election that returned a hundred and eighty-four Liberals (a new record for the Canadian House of Commons) and only thirty-nine bedraggled Conservatives, who had chosen to be known temporarily as the National Government Party.

Mackenzie King had campaigned on a platform of national unity. Conservatives hadn't dared to come out for conscription— these were the days of *Sitzkrieg,* and even the English felt no urgency about compelling men to enlist for overseas. For an interval it was possible to suppose, as King appeared to do, that all Canada spoke with one mind.

This illusion did not survive the spring of 1940. National registration in July was only a beginning—too much for Camillien Houde, it was far too little for English Canada. After a press campaign for all-out conscription that lasted a year and half, Mackenzie King called a plebiscite, not to authorize overseas conscription but to release the Government from the promise not to impose it. King hoped for a "yes" vote in Quebec of thirty per cent—"it might even reach thirty-five," he noted hopefully on the eve of voting day. J. Arthur Mathewson, provincial treasurer in the Godbout Government, was even more optimistic. He told his friends a majority in Quebec would vote "yes," and offered to bet one dollar for each percentage point by which the "yes" vote fell below fifty. Luckily for him, he did not bet with many people. In fact Quebec voted "no" by seventy-one per cent to twenty-nine. Since Quebec in 1941 was only eighty per cent French-speaking, this meant that seven out of eight French Canadians voted "no." Outside Quebec, the vote was eighty per cent "yes"; the over-all national breakdown was sixty-four to thirty-six per cent affirmative, or almost two to one.

When the King Government accepted the all-Canadian "yes" as a release, Quebec felt betrayed. P. J. A. Cardin, last survivor of the Big Three from Quebec in the King Cabinet (Fernand Rinfret had died in 1939, Ernest Lapointe in 1941) resigned his portfolio with a bitter speech. He himself had campaigned for a "yes" from Quebec, but he thought the failure to get one should be taken as decisive. The pledge of "no conscription" had been a pledge to French, not to English Canada, since the English had been in favor of conscription all along, and "you cannot extinguish a debt by consent of the debtor alone."

But though Cardin resigned from the Cabinet he did not cross the floor to join the Opposition. Few Liberals did, and those few were mavericks who had long been restless anyway in the Liberal caucus. The majority from Quebec remained aware that to exchange a Liberal for a Conservative regime (or an English-speaking coalition of both parties, as in 1917) would be a jump from a lukewarm frying pan to a very hot fire.

The Liberals' "conscription" measure, Bill 80, imposed compulsory service for home defense only—conscripts could not be sent outside the northern half of the Western Hemisphere without a further reference back to Parliament. Home-defense conscription proved adequate to keep up the flow of reinforcements before D-Day, since in other provinces most boys who got their conscription notices "went active" at once. In Quebec they mostly didn't. In Quebec even home-defense conscription was not too rigorously enforced—by February 1944 there were 6200 deserters in the Quebec Military District out of a national total of 11,094, or more than all the rest put together.

Nevertheless, there were some ugly incidents. In May of 1944 a Royal Canadian Mounted Police party went to the little village of St. Lambert on the Chaudière River, looking for a young man named Georges Guenette who had been listed as a deserter ever since conscription began. He had been living quietly on his father's farm. On that May morning when the police arrived, Guenette *père* shouted a warning and the boy started to run. One of the constables fired a shot, which he said afterward was aimed at the ground; if so, the bullet must have ricocheted off a rock, for Georges Guenette fell dead.

That was the only such incident that ended in a fatality, but there were many of a minor nature—street fights between servicemen and civilians, sporadic cases of arson or sabotage, and a chronic underlying mood of mutual suspicion and dislike. A political party called the Bloc Populaire was formed in 1942 in the wake of the plebiscite campaign, ostensibly dedicated to various social objectives but primarily to fight against conscription. I remember one of its speakers, a fiery young redhead named Jacques Sauriol, before a Sunday afternoon audience in the village of Ste. Eustache:

"French Canadians are against the war—law or no law, police or no police. The RCMP will have a hard time persuading us, at pistol point, that England is fighting *pour la civilisation Catholique.*"

Another French-Canadian nationalist, in a private talk about the same time, elaborated the same theme:

"Show me an Englishman who lives in a part of the world captured by a German Empire two hundred years ago, who now is compelled to put on a German uniform, take orders in German (which he doesn't understand), and be sent off to a foreign country to fight and die for the triumph of that German Empire. I'd like to meet that Englishman. We would understand each other perfectly."

The Bloc Populaire never had a chance to show its true strength among the people of Quebec. The next federal election didn't come until 1945, when the war in Europe was already over. Conservative Leader John Bracken, to the delight of the Liberals and the utter consternation of his own supporters, had come out in favor of conscription for the continuing war in Japan —which even English Canadians didn't want. Once again the Liberals had become the lesser of two evils, or perhaps the least of five.

And so the Bloc Populaire was able to elect only two of its thirty-seven candidates in 1945, and got only thirteen per cent of Quebec's popular vote. The figures are misleading. Quebec's movement of protest was much stronger than that. No fewer than one third of Quebec electors voted against both the old parties. Conservatives entered only twenty-nine candidates among Quebec's sixty-five seats, and of these only one was elected. Other men who had been Conservatives all their lives ran as "independents" and gathered almost a fifth of the popular vote, though only four of them won. Obviously, if the Liberals survived in Quebec it was strictly *faute de mieux*.

The most that could be said was that World War II had done less damage to the fabric of the nation than World War I did. Where 1917 had left a gaping wound in Canada's body politic, 1942 and 1944 left only a bruise, a wound beneath the skin. But even it took more years to heal than most Canadians realized at the time.

There were other wounds of 1914–19 which were also no more than bruises in 1939–45. No jobless veterans were begging or rioting in the streets after World War II. No counterpart of the Winnipeg general strike came in 1946. [—the nearest approach, the Ford strike in Windsor in the autumn of 1945, was fought not for wages but for union recognition, and the union won.]

These gains over the previous generation were not accidental, but neither were they wholly planned. They were the fortunate results of a series of warnings that began at the very height of the feverish wartime prosperity, and that were heeded by the prudent politicians then in power.

II

Memories of Hardship:
The Birth of the Welfare State

ONE OF THE MORE OPULENT department stores of Montreal used to display in a show window on Sherbrooke Street, during the winter of 1942–43, a quotation from a wartime speech by King George VI: "We are all in the front line now." The words had been true enough of His Majesty's immediate audience, the people of Britain during the blitz. The Montreal merchants saw no irony in the fact that they presented his words, printed in white on a scarlet plaque, as the centerpiece in a window display of mink coats and stoles.

Ironic or not, it was a not too unfair symbol of the hardships of war, for those of us in Canada who were able to stay home. We had never had it so good. Canada was as close to full employment as it is possible to get—nobody able and willing to work lacked a job. Wages, like prices, were under government control, but they were adequate by the standards of the time— $31.75 a week was the average for males, which was $9.52 more than the average in 1939. Also, more people were working full time. Annual as distinct from weekly earnings were almost half as high again as they had been when war began. Hotels were continuously crowded, trains packed, liquor stores filled with queues of customers in spite of liquor rationing. A few things like white shirts were hard to find in the shops, but every necessity of life was in ample supply.

It was easy for busy men in Ottawa to assume that any people so bountifully endowed with this world's goods must be content. But this complacent assumption left several things out of account, and one of them was the Great Depression. Those years of poverty and neglect, of hunger and despair had left behind a legacy of resentment which became more intense, not less, in the sudden affluence of wartime. Maxime Raymond, the founder of the Bloc Populaire, used to say bitterly: "They had no money to help the unemployed, but when it was a question of going to war, then they knew where to find the money." It was true.

Nobody will ever know just how many Canadians were employed during the Great Depression, because in those days no serious attempt was made to keep accurate figures. In answer to an MP's question the Labor Department said, rather superciliously, that "provincial and municipal expenditures for relief are not recorded with the Dominion Government"; federal relief costs, for jobless city men and drought-stricken farmers combined, were $322 million for the whole decade, 1930–40. Another statement by the Minister of Labor, just before the war, put the total number of people receiving direct relief at 600,000, but this was admittedly an estimate, not a precise figure.

How accurate these estimates were may be guessed from a contrast. In 1933, when jobless men by thousands were riding the brake rods of freight trains from coast to coast in a vain search for work, Ottawa's figure for those "registered" as seeking employment was only 665,121. In 1944, when labor was so scarce that selective service machinery was being used to force men out of non-essential and into essential jobs, the comparable figure was no less than two and a half million! True, the second figure was exaggerated upward as much as the former was exaggerated downward—it included everyone who changed jobs, every applicant for new employment, and a host of other fringe cases. Nevertheless, the contrast gives a clue to how little the federal authorities knew, or seemed to care, about unemployment when it was at its worst.

If the federal authorities thought (as they seemed to do, for a while) that the people of Canada had forgotten their decade of depression, or forgiven the men who had done so little about it, they were soon to receive a number of rude reminders. The first came in December 1942, in one of the Gallup Poll's quarterly reports on the state of Canadian political opinion.

Liberals, who had got more than half the votes cast in 1940 and thought they had been gaining rather than losing in the meantime, learned that their support had dropped to thirty-six per cent. That, however, was not the most dismaying feature of the poll. What disconcerted the Liberals most was to find the socialist CCF, which in the 1940 election had polled only eight and a half per cent of the popular vote, now recorded at twenty-three per cent, only one point below the Conservatives.

Politicians are always suspicious of public opinion polls, especially those that go against them, so there was a certain amount of skepticism about this one. It was dispelled within six months. In the key province of Ontario, where a Liberal Government had been in power for nine years, the Liberals were reduced from sixty-three seats to fifteen, and the status of a splinter party. The Conservatives squeaked into office with less than an over-all majority, and the official Opposition (with only four fewer seats than the Government) became the socialist CCF (Cooperative Commonwealth Federation).

If further evidence was needed that the mood of Canada was swinging left, it came the following year. The prairie province of Saskatchewan, which with only one brief exception had been Liberal ever since it became a province in 1905, threw out its Liberal Government in the summer of 1944 and installed the CCF in its place.

But the federal Government did not wait for this final and clinching evidence before starting to do something about it. Partly by coincidence, partly by design, Mackenzie King's ministers began to set in motion things which in retrospect seem rather commonplace now, but which were revolutionary in their day. Unemployment insurance (introduced in 1940) had made relatively little impression because it came too late to affect the massive unemployment of the thirties. What was now planned and promised went a great deal further.

It happened that, during the first half of 1943, Mr. Justice

Charles P. McTague, who had left the Supreme Court of Ontario
to become chairman of the War Labor Board, was preparing a
report on a national labor relations code and, in particular, on
modifications in the Wage Stabilization Order. It was obvious
that wage control was an essential component of price control,
but it was equally obvious that an hourly wage that would bring
comfort and even affluence to a bachelor would still be less
than adequate for a man with ten children. Mr. Justice McTague
suggested that this gap be bridged by the payment of a family
allowance, a flat sum per month for each child.

The McTague Report went to Cabinet in September 1943. The
Cabinet reaction was mixed, to put it mildly. Even Mackenzie
King, who to his dying day fancied himself a radical advocate
of the economic underdog, exclaimed that "to tell the country
that everyone was to get a family allowance was sheer folly; it
would occasion resentment everywhere." Other, more conservative
ministers were less restrained in their language.

But meanwhile, pressures in the opposite direction had been
building up from several sources. Canada was not the only country
to feel a certain irony, a certain embarrassment, in the fact that
men were now being called upon to fight and die for a fatherland
which had hitherto shown little interest in their welfare. In
Britain Sir William Beveridge had come out with the Beveridge
Report on Social Insurance, another of those documents which
look commonplace only in retrospect; it proposed universal and
compulsory insurance against the universal risks of disability, old
age and unemployment. "Womb-to-tomb" security it was called,
with a sneer that was believed at the time to be devastating.
Sir Alan Herbert wrote a sardonic little rhyme for *Punch*, which
ran in part:

> *Oh, won't it be wonderful after the war—*
> *There won't be no war, and there won't be no pore.*
> *There won't be no sick, and there won't be no sore,*
> *And we shan't have to work, if we find it a bore. . . .*
> *Now there's only one question I'd like to explore:*
> *Why didn't we have the old war before?*

What was meant as a sneer survived as a good question: If, as Maxime Raymond kept saying, "they know where to find the money" for war, why could it not be found for peace? The Beveridge Report reduced the cost of social insurance to fairly precise figures, modest compared to the colossal sums that were being spent for victory. Why would it be impossible to raise such amounts in a free peacetime economy?

Reading the Beveridge Report and noting the warmth of its reception at home and abroad, the Mackenzie King Government quickly and quietly ordered one for Canada. Dr. Leonard Marsh, a McGill social science professor, was commissioned to prepare a report on Social Security for Canada. He managed to produce it in a few weeks of eighteen-hour days, recommending old-age pensions, family allowances, health insurance plus disability allowances, and every other element in a complete protective system of social insurance. This was transmitted to Cabinet on February 17, 1943.

Some of Marsh's figures make strange reading today. Old-age pensions, first introduced some fifteen years before over the horrified protests of the Canadian Senate, amounted to a maximum of twenty dollars a month, payable only to those who could prove themselves in need. Other income was permitted up to a ceiling of one hundred and twenty-five dollars a year, so that the most a pensioner could enjoy was three hundred and sixty-five dollars a year or precisely one dollar a day.

Even though the federal treasury paid three quarters of the cost, administration of the pension was left wholly to the provinces, and it was provincial officials who determined eligibility. Restrictions were severe. Not only must the pensioner be without other means, he must also be without close relatives who, in the opinion of the competent authorities, *ought* to be supporting him whether or not they were actually doing so. Similarly, any property he owned was assessed for whatever income it *should* be providing, whether or not it did produce any income at all.

Provincial authorities varied in the strictness with which they applied the restrictions, and it was usually the poorest provinces

that were most severe in applying the rules. Thus the average
pension actually paid, in 1941, varied from $11.25 a month in
Prince Edward Island and $14.81 in New Brunswick, to $18.62
in Ontario and $18.97 in British Columbia. (Alberta and British
Columbia started in 1942 to pay supplementary allowances from
provincial treasuries of up to ten dollars a month, in cases of
need.)

As for health insurance, it too was a provincial matter of which
little or nothing had been heard for years. Like every other kind
of welfare legislation, it was part of the Liberal platform adopted
in 1919 (his speech for that particular plank was a big factor
in winning the party leadership for Mackenzie King) but progress
since then had shown the speed of a glacier. Except for the
twenty-dollar pension in 1927 and the Unemployment Insurance
Act thirteen years later, nothing at all had changed.

The atmosphere of 1943 was more conducive to action than
that of any time since the previous World War. A draft bill for
health insurance was prepared for the Special Parliamentary Committee on Reconstruction and Rehabilitation. The National Liberal
Federation executive, meeting in September, came out for a comprehensive social insurance program, a shelf of public works as a
reserve against times of depression and unemployment, a rise in
the non-contributory old-age pension, and other similar welfare
measures.

This program was not adopted without a fight. Ministers like
James G. Gardiner, big-L Liberals who were conservative with a
small *c*, argued fiercely that the party's reverses in Ontario had
not meant a protest against the cruelties of *laissez-faire* economics,
but precisely the opposite—a revolt against "wartime controls"
and in favor of "free enterprise." But Liberal Young Turks led
by Brooke Claxton, not yet a minister but already the Prime
Minister's parliamentary assistant, carried the day against the old
guard and determined the party's future for a decade or more.

Most of the components of their Brave New World lay in
the provincial field of authority, and could be carried out only
in collaboration with the provinces. But there was one major step

that was wholly within Ottawa's competence, and on it, work
began at once. When the next session of Parliament opened on
January 27, 1944, the Speech from the Throne announced that a
bill would be shortly introduced for the payment of family allowances to all Canadian parents.

The first reaction of the Conservative Opposition was cautious.
Gordon Graydon, who was Leader of the Opposition because
Conservative Leader John Bracken had no seat in the House,
attacked the government only for the "omissions" in its proposed
social welfare legislation; he was careful to add that he had no
criticism in principle of "this long-overdue program." But when
the family allowance bill was introduced in June, other Conservatives were not so prudent.

John Bracken said in a public statement that the family allowance, already known as the Baby Bonus, had "all the earmarks
of a political bribe." George Drew, Conservative Premier of Ontario, heartily agreed. "I assure you," he said in a province-wide
radio broadcast, "that the Government of Ontario intends to do
everything in its power to make sure that this iniquitous measure
does not go into effect." And why was it so iniquitous? Because,
among other things, it would redistribute public funds in favor
of those who had failed to do their duty during the war.

Just in case anyone should not realize who these favored slackers
might be, Dr. Herbert A. Bruce, Conservative MP for Toronto-
Parkdale, made it unequivocally clear: the Baby Bonus was "a
bribe of the most brazen character, made chiefly to one province
and paid for by the taxes of the rest." The province of Quebec,
"because of its large families, will derive the greatest benefit from
this measure, at the expense of the other provinces and particularly Ontario, which pays one half the taxes of Canada." Thus
the bill would result in "bonusing families which have been unwill-
ing to defend their country."

But there were men in the Conservative caucus in Parliament
who listened to these strident cries with horror. John Diefenbaker,
for one, made it clear to his fellow MPs that, no matter what
the caucus might decide as party policy, he himself was going to

vote in favor of the bill. Howard Green of Vancouver South
announced the same intention. One by one, other members joined
them until the caucus was almost unanimous—but unanimously
against the stand taken by the party's leader.

When the debate on the family allowance bill began Gordon
Graydon, obviously somewhat embarrassed, argued that it was (or
anyway might be) unconstitutional, and moved it be sent back
to a committee for further study. The amendment was ruled out
of order, as Graydon must have known it would be. Thereafter,
every Conservative speaker with the exception of Dr. Bruce, while
criticizing the bill in detail, announced his intention to support
it in principle.

Debate on second reading ended on July 28. The Conservatives
would gladly have let the bill go through without a recorded
vote, but they knew the gleeful Liberals would never let them
off so easily, so they came into the chamber prepared. Dr. Bruce,
who could not be persuaded to vote in favor of the bill, was
at least persuaded to stay away. And so, when the Liberals demanded and got a recorded vote, it was solemnly counted by
the Clerk of the House: ayes, one hundred and thirty-nine; nays,
nil. But the Liberals still contrived to have the last word. William
Golding, Liberal MP for Huron-Perth, Ontario, rose with a straight
face to explain why he had not voted: "Mr. Speaker, I was paired
with the honorable member for Parkdale (Dr. Bruce). Had I
voted I would have voted for the motion."

Meanwhile, the Mackenzie King Cabinet had begun its preparation for a general election. A vice-president of the Cockfield
Brown advertising agency moved to Ottawa early in 1944 and
started work on a series of campaign advertisements offering womb-
to-tomb security—old-age pensions, health insurance, subsidized
housing, the lot. In fact the election was not called until June
1945, but the welkin was ringing with promises for many months
before.

Fulfillment of the promises was slower. Canada had to wait
seven more years for a flat-rate pension to all old people without
means test, and twenty-two for a contributory system. Hospital

insurance didn't arrive in most provinces until the 1960s, and health insurance is still in the future. But when all the cynical remarks have been made, it remains a fact that the social welfare programs introduced at the end of World War II have transformed Canada.

Family allowances at the start distributed about $190 million a year—less than a third of what they amount to now, but more than the total federal outlay for relief from 1935 to 1939 inclusive. Old-age pensions in 1945 cost the federal Government only $33 million, or presumably $44 million for all contributing governments; they are now running around $75 million *a month*. In the earlier postwar years such things as veterans' re-establishment credits, housing loans, cashed-in Victory Bonds, and so on released a volume of purchasing power that Canada had never known before. Employment was high, but for those who didn't have jobs the unemployment insurance fund had been built up during the war to a quarter of a billion.

More was promised if necessary. On April 12, 1945—by coincidence, it was the last day in the life of President Franklin Roosevelt, the father of the New Deal—the Canadian government published a White Paper on Employment and Income which was, in effect, a blueprint of the postwar economy. The theories of Lord Keynes, which now seem conservative but then were still radical, were to be wholeheartedly adopted. Massive investment of public money was to be used to offset the downturns in the business cycle; taxation for surpluses in good times would keep the national debt from expanding beyond tolerable bounds.

It is still too soon to be dogmatic about what these new policies achieved. The only certain thing is this: *something* changed Canada. Twenty years and several "recessions" later, we still have not had another depression. The rate of economic growth has varied, but growth itself has never stopped. Employment has been easier to find in some years than in others, but the unemployed are no longer destitute; even a fairly severe recession no longer creates a distress situation.

As time went on the radical governments became more conservative while the conservative governments became more radical, and things were now taken for granted by left and right alike which had been slogans of conflict a few years before. The voltage went out of the arguments about economic and political systems. If the result was not a unified country, it was at least the removal of one cause of disunity—the one which had seemed, in the previous decade, to be the gravest of all.

For the whole period since World War II began, the very phrase "national unity" suggests the chronic strains and tensions between English and French Canadians. It's easy now to forget that for the whole period between the wars the dangerous strains and tensions were between two quite different groups, a division that had nothing to do with language or race—the division between the rich and the poor.

III

Political Fissions: The Luxury of Dissent

CANADA'S POLITICAL SYSTEM is founded, perhaps appropriately, on a contradiction in terms.

The British North America Act proclaims, in writing, that the Canadian Constitution shall be "similar in principle" to the British. But the British Constitution is not written. It is a millennium's accumulation of precedent and tradition, at once flexible and durable, molded to and by the British national character. The Canadian Constitution is written, dogmatic, rigid but vulnerable to legalistic casuistry, originally (and to some extent still) a product of bargaining among scattered colonies whose national character did not exist. Small wonder that a century's use has transformed the Candian system from one "similar in principle" to the British into one that is peculiar if not unique.

True, the basic machinery is much the same. The Cabinet is responsible to a Parliament that must be elected not less often than every five years, but can be dissolved at any time on request of the Prime Minister. (In practice, in both countries, the usual length of a Parliament is about four years.) Defeat in the House of Commons, on a major issue, compels the Government to hold a general election and submit to the judgment of the people; this happens seldom in either country, but in Canada it happened in 1925 and again in 1963. Parliamentary rituals, though not identical, are similar. But traditions and practices are sharply different. In Britain, a unitary country, the Prime Minister may choose the men he thinks most able to form his Cabinet. In Canada the Prime Minister must choose at least one minister from each province (unless, as often happens, his party has no elected members in one or more provinces). He must keep a traditional balance between English and French, Protestant and Catholic, east and west. By a tradition still new but already stern, one minister should be a woman. An obvious result is that a federal Cabinet always includes some members less able than other MPs who, because they come from the wrong city or the wrong religion, must remain backbenchers.

Another difference is the structure of political parties. The two strongest in Canada, Liberals and Progressive Conservatives, inherit their names from Britain but not their natures. Canadian parties, unlike British, do not represent social classes.

What they do represent is hard to say. The major parties, the only ones ever to hold office nationally, do not represent anything in particular. They differ in historic origins—the Liberals are descended from Reformers of the nineteenth century, Conservatives from the Tories who then supported the Establishment—but this distinction has vanished from all but the vocabulary of political invective. Some Conservatives still call Liberals "crypto-republicans," some Liberals call Conservatives "puppets of Big Business" or "colonialists," but nobody takes this kind of talk seriously any more. Today no difference between the major parties can be defined in general terms that both would accept. Each tries to appeal simultaneously to all five regions, all religions, all ethnic groups, all income brackets. Both rely mainly on the same contributors for funds.

But Canada also has four minor parties, often miscalled "splinter" parties, and among them the differences are considerable. None has yet developed nation-wide strength, but each is formidable in certain regions.

Social Credit is in some ways the most formidable of the four. Never powerful in federal politics, it nevertheless holds office in two provinces, Alberta and British Columbia. In Alberta it has been in power since 1935 and still seems unbeatable. In British

Columbia it has not been seriously threatened with defeat since it was first elected in 1952.

As a philosophy or socio-economic theory, Social Credit was developed in the 1920s and early 1930s by an Englishman, Major C. H. Douglas. Its principal tenet is currency reform—a currency based on the productive capacity of the nation rather than gold, a "social dividend" to all citizens which would maintain purchasing power while inflation would be averted by a "just price." Douglas' theories sound less heretical now, in these days of Keynesian economics and anti-cyclical budgeting, than they did in the 1930s, but they have never convinced any economist of national repute. Also, Douglas had a paranoid streak. He tended to believe the world's ills were the work of a vast conspiracy of international bankers allied, for some unexplained reason, with international Communists and "international Zionists," a euphemism to disguise his anti-Semitism.

Douglas' followers might now be forgotten along with the Technocrats, the Townsendites, the Single-Taxers, and the many others who were about to save the world in the 1930s, if Douglas' monetary theories had not caught the eye and imagination of a radio preacher in Alberta, William Aberhart. As founder and dean of the Calgary Prophetic Bible Institute he had built up a tremendous following on the farms and ranches of Alberta, and his adoption of the Douglas doctrine gave it instant appeal.

This was in 1932. Depression and drought were bringing widespread misery to the prairies. When in 1934 a scandal broke out involving Premier J. E. Brownlee, the United Farmers Government which had ruled Alberta since 1921 fell to pieces. Aberhart and his new Social Credit Party swept into office in the general election of 1935, and have been invincible ever since. On Aberhart's death in 1943 the leadership devolved upon his ex-pupil and protégé Ernest C. Manning, who had become Aberhart's provincial secretary at the age of twenty-seven and who at fifty-nine gives no sign of any loss of political potency.

Social Credit in practice under Aberhart and Manning has

shown no resemblance to the Social Credit of Douglas' theory. Aberhart tried to put the theory into effect in his first few years of power, but found it went beyond provincial jurisdiction under the British North America Act. Thirty-seven of his statutes were either ruled unconstitutional by the Supreme Court of Canada and the Privy Council in London, then the Commonwealth's final court of appeal, or else they were disallowed by the federal Government in Ottawa. Thus frustrated in attempt to make Social Credit an actuality, Aberhart and Manning settled down to give Alberta "sound," honest, and rather conservative administration, to the apparent satisfaction of practically everybody. The wartime boom brought prosperity, which was maintained after the war by the discovery of oil. Manning's more devout followers believe that Alberta's present affluence is literally the work of God—that the oil wealth, which had been there since Paleozoic time, was not revealed to sinful men until a godly government was there to exploit it.

In British Columbia the history of Social Credit is shorter and less theological. Premier W. A. C. Bennett was a Conservative, ex-candidate for the provincial Conservative leadership, until a few months before the election that brought the Social Credit Party to office. Its victory was caused by the collapse of a Liberal-Conservative coalition, originally formed to head off the threat of Canada's socialist party, the Cooperative Commonwealth Federation.

Cooperative Commonwealth Federation was the unwieldy name (normally shortened to CCF) of a left-wing group formed in 1932 by an alliance of various labor, farmer, and cooperative organizations plus a rather academic society of intellectuals called the League for Social Reconstruction. The founding conference was held in Calgary in August 1932, but the meeting more often described as the birthplace of the CCF was its first party convention in Regina, Saskatchewan, the following year. This was the rally that produced the CCF program better known as the

Regina Manifesto, a fourteen-point platform that ended with this ringing paragraph:

"No CCF Government will rest content until it has eradicated capitalism and put into operation the full program of socialized planning which will lead to the establishment in Canada of the Cooperative Commonwealth."

The responsibilities of twenty years of office in one province, Saskatchewan, plus observation of socialism in other countries and also, no doubt, the normal effects of advancing age have somewhat tempered these high ideals. But they were certainly the mood of the moment at the Regina convention of 1933, and they still express the political aspirations of the CCF. Perhaps the phrase "to eradicate capitalism" has now become too strong, but "the Cooperative Commonwealth" is still the ideal.

Chief founder and first president of the CCF was James S. Woodsworth, a former Methodist minister who had been an MP on the Labor ticket since 1921, and whose memory still commands a respect amounting to reverence. As a lifelong pacifist he could not accept his party's support of the war in 1939, and he abdicated the leadership at that time, but the parting came without rancor or any loss of mutual regard. His successor was his former chief lieutenant, M. J. Coldwell, who remained CCF leader until after his personal defeat in the election of 1958.

As its name suggests, the CCF was intended to be a federation of farmer and labor groups, but in its first years it elected few Labor members. Woodsworth himself was succeeded, after his death in 1942, by another labor MP, Stanley Knowles, in his riding, Winnipeg North Centre, and a few union men were elected from the east and west coasts. But the backbone of the party from 1935 to 1958 was its farm bloc from Saskatchewan.

The Diefenbaker sweep of 1958 wiped out this rural strength; the remnant of the CCF was mainly labor. In 1961 a formal attempt was made to unite, once again, the farm and labor movements, and the old CCF became the New Democratic Party (NDP), which drew its financial support mostly from labor but hoped to draw electoral support from both. At least in the early years, the hope proved vain. The NDP won twenty-one seats in the election of 1965, a total it had only once exceeded in the past, but its members did not include a single farmer.

The other two minor parties are French Canadian and operate only in Quebec, yet they have nevertheless their own significance in federal politics.

Ralliement des Créditistes was the title adopted by the Quebec wing of the Social Credit Party after it split from the group led by Robert Thompson of Alberta, after the election of 1963. Like the western Social Crediters (or Socreds as they are called), the Créditistes do not lean heavily on monetary theory. A favorite slogan of their leader, Réal Caouette, in the 1962 election was "You don't have to understand Social Credit in order to vote for it." Another slogan, even more effective among the disgruntled poor of Quebec, was "What have you got to lose?"

Caouette came back from the 1962 election with twenty-six Quebec seats. Thompson, the party's "national leader," had only four. The English-speaking tail continued to wag the French-speaking dog for the short Parliament of 1962–63, but this could not be expected to last. When the break came, only a handful of French-speaking MPs stayed with Robert Thompson, and all were defeated in 1965. Only nine of Caouette's party survived the 1965 election, and in 1966 it dropped to eight when Gilles Grégoire, his chief lieutenant, also broke away and became an independent. His differences with his former colleagues were apparently more personal than ideological, for all are French-Canadian nationalists whose ideas vary mainly in intensity.

Union Nationale is the name of a Quebec party founded in 1935 by a rebel group of Quebec Liberals, dissatisfied with the aged and corrupt regime then in power, and the Quebec Conservatives led by Maurice Duplessis. It routed the provincial Liberals in 1936, lost power again for the duration of World War II, but came back in 1944 and remained unbeaten until after the death of Duplessis in 1959. In Quebec provincial politics it replaces the Progressive Conservatives, who have no provincial organization in Quebec.

The Union Nationale has no federal arm and no federal ambitions; it is a Quebec party pure and simple. But from time to time, and in various ways, it has more impact on federal politics than many a party, living or dead, which has nourished ambitions to rule all Canada.

IV

How the Cold War Started—in Canada

ONLY PEOPLE BORN BEFORE 1914 can remember the numbing shock of August 23, 1939. On the eve of his invasion of Poland, Adolf Hitler concluded a pact of non-aggression and mutual assistance with Josef Stalin, and shattered the illusions of a generation.

It is difficult now, after twenty years of Cold War, to recapture the image of the Soviet Union that existed in the minds of young radicals in the 1930s. We were not quite as naïve as we are sometimes made out to have been—the twists and turns of the Communist Party line, the Moscow purge trials that began in 1937, all contributed to a certain cynicism and wariness toward the real Party man. But we still regarded Communists with something like the mixture of awe, admiration, and mistrust that Roman Catholics seem to feel for the Jesuits. They might be unscrupulous on behalf of the cause, and therefore not quite liked or trusted by ordinary folk, but at least they were wholly dedicated men who were, after all, on the right side fundamentally.

The pact with Hitler contradicted all that. Communist tirades and Communist-led strikes against the "imperialist war" went on for two years, until the hot June weekend in 1941 when Hitler's armies struck without warning at his "ally," the Soviet Union, and Communists overnight became the most strident of all advocates of all-out war.

Two years are not long enough to erase the impressions and emotions of a decade—especially a decade that included the Great

Depression, the Spanish Civil War, and the shameful pact of Munich. Whatever memories of betrayal lingered through the summer and autumn of 1941, when the Germans were sweeping the Red Army before them, were dispelled by the heroic resistance and the successful counterattacks that came with the Russian winter. The Russians were our glorious allies. Even in right-wing circles, Communists became respectable.

Feelings of guilt about Munich were augmented by similar feelings about the long, slow buildup that preceded the second front. Victories in North Africa and Sicily, advances in Italy were all very well, but these were side shows in which relatively few men were engaged. On the eastern front, Red Army casualties ran into millions—but so did German. A wry little joke became current in 1943:

> First Commuter, looking up from newspaper: "We seem to be doing a bit better lately."
> Second Commuter: "You speak English remarkably well, for a Russian."

If there were any who foresaw the future with accuracy (and there were a few) they found it prudent to keep quiet. Had anyone prophesied in public, in 1944, that within five years the Western powers would be forming an alliance with the Germans against the Russians, he would have been imprisoned without trial under the Defense of Canada Regulations.

This euphoria about Stalin's Russia persisted for at least a year after the end of the war. It survived the bitter wrangling at San Francisco where the United Nations Organization (UNO, as it was then called) was brought to birth. It survived, at least for a while, the rigid and acrimonious partitions in Germany and Berlin, Austria and Vienna, Venezia Julia and Trieste.

As late as March 1946, when Sir Winston Churchill at Fulton, Missouri, coined the most memorable of postwar metaphors ("From Stettin on the Baltic to Trieste on the Adriatic, an Iron Curtain has descended across the continent of Europe"), he raised an angry storm. His immediate audience was cool, press reaction was reproachful, and a thousand members of the CIO turned out to picket his speech in New York a few days later.

Just two weeks after Churchill's Fulton speech, Prime Minister Mackenzie King rose before a packed House of Commons to remove the veil of secrecy from a series of events in Ottawa, Montreal, and Chalk River, Ontario. The facts then made known to the public had been known to authorities in Ottawa, Washington, and London for six months, and they altered the relations between the Soviet Union and the West for decades to come.

Of the several dates that might be chosen as marking the beginning of the Cold War, one of the more plausible is September 5, 1945, the sultry Wednesday evening in Ottawa when a short, stocky, blond Russian named Igor Gouzenko walked for the last time out of the office in the Soviet Embassy on Charlotte Street, where he had worked as a cipher clerk since 1943.

Under his shirt, carefully distributed so as not to bulge or crackle, Gouzenko was carrying several dozen documents of varying size and thickness. When he got back to the little apartment in Sandy Hill where his pregnant wife was waiting for him in an agony of fear, the documents were soaked with sweat, not only because of the unseasonable heat wave. Gouzenko was just as frightened as his wife, and with good reason. The papers he had carried away from the Soviet Embassy were messages to and from Moscow, and other extracts from the secret files, which proved the existence of an espionage network in the lower and middle echelons of the Canadian government, which was passing out secret information to the Soviet Union.

Gouzenko was not the first, though he did become the most famous, of Soviet defectors to find refuge in Canada, but the history of his predecessor was not reassuring. Just before the war a Soviet general named Alexei Krivitsky, who had fled the purges by which Stalin was then decimating the senior ranks of the Red Army, came first to the United States (where he sold his story to the *Saturday Evening Post* for a handsome sum) and then settled in Montreal.

Under the name of Alex Thomas, Krivitsky lived as unobtrusively as possible with his wife and their seven-year-old son in an inconspicuous stucco house in the suburban village of Hudson Heights. In spite of his best efforts, though, he did not succeed in avoiding notice. Even casual acquaintances were struck by the fact that a refugee (from an unspecified Baltic country, he let it be known) could live in such comfort and even luxury with no job. Moreover, those who came to know the whole "Thomas" family were aware that for some strange reason the wife lived in a state of constant terror. Her husband was apologetic about her, and spoke vaguely of her "nerves," but she did not look like a nervous woman. Rather, she looked like a strong, healthy, practical girl who was scared half out of her wits.

She had cause to be scared. On at least one occasion Krivitsky was spotted by a Montreal Communist at a public meeting there. When, against the advice of the RCMP, he took his family to New York in 1941, Soviet agents were ready for him. Very shortly thereafter, he disappeared one evening; his body was found a few days later in a cheap hotel room in Atlantic City. Officially it was suicide, but the RCMP knew it was murder, and, no doubt, Igor Gouzenko feared the same.

Gouzenko and his wife and child had lived in Canada, by that time, for only two years. Before coming, both had had the customary "double indoctrination" about life in capitalist countries— first the standard picture given to all Soviet school children, of existence in the hell of wage slavery and capitalist exploitation; then the counterbriefing before they left Russia, to prepare them for the somewhat different reality they were about to see with their own eyes. By his own account in his autobiography (entitled *This Was My Choice* in Canada, *Iron Curtain* in the U.S., published in 1948) the counterbriefing was never very effective in Gouzenko's case; almost from the moment of his arrival he was struck by the contrast between what he had been told and what he could see before him. Even more he was struck by the contrast between the living conditions of Canadian wage slaves and those in the Soviet workers' paradise.

"During two years of life in Canada, I saw the evidence of

what a free people can do," he said later in his formal statement
to the Royal Commission on Espionage, 1946. "What the Canadian people have accomplished and are accomplishing here under
conditions of complete freedom, the Russian people, under the
conditions of the Soviet regime of violence and suppression of all
freedom, cannot accomplish even at the cost of tremendous sacri-
fices, blood and tears. . . . Convinced that such double-faced
politics of the Soviet Government toward the democratic countries
do not conform with the interests of the Russian people and en-
danger the security of civilization, I decided to break away from
the Soviet regime and to announce my decision openly."

But on the evening of September 5, 1945, he found this decision
very difficult to carry out. The decision itself had been forced
upon him by the news, almost exactly a year before, that he and
his wife were to be recalled to Moscow. This first announcement
was followed by a reprieve of several months—because the Ottawa
embassy was short of staff and because Igor Gouzenko had been
leading his class in the study of English and otherwise performing
his duties satisfactorily, he was to remain at his post "for the
time being"—but Igor and Anna Gouzenko made up their minds
then, in the autumn of 1944, that come what might they were
going to stay in Canada. It was in preparation for this break
that Gouzenko began, during the ensuing year, to mark certain
documents for removal from the secret files of the Soviet Embassy.

The files themselves were so secret that even the ambassador
did not have access to the barred-off rooms where they were
kept. Ranks in the embassy were, and no doubt still are, purely
nominal. The head of the Red Army spy ring, Colonel Zabotin,
was listed in the diplomatic corps as a military attaché, but his
two principal aides, both commissioned officers of Red Army
intelligence, were described on the embassy staff as a chauffeur
and a doorman. (Members of the intelligence service got a sharp
rebuke from Moscow when, by some oversight, the ambassador
was allowed to learn of one project on which they were engaged.)
Igor Gouzenko was only a cipher clerk, but he was a trusted
one.

The documents he had earmarked for removal, over a period of many months, were messages from or about Canadian agents in the Soviet espionage service. Just how many names they contained has never been revealed; some were those of innocent people, mentioned without their own knowledge, and others were cover names for agents still unidentified. But the documents were the primary evidence whereby about two dozen people were named in the report of the Royal Commission on Espionage, most of whom were tried and half of whom were convicted.

Gouzenko's story was such a bombshell that he had great difficulty persuading anyone even to listen to it, let alone believe it. This after all was 1945: the Russians were our glorious allies, who had broken the back of Hitler's armies at Stalingrad, and though the prolonged acrimony of the United Nations' founding conference at San Francisco had already rubbed some of the bloom off the wartime friendship, there was still a great reluctance to think of the Soviet Union as an enemy. Prime Minister Mackenzie King admitted, months later, that his first thought when he heard about the affair was that "Gouzenko should be told to go back to the Soviet Embassy with the papers he had in his possession." The Prime Minister added a very characteristic comment: "This was a case where we could not be too careful or too cautious." The result of Mackenzie King's caution and care was that the Gouzenkos were nearly kidnaped by Soviet agents.

Their first thirty-six hours of "freedom" were a nightmare. Igor Gouzenko walked out of the embassy for the last time shortly before 9 P.M. on September 5. He didn't dare go to the police, naturally assuming that they would merely turn him over to the Soviet authorities, but he thought he could protect himself by telling his story to a newspaper, so he headed for the Ottawa *Journal*. To his horror, the most senior editor he could find on night duty looked at him with no sign of interest and suggested he talk to the Royal Canadian Mounted Police.

Gouzenko did go to the RCMP, though with great misgiving, and asked to see the Minister of Justice on "extremely important" business. It was then nearly midnight; the constable told him to come back in the morning. After a sleepless night he did so—to be told that the minister was "unable" to see him. Back he went to the Ottawa *Journal,* where this time he got a longer and more sympathetic hearing but the same answer in the end: "I'm sorry, but we can't do anything for you." A girl reporter said apologetically: "Your story just doesn't seem to register here. Nobody wants to say anything but nice things about Stalin these days."

The Gouzenkos tried the RCMP again, then the Crown Attorney's office, then another newspaper. Finally, exhausted and terrified, they went home—where they noticed two strange men keeping watch on their apartment. Within minutes, a knock sounded on their door and a harsh voice called "Gouzenko." Igor recognized the voice—it was Lieutenant Lavrentiev, Zabotin's chief aide and pretended chauffeur.

Luckily for him and for Canada, Gouzenko did not answer the door. When they heard Lavrentiev leave, he and his wife went next door and begged shelter of a neighbor—an RCAF sergeant who listened to their story somewhat incredulously, but decided to help them. He called the Ottawa city police, who undertook to watch the building for the night. When a squad from the Soviet Embassy arrived about midnight and broke into the Gouzenko apartment, the Ottawa constables simply arrested them for burglary.

That did it. The Russians were never actually prosecuted, of course—they had diplomatic immunity, though it cost them some embarrassment to establish it. But at last the Canadian authorities were convinced that Gouzenko was telling the truth and was not, as they had first suspected, either a lunatic or a fraud. The RCMP had put a watch on him from the first (they had not been as indifferent as Gouzenko thought), and now they took him under their protection in earnest.

For nearly six months nothing seemed to happen at all. Prime Minister Mackenzie King announced his intention of taking a trip to Britain, to renew his acquaintance with the new British Prime Minister Clement Attlee and to "obtain information at first hand about conditions in Europe generally." Before taking ship from New York he also paid a weekend visit to Washington, to meet the new President Harry Truman. The party leaders in the House of Commons were more than usually unctuous in expressing their approval of this prime ministerial journey, because Mackenzie King had given them a rough idea of the real reasons for his trip. He was away for a month, and on his return went back to Washington for another brief visit while Prime Minister Attlee, by a coincidence that struck nobody as odd at the time, flew out from London. Nothing was made public of what the three statesmen said to each other.

Meanwhile, in a summer cottage beside a small lake in the Gatineau Hills, RCMP officers were questioning and requestioning Igor Gouzenko. As the bright autumn days grew shorter and cooler they sought out other quarters in town for the Gouzenko family; Anna went to hospital to have their second child (where, to her horror, a fellow patient recognized her, but was apparently satisfied by her protest that it must be a case of mistaken identity). Except for such occasional and random accidents, the Gouzenkos disappeared from ordinary life and from everyone they had ever known, into a kind of limbo of pseudonymity in which they have dwelt ever since.

The reason it took so long to question Gouzenko was not that the RCMP doubted his word, but that his information was tantalizingly incomplete. Except for the various spymasters on the staff of the Soviet Embassy, he had never actually seen any of the agents whose work he was revealing. All were known to him merely as names, including fictitious "cover" names; in some cases he knew the real name of the agents too, in others he did not (some have never been identified to this day). It took months of patient checking and cross-checking to make certain who were these Canadian Soviet agents and where they could be found.

Early in October an Order in Council was passed authorizing the Acting Prime Minister (Mr. King was in Britain) or the Minister of Justice to order the detention of suspected spies "in such places and under such conditions as the Acting Prime Minister or the Minister of Justice may from time to time determine." But it was not until four months later, on the morning of February 15, 1946, that the authority was exercised in predawn raid that roused twelve men and two women from their beds in Ottawa and swept them off into custody.

It was thought necessary to hold them incommunicado. One Cabinet minister, talking about the incident a few weeks later, explained the reason for this with rather startling candor: "If we had let them see a lawyer, he would have told them not to talk." Since they did not have the benefit of counsel some of them did talk, though others did not. The results were curious.

Kathleen Wilsher, private secretary to the British High Commissioner in Ottawa (then the Right Honorable Malcolm Macdonald), was found guilty of passing secret information to the Soviet Embassy through a contact man named Eric Adams. She was sentenced to four years in the penitentiary. Adams, accused of receiving the information that she was convicted of transmitting, was acquitted. Kathleen Wilsher had freely told on herself, in her examination by the Royal Commission, without benefit of counsel; later she was a most recalcitrant and silent witness at Adams' trial.

By far the biggest fish to be caught in the Gouzenko net was Dr. Alan Nunn May, the British physicist who came to Canada to work with Dr. John Cockcroft and other distinguished scientists at the wartime nuclear research projects in Montreal and in Chalk River, Ontario. Nunn May was a Communist of some years' standing when he came to Canada, and was known to the central authorities of the Communist International in Moscow; Canadian agents were directed to get in touch with him. From him, within days of the American attack on Hiroshima and the first public revelation of nuclear weapons, Colonel Zabotin had obtained a sample of uranium oxide and some additional information about the "Manhattan Project" (the wartime code name for the making of the first atomic bombs). Nunn May was arrested in Britain, tried and convicted there, and sentenced to ten years in prison.

It's not easy to determine, in the perspective of two decades, how much good to the Soviet bloc and harm to the Western alliance were done by the spy ring's activities. Alan Nunn May, who freely admitted at his trial what he had done in Canada, said the only information he had given was "published or about to be published," and indeed the Smyth Report on the atomic bomb, which came out in the summer of 1945, was a fascinating and extraordinarily detailed account of how the new "absolute weapon" had been devised and developed. Whether the U.S.S.R. would have been able, without Nunn May's help, to explode its own nuclear device by 1949, only the Soviet government could possibly know. It seems a safe guess that, at most, the Soviet achievement would merely have been postponed a few years. "The only important secret of the atomic bomb was the fact that you can make one," a Canadian scientist remarked at the time. "Once you know for sure that it's possible, and not a waste of money, any good physicist can figure out ways of doing it."

So far as is known to the public, the other information transmitted to Moscow was trivial. The Montreal chemist Dr. Raymond Boyer passed along the formula of a process which he himself had devised. It was a new way of making an explosive called RDX. The explosive was first invented in 1905, and was well known to the Germans as well as to all the Allies; this Canadian discovery was merely a different method which, in the official Canadian opinion, was an improvement. The British and the Americans considered the suggested change but decided not to bother with it. When the question of telling the Russian allies about it came up, Canada's Munitions Minister C. D. Howe was in favor of passing on the information, but the Americans objected, and it was not passed on.

Boyer felt very strongly that this was a wrong decision. An idealist of independent means, he had had close association before the war with the Communist Party in Montreal, and had given it occasional donations of money. But he insists that he was never a Party member, and to prove it he cites a fact of which the Royal Commission refused to take note in its report. The fact was that he had been a supporter of the war against Hitler between 1939 and mid-1941, the period when the Communist Party was bitterly denouncing the "imperialist war" and organizing strikes and sabotage against it.

Boyer instead offered his services to the country. He was assigned to a McGill research project for munitions development, and he refused on patriotic grounds to accept any salary for the job. Dr. F. Cyril James, then principal of McGill, recalls that a salary was paid to Boyer anyway, but that he used to send the checks back. Characteristically, he forgot to tell the Income Tax Department that he was doing so, and for several years paid the heavy wartime taxes on income that he never received.

During this time his relations with his Communist friends were somewhat cool, but they were fully restored when Hitler invaded Russia and the Communists became instant patriots in all Allied countries. It was not surprising that he came into close touch with the Canadian agents of the spy ring. Nor was it surprising that, when his own new formula for RDX was kept from the Soviet Union on American insistence, he should decide to pass it on himself on his own initiative. The decision was nevertheless a violation of his oath of secrecy, and of the Official Secrets Act; Boyer was one of those found guilty, largely on his own testimony, and sentenced to four years in penitentiary.

Boyer's case, unique in detail, was typical in character of the Canadian spy ring. All but one of the Canadians involved were Communists or sympathizers. (The exception was the passport clerk who, according to the Royal Commission, accepted a bribe of three thousand dollars to issue a false passport. The man named in the Commission report was acquitted at his trial, but the evidence was strong that *somebody* in the passport office made this deal. According to the Royal Commission, he originally asked five thousand dollars, but Moscow said this price was "fantastic" and he settled for three thousand.)

But the other Canadian agents were idealists, pathetic ones in some cases. They offered their services without pay. When small amounts were pressed upon them (it is standard Soviet practice that agents should be persuaded to accept money and sign receipts for it) they either refused with indignation or, in some cases, accepted with reluctance and misgiving. Kathleen Wilsher, who as private secretary to the British High Commissioner was providing a steady flow of secret dispatches from London, had great scruples about taking twenty-five dollars to cover her expenses for a trip to Montreal; she kept a record of every penny she spent, and put the balance in a separate bank account.

Little Emma Woikin, a cipher clerk in the Canadian Department of External Affairs, gave information to the Soviet Union because "I have a feeling of love for that country" where her parents had been born. Her native Canada seemed to her a much harsher land. "There was a time when I was quite poor, and my baby died because we had no medical care, and nobody seemed to care. My husband was sick, and nobody seemed to intervene at all." In the Soviet Union she had been told, "there is hope for the poor, or something." Mrs. Woikin had been passing secret dispatches to the Soviet Embassy for months before she finally, and reluctantly, accepted a "gift" of fifty dollars.

Aside from the passport clerk, Alan Nunn May took the most money of all those exposed by Gouzenko. In the rather pompous words of the Royal Commission, he received "at least seven hundred dollars, plus two bottles of whisky." Hardly a lavish reward for putting his career and his liberty in danger.

To Igor Gouzenko himself the affair brought large rewards and heavy penalties.

The rewards began with an outright gift from a rich Ottawan, Frank Ahearn, who gave him a fully paid-up government annuity of a hundred dollars a month for life, in token of the Canadian people's gratitude. This of course he still has, but a hundred a month bought nearly twice as much in 1945 as it does now.

Then he sold his autobiography, *This Was My Choice*, first to a publisher and then to Hollywood. It was of course a collaboration, but the total that Gouzenko himself received was something over a hundred thousand dollars. It must have seemed an inexhaustible fortune, to a young man who had never had more money than his monthly stipend, but as things turned out it was not. Most of it was spent by 1954, when Gouzenko finished the novel he'd been working on for years and, to everyone's surprise, won the Governor-General's Medal for the best Canadian novel of the year.

Again there was a translator to pay, but again, too, there was a sale to Hollywood. Altogether, according to a statement by his wife Anna in a newspaper interview in 1965, Gouzenko got sixty thousand dollars for his prize-winning, best-selling *Fall of a Titan*. But, said Anna wistfully, "he blew it. My husband is no businessman." In 1963 he was sued by one of the chartered banks for recovery of a two-thousand-dollar loan. The suit was settled out of court. Through the combined efforts of the Government and some friends he got his debts paid, and a pension of fifty dollars a month for each member of his now considerable family was arranged—enough for the necessities of life, though not for comfort.

For all these things he paid the penalty of a fugitive's existence. He has never held a job for long, fearing recognition whenever he stays long in one place. The Soviet fatherland has not forgotten him—in 1965 an American traitor confessed, among other things, that his Soviet employers had sent him to Canada to see if he could find out where Igor Gouzenko was living. (He failed.) But although the Russian attempts to find Gouzenko seemed rather halfhearted, he himself feels sufficiently insecure that he lives in constant apprehension, and seems to have given up all hope of a normal, stable existence.

One of his consolations has been the glowing paragraph of tribute, and the acknowledgement of his services to Canada's security, in the report of the Royal Commission. Another service that may or may not be a consolation, and of which indeed Gouzenko may not even be aware, was his contribution to the Canadian sense of nationhood. To find themselves spied upon, to learn that some of their own fellow-citizens had become agents of an unfriendly foreign power, was a shock to Canadians—but a unifying shock. Unlike the exposure of Alger Hiss in the United States two years later, it brought self-confidence rather than self-doubt. Canada's spies had proved to be rather pathetic little creatures, dealing mainly in trivial little secrets and now exposed to a structure of authority which itself had never been involved. On the whole, a maturing experience.

V

The Nuclear Club, and How Not to Be a Member

CANADA'S CONNECTION WITH the atomic age began a dozen years before the atomic age itself. It may be dated from May 16, 1930, when a French-Canadian prospector named Gilbert LaBine found a rich deposit of pitchblende on the shores of Great Bear Lake, in the Northwest Territories.

LaBine was vice-president and managing director of a company called Eldorado Gold Mines Limited, which sounds more imposing than in fact it was. Eldorado in those days consisted of Gilbert LaBine and his elder brother Charles, a couple of self-made prospectors who had started as laborers in the silver mines of Cobalt in 1905, and had operated on the fringes of every mining boom in Canada during the first quarter of this century, never making a fortune but always doing moderately well. During the middle twenties, when stock was easy to sell, they had raised half a million dollars to develop a gold-mining claim that Gilbert had staked in Manitoba. The gold quartz vein petered out before the money did, and Gilbert LaBine flew north in 1929 to look for better prospects for investing what they had left.

Since he had gone to work at fifteen after only one year of high school, it's remarkable that LaBine was even aware of the value of pitchblende, let alone able to recognize an outcropping of it. However, he had for years been spending his winters improving his knowledge of geology; he knew what pitchblende looked like. And he knew that the world price of radium ran as high as a hundred thousand dollars a gram—just the kind of price to make it worth while developing a mining property that lay fifteen hundred miles by water from the nearest railhead, and probably another three thousand from a refinery. Actually this price turned out to be artificially high, maintained by the near monopoly then enjoyed by the mines of the Belgian Congo; it dropped to twenty-five thousand when Eldorado entered the market, so the LaBine brothers' enterprise never did become sensationally profitable. After operating on a fairly modest scale during the thirties they shut down the mine in July 1940, intending to leave it closed until the end of the war and the return of normal conditions.

But meanwhile, unknown to the LaBines, Canada was being drawn into the new world of nuclear physics by quite different avenues and circumstances.

Most of Britain's top physicists were urgently engaged, during the first years of the war, in developing and perfecting radar (which was the salvation of Britain when Hitler's V-1 bombs were set flying toward England in the summer of 1944). Some, however, were reserved for another task that might have become even more urgent—the deadly race to produce the atomic bomb.

The United States, even though neutral, had also got into the nuclear race as early as October 1939, when Albert Einstein signed the famous letter to President Franklin Roosevelt recommending the program of research that led to atomic weapons. The Einstein letter moved the United States Government to allot the magnificent sum of six thousand dollars to the project—a modest beginning for what turned out, eventually, to be the most expensive scientific experiment ever conducted.

Just one year, almost to the day, after Pearl Harbor, the Italian refugee Enrico Fermi achieved the first chain reaction in his crude reactor in a converted squash court in Chicago—December 2, 1942, the true birthday of the atomic age. By coincidence it was the same day that a joint British-Canadian research team moved into absurdly inadequate quarters in a run-down mansion in Montreal. Britain had decided to move her whole nuclear program to Canada, for three reasons—to get it out of bombing range, to take some pressure off Britain's overtaxed industrial system, and to be near the American team in Chicago and New York.

Canada had already developed a modest atomic research program of her own. Dr. George C. Laurence, now president of the Atomic Energy Control Board but then a young physicist on the staff of the National Research Council, had borrowed half a ton of uranium oxide from Gilbert LaBine in the spring of 1940, for a series of experiments and observations of neutron behavior. Laurence's equipment was laughably crude, really no more than a large paraffin-lined bin filled with ten tons of calcined petroleum coke, in which he had buried packages of uranium oxide, uniformly spaced. (Inquirers were told that the bin was for storage of surplus materials from a nearby laboratory.)

But Laurence's aim, as he explained in an article written after the war, was "to determine, by measuring the behavior of neutrons in this small quantity of material, whether a great release of atomic energy could be produced in a large quantity of the materials, and if so, what was the minimum quantity necessary for the purpose."

When, at the suggestion of British physicist R. H. Fowler, Laurence went to the United States for talks with Enrico Fermi and other physicists working there, he found that they were engaged on very similar problems. At that stage, even their equipment was not much more elaborate than Laurence's glorified coke bin back in Ottawa. They were all members of the same intellectual fraternity, and when the British team moved to Canada it was natural that a Canadian team should join them.

Sharing out the work between the Anglo-Canadian group in Montreal and the American groups in New York and Chicago, was more difficult. Much of 1943 was spent in fruitless and frustrating discussions that led nowhere. But after the 1943 summit conference in Quebec City, where not only President Roosevelt and Prime Ministers Churchill and King but most of their military and scientific advisers met, a three-nation coordinating committee was set up and the Canadian share of the program got under way.

On January 28, 1944, came the junction of the two paths that had led Canada into the atomatic age. C. D. Howe, Minister of Munitions and Supply, made an announcement in the House of Commons that only a handful of Canadians could understand, but that even the uninitiated could recognize as important:

"As a necessary means for the more effective prosecution of the war, the Government of Canada has acquired all properties and assets of Eldorado Mining and Refining Limited, by expropriating all the capital shares of the company. . . . The president, directors and officers of Eldorado Mining and Refining Limited have been invited to continue to act in their present capacities and have agreed to do so. There will be no change in existing arrangements affecting the employees. . . . I regret that for reasons of secrecy I am unable to give the House any further information on this subject. In the interests of military secrecy I hope that no questions about this matter will be asked."

MPs and reporters alike respected the request. It was obvious, to anyone who remembered the news stories of the late thirties about the first successful attempts to split the atom, that this expropriation of Gilbert LaBine's "radium mine" had something to do with atomic energy, but few cared to ignore such a warning from the Minister of Munitions in wartime, and the few who did inquire were firmly and even sternly discouraged. By 1945 the expropriation of Eldorado had been almost forgotten. When on August 6 of that year the whole world was astounded to hear about the bomb that destroyed Hiroshima, Canadians were almost equally astonished to discover that a nuclear research project had been in full swing in their own country for about a year and a half, and one of the three nuclear reactors in the entire world was about to go into production on the banks of the Ottawa River.

About three hundred scientists had been at work on it, some of them for three years or more. Not all were nuclear physicists. The machinery of a nuclear reactor is not too complicated in principle. The complicating factor is that every operation, however simple in itself, has to be conducted by remote control through protective screens of reinforced concrete. Automation in 1945 was neither as commonplace nor as far advanced as it is now, and in the field of atomic research nothing had yet been learned by experience—nothing quite like this had ever been done before, anywhere.

The task assigned to Canada was to try one of the two known methods of making plutonium, the artificial radioactive element which was the stuff of one of the first atomic bombs. The other method, which looked as if it would be quicker and easier, was undertaken by the United States, using graphite as the moderator in the nuclear reactor. The Canadian plant was to use deuterium oxide—"heavy water."

Whether the "heavy water" reactor has any advantages over the more common graphite pile is not for the layman to say (it was the subject of a bitter altercation among Canadian nuclear scientists in the early 1960s). The important thing was that the Canadian plant at Chalk River, combined with the fact that Canada then had practically all of the free world's known resources of uranium ore, gave Canada a place at every table where the early decisions about nuclear policy were made. It gave Canada a degree of access that other countries did not have to the "atomic secrets" of the United States and Britain—though in the early postwar days that access was very limited indeed, for the U.S. appeared to consider itself the sole repository of nuclear knowledge and to think it could remain so if the Russians could be prevented from "stealing" the "secrets." But the Russians themselves encouraged this notion by their espionage activity, and the exposure of Alan Nunn May in Canada and, later, Klaus Fuchs in Britain seemed to justify American caution.

Canada did not object too strenuously to the American policy of secrecy. In Ottawa as well as in Washington it was accepted that the "proliferation" of nuclear weapons would be a calamity of the first magnitude. Ottawa wanted to set an example, as ostentatiously as secrecy itself would allow, of a small nation which had a nuclear capability but which voluntarily forswore the possession or manufacture of nuclear weapons.

So Canada took part in all the attempts to set up international control of atomic energy. General Andrew G. L. McNaughton, a former president of Canada's National Research Council and the first commander-in-chief of the Canadian army overseas in World War II, was appointed Canada's representative on a United Nations commission for atomic control. He and a brilliant staff worked very hard devising plans for international control systems, though in retrospect what they produced looks as naïve and absurdly hopeful as the Kellogg Peace Pact of 1928. All nuclear materials were to be put under the control of an international authority. UN inspectors were to have free access to all corners of all countries to make sure that these materials were being used for peaceful purposes only. Naturally the Soviet Union, which did not permit free travel within its borders even to its own citizens, would have nothing to do with these proposals. It's an interesting speculation whether, if the Soviet Union *had* accepted them or even pretended to, any Western nuclear power (or would-be nuclear power) would have accepted them too.

Naturally General McNaughton and his men knew that their plans had no chance of immediate acceptance. What shored up their optimism was the belief that they had plenty of time. In those days the American monopoly of nuclear power appeared to be, if not a permanent thing, at least likely to endure for a long time.

Even the British, who had been part of the "Manhattan Project" that made the atomic bomb and who at the outset knew far more about nuclear physics than the Americans did, were running into massive and costly problems in building nuclear power reactors. (To their furious indignation, their ex-allies in the United States were prevented by postwar secrecy laws from telling the British how to solve these problems, many of which had been surmounted while the two countries were still part of one wartime team.) Aside from their actual experience with atomic energy, the British had as large a supply of highly trained physicists and highly skilled technicians as any country on earth at the time—or so it was supposed. Obviously, if nuclear power was proving difficult for the Britsh, it would be impossible for the primitive Russians. I remember a conversation in late 1947 in which General McNaughton guessed it would take them decades to catch up: "Even if they had enough physicists, which they haven't, they simply haven't got enough plumbers." This opinion was widely shared—even the most pessimistic prophets thought the Russians would need three to five years, and a commoner guess was twenty. It took them two.

Explosion of the first Soviet nuclear device in 1949 changed the very nature of the problem. What had been a relatively calm contemplation became a matter of urgency and of dread; talk of disarmament went on halfheartedly while rearmament proceeded at rates of speed and expenditure that had never even been imagined before in what was still (despite Korea) called peacetime. As H-bomb followed A-bomb and Sputnik followed SAC, and solid-fueled Minuteman missiles were buried in tunnels that guaranteed a retaliatory shot no matter how little might be left of the United States, the whole subject of nuclear weaponry took on an air of lunacy.

Canada, still rather primly outside the Nuclear Club (not that anyone was pressing her to join), continued to be the major source of nuclear fuel. Eldorado began to peter out in the fifties, and was finally closed and virtually abandoned in 1960, but meanwhile new discoveries made it clear that the great pre-Cambrian Canadian Shield contained as much uranium as the world was ever likely to need. Names like Blind River and Beaverlodge became familiar. Modern towns like Elliott Lake and Uranium City sprang up out of nothing in the wilderness, carried to affluence by the uranium boom and then, overnight, to virtual destitution when the boom ended with the decade of the fifties.

The moral contradictions and paradoxes of the atomic age are clearer now than they were in 1945—the questions, that is, not the answers.

Canada built a nuclear reactor for India in the fifties, and in the sixties undertook to do the same for Pakistan. Both, of course, are built under the strictest guarantees that they will be used for peaceful purposes only, and there is no reason to doubt that the present governments of both countries will observe this undertaking. But with China newly become a nuclear power, and already once an aggressor against India, it is too easy to imagine a military take-over government in Delhi (if China were again to invade and India again to be defeated) which would hardly feel itself bound by the pledge of a predecessor for which it was in no way responsible. Any nuclear reactor can be used for either peaceful or military purposes, and nothing short of very close inspection can tell which is which at a given moment.

Also, France has become a nuclear power and potentially a major customer for Canadian uranium. The French want Canadian uranium for peaceful purposes only—because, they explain, they already have all they need for their modest military program. But they refuse to make any promises or accept any stipulations that are not also required of the British and the Americans; France must be accepted as a nuclear power and treated like other nuclear powers. The French also point out with Gallic logic that since France *has* a nuclear weapons program and has every intention of maintaining it, just as the United States also intends, it really doesn't matter whether any one stockpile of uranium is used for the military or the civilian program.

Canada has prepared to meet this dilemma by stipulating that henceforth *all* sales of Canadian uranium shall be for peaceful purposes; the previous exemptions for Britain and the United States are eliminated. This drew no objections from the British and the Americans because they too, like France, have all the uranium they need for their military programs. But since the Americans are no more likely than the French to accept any thoroughgoing Canadian inspection of their use of Canadian uranium, the whole concept of atomic control seems to have been considerably diluted.

Probably this was inevitable. Once China became a nuclear power, all hope of controlling nuclear weapons through any international agency faded—since China is not a member of any organization that includes the United States. And any control system that omits or ignores the largest nation in the world is obviously unrealistic. For Canada as a supplier of uranium, it will be more and more difficult to refuse orders on which the employment of whole cities and even regions may depend, in order to maintain lip service to a non-existent system of nuclear control, or to combat a process of nuclear proliferation that is taking place anyway.

Yet the Quixotic idealism that underlay Canadian policy had a bearing on the developing sense of Canadian identity. The new nation had a belief in its own purity which, for the time being at least, obscured its perception of material advantage. This was not the first, and is unlikely to be the last, occasion when illogical scruples on Canada's part exasperated more pragmatic allies—all the more because, at other times and in other ways, Canada would press its own claims to special privilege as brassily as any other. Nevertheless, the scruple about nuclear weapons was neither unreal nor ignoble, but a part of national character in which the nation has a right to take pride.

VI

The Long Boom and the Brief Bust

IT WAS BEGINNING to get dark by four o'clock on that cold February afternoon, and many of the officials, leading citizens, and curiosity-seekers had gone home, but about five hundred hardy souls were still there when the big moment came. Leduc Number One, the hundred and thirty-fourth well to be drilled by Imperial Oil Limited in western Canada, sent "a beautiful ring of black smoke floating skyward" and, incidentally, took a vast weight off the mind of Vernon Hunter, the man in charge of the drilling crew. "Dry Hole" Hunter and his men had spudded in the Leduc well three months before, and they were almost a mile deep when they got convincing evidence of oil.

"That's the last time I'll ever predict when a well will go into production," Hunter said later. They had brought up enough showings of oil to warrant a production test on February 3, 1947. Asked how long the test would take, Hunter answered casually, "About ten days." Then, to his horror, he discovered that Imperial Oil's public relations staff had taken him literally at his word. Hordes of press and radio reporters, an array of Imperial Oil executives, and provincial politicians including the Minister of Mines, N. E. Tanner, were invited to the bald prairie of Leduc, thirteen miles southwest of Edmonton, to watch Imperial strike oil on February 13. By some miracle, the strike actually took place on schedule.

It was not, of course, the first discovery of oil and gas in western Canada. The fur trader and explorer Peter Pond noted seepages along the Athabaska River as early as 1788. In 1912,

William Stewart Herron, the oil pioneer of Turner Valley, persuaded two Calgary businessmen to finance a search for oil by taking them to a rock fissure where gas was escaping, touching a match to the gas leak, and frying them a plate of ham and eggs.

There are still (or were until recently) about three hundred producing wells in Turner Valley. During the war they reached a peak output of nearly ten million barrels a year, which at that time was ninety-five per cent of oil production in all Canada. But the record of Turner Valley was a record of boom and bust. Even its discoverer Herron was alternately rich and poor all his life, making fortunes in each successive boom and losing them in the subsequent collapse of speculative values.

This may be one reason why the Leduc strike made relatively little impression at the time. It was front-page news for a day, even in eastern Canada, but for no longer. By February 15 it was buried deep in the financial pages of Toronto, which recorded only "a mild flurry in western oils" as a result of the discovery which was to change the whole face and nature of the Canadian prairies, and even the identity of Canada itself.

Another reason was that Alberta had few oil millionaires. Most Alberta farmers owned only surface rights to their land. Mineral rights were held either by the Crown (i.e., the Social Credit Government of Premier Ernest Manning) or by the original corporate owners, the Canadian Pacific Railway or the Hudson's Bay Company. Mike Turta, the farmer on whose land Leduc Number One was drilled, was getting a rental from Imperial Oil of only fifty dollars per acre per year for the small bit of his farm on which the drilling crew was working, and this was typical.

There was, of course, immediate prosperity in the region. Shopkeepers doubled and tripled the volume of their trade. Hotels and rooming houses became permanently chock-a-block. Farmers could make eighteen or twenty dollars a day, in a normally slack season, hauling drill crews to and from their drilling sites through the sticky Alberta mud, with the horse-drawn rigs that were still the best means of coping with gumbo.

But the face of the land changed slowly, because the people themselves were slow to change. In September of 1948, eighteen months after the Leduc strike had brought its well-kept promise of riches, I called on a Leduc farmer whose cash take for the previous twelve months had been something over three hundred thousand dollars—all "income" for practical purposes, but two thirds of it legally "capital gain" and therefore tax free.

He was carrying in an armload of wood for the kitchen stove when I arrived. He and his wife had bought a gas stove, to be connected eventually with the great reservoir of natural gas beneath their feet, but he hadn't got round to connecting it yet—it stood in the kitchen, still in the plastic wrapping in which it had come from the warehouse. They had no dishwasher or any other modern household appliance. Neither had they any hired help, indoors or out.

"I've never worked as hard as I have this summer," the farmer said. "Couldn't get any help for love or money, so I had to run the farm alone."

But with all that money coming in, why keep on working? Why not just retire?

It was clear that the question struck him as immoral. "I'm not forty yet," he said. "A man can't play all the time. This is the only work I know, and the kind I like best."

He was still driving the car he had owned for five years, and wearing the same clothes. A provincial government official, speaking half in amusement and half in exasperation, told me: "These people won't spend a cent more than they need to, no matter how much money they get. They won't even put it in the bank, for fear the income tax department will catch up with them. They just stuff it into the mattress, as they've always done."

Mattresses in rural Alberta would be rather lumpy by now if this local folkway had gone unchanged. One recent estimate put at six billion dollars the total new investment brought to Alberta by the oil boom in its first seventeen years. The figure doesn't mean much, since inclusions and exclusions are bound to be highly arbitrary, but by any standard the capital inflow was colossal. In 1948 alone, sixty-eight new industries were established in Edmonton. In the first five years after the Leduc strike, retail sales doubled. The city still looked like the drab market town that was the capital of a bankrupt Alberta in the thirties, but the economic yeast was stirring long before it showed.

A similar delayed reaction took place within the Social Credit Government. It was made up of men who ten years before had been thought to be, and had thought themselves to be, radical reformers bent on shattering a sorry scheme of things in the Canadian economy, and remolding it nearer to the heart's desire. But when first the war boom, then the oil boom brought Alberta wealth undreamed of, they reacted like the canny farmers and small townsmen they were and are.

They remained puritanically honest. Despite recurrent gossip about petty graft here and there, Alberta's public men have gone through two decades of fabulous temptation without a single major financial scandal having been revealed or even hinted at. Premier Ernest Manning has continued, during thirty-odd years as a minister of the Crown, his true vocation as a Baptist minister, preaching each week to an enormous radio congregation. His simple, total integrity astounded and delighted the hard-bitten oil men who flocked into Alberta from 1947 on.

"I've dealt with governments all over the world, buying oil leases and so on," one of them said to me in 1948. "This is not only the most honest government, it is the *only* honest government I've ever had to do with. And I can't tell you what a pleasure it is!"

Small wonder that these ex-radicals became the darlings of ultraconservatives—with whom, both parties found to their mutual surprise, they had much in common. Simple honesty in financial matters was only one ideal they shared. In practice, the Social Crediters also adopted as a matter of course the conventional wisdom of the small businessman.

Their first preoccupation was to pay off the provincial debt, even though money was the only thing visibly decreasing in value during the postwar inflation. Only gradually and very late did they begin to put massive amounts of the province's new wealth into tangible, inflation-proof assets like schools and roads (Alberta's were probably the worst in Canada, at least until Newfoundland entered Confederation in 1949).

And long after the Manning Government had become by any common-sense standard the richest of all provincial regimes, it retained the psychological attributes and attitudes of poverty. It even succeeded in convincing other governments that this illusion was reality. Right up to the re-examination of fiscal resources that began in the early 1960s, Alberta remained a "have-not province" receiving "equalization payments" from the federal treasury, to compensate for its lack of a "fair share" of income and corporation taxes.

Nevertheless the money was in fact pouring in, however invisibly. This turned out to be a fact of crucial importance, because Canada during 1947 was running into a financial crisis of the first magnitude unbeknownst to any Canadians except a handful of economists, but no less inevitably for that.

By coincidence, the first public warning was sounded in February, the same month in which Leduc Number One inaugurated the new era in Canada's economic destinies. Graham Towers, governor of the Bank of Canada, said in his annual report: "Canada cannot continue indefinitely to sell on credit in overseas markets, while incurring a substantial cash deficit in her balance of payments with the United States."

Nobody paid much attention. The only kind of postwar economic trouble that was anticipated by the conventional wisdom was the postwar depression that was supposed to follow the postwar boom, just as it had in 1921. Unemployment was predicted for all the war-swollen industries, as soon as the "artificial demand" of the immediate postwar period had run its course. So long as the boom itself continued, with high employment and high cash incomes, we assumed that nothing very serious could happen to our economy.

So parliamentary correspondents in Ottawa were surprised, on November 17, 1947, at the elaborate arrangements made for release of the General Agreement on Tariffs and Trade (GATT). We knew it was important, of course. A prestigious team of economic experts had been in Geneva for seven months negotiating it, and the fact that it was now to be signed was the greatest step toward freedom of trade, perhaps, since Britain's repeal of the Corn Laws a hundred and one years before.

Nevertheless, we were somewhat mystified by the ostentation of secrecy in releasing the news. Arrangements were to be the same as those for Budget Night—the "locked room" in the House of Commons, which reporters might enter whenever they liked but might not leave again until a stipulated time, and in which they could read, digest, and discuss with officials the documents that they would not be allowed to communicate until the release time came.

Once inside the locked room we soon found out what the fuss was about. The real news for release that night was not the Geneva Agreement at all. It was the much more sensational fact that Canada, though a signatory and a fervent supporter of GATT, was being compelled to take immediate advantage of GATT's escape clauses. Far from setting out on a new era of freedom of trade, Canada was announcing a drastic emergency program of trade restriction and exchange control.

D. C. Abbott, then Minister of Finance, was to announce the new restrictions by radio at the same time as reporters' dispatches were to be released—"taxation by radio," the Conservative Opposition called it, when the emergency program was finally debated in Parliament almost a month later. It was certainly an extraordinary procedure, and could hardly have been adopted had not six years of war got Canadians so well used to extraordinary procedures and emergency programs.

The reason for this program was paradoxical but clear enough. In the middle of the most feverish prosperity the country had ever known, Canada had run out of money. We were doing more business than ever before, more than Canadian producers had ever dreamed of, and we were doing it with old familiar customers—yet the result was that we were on the brink of national bankruptcy. Abbott summed it up in one sentence: "We've been living beyond our customers' means." We were like a merchant doing a roaring trade with people who all had charge accounts; we could feel enormously prosperous until it came time to settle with the wholesaler.

The customers were mostly in Britain and Europe, and in the early postwar years they had no money. They wanted to buy everything Canada had to sell—but on credit. On paper, Canada had had a foreign exchange surplus of $600 million in 1946, but postwar credits and direct grants-in-aid to overseas countries came to $860 million. Canadian reserves were therefore depleted by about a quarter of a billion dollars during the year.

That was only the beginning. All through 1947, Canada's imports from the United States, all paid for in cash, went on increasing. Canadian exports, still mainly on credit, had stayed about the same.

Even on paper, we didn't quite break even in 1947. The bookkeeping deficit in Canada's balance of payments for the first eleven months was $15 million. On top of that we had a net outflow of capital to the United States, and a total of more than half a billion of unrequited exports. (Canada's postwar loans to Britain and other allies totaled $1.8 billion, compared to an American total of less than $8 billion—i.e., Canadian loans in proportion to national income were about four times as large as the American in the first years after the war.) The result was that Canada's foreign exchange reserves, which on VJ-Day had been $1.5 billion, were below $500 million by mid-November 1947, and plunging toward zero at the rate of about $75 million a month.

They plunged all the faster because Canadians had more money to spend than ever before, and spent it on American consumer goods. (Even those "made in Canada" had large components of imported American parts.) Douglas Abbott's Budget speech that spring had announced a budgetary surplus for 1946–47 of $352 million. This reduced the national debt to only $13 billion, no more than one year's gross national product, and it justified massive reductions in the personal income tax. The average tax cut was twenty-nine per cent, but that figure is misleading—in the lower brackets the reduction was as much as fifty-four per cent of a tax rate already cut, the year before, from its wartime peak. Add the various demobilization and re-establishments grants to the returning war veterans, and the cashing in of Victory Bonds by civilians, and you get a pressure of buying power like nothing that had ever been known in Canada before.

And so Canadian imports from the United States, which before the war had run around $500 million a year, shot up to a billion and a half in 1946 and two billions in 1947. By July the Canadian deficit with the U.S. was half a billion for the half year—despite the fact that the hard-pressed British managed to pay American cash for $200 million worth of food, in addition to what they got under Canadian loans to Britain.

Something had to give. Britain, as she had undertaken to do when Lend-Lease terms were negotiated with the U.S. during the war, had returned briefly to a convertible sterling in the summer of 1947. Within days, there developed such a run on the pound that currency restrictions had to be hastily reimposed to protect a badly impaired British reserve. Evidently there was no hope of replenishing Canadian reserves by asking overseas buyers for sufficient amounts of convertible cash. There was equally little hope of switching our purchases of consumer goods from American to overseas suppliers—the overseas suppliers were unable to make enough for their own needs, let alone for export.

Those were the reasons for the new program of restrictions in Canada, and they were clear enough. But even after they had been explained, the program itself hit most Canadians like a thunderbolt from the blue.

Imports of household appliances, of luxury goods like toys and jewelry, and even—harshest blow of all—of fresh vegetables and most fruits were forbidden. Many other common household goods were put on strict and limited quotas. A federal agency under C. D. Howe, the wartime Minister of Munitions and Supply, was set up to license the import of capital goods. Howe's office had absolute and arbitrary authority, under the emergency powers enacted for the orderly liquidation of wartime controls. What Howe thought necessary or desirable came in; what he didn't stayed out.

Reading these ghastly details in Parliament's locked room on that November night, reporters wondered if the Government could survive. The 1945 election had given it a majority of only five over the combined Opposition. True, until now the Opposition never had combined. It was a motley lot of Bloc Populaire and "independents" (ex-Conservative, mostly) from Quebec, Social Crediters from Alberta, socialist CCF from the prairies and British Columbia, as well as the sixty-seven Progressive Conservatives who were its main body. But surely, we thought, this grim austerity program would unite the Opposition if anything could, and perhaps even detach the three or four rebellious Liberals whose switch of allegiance would then be enough to bring the Government down.

But the Opposition proved to be united only in its customary ineptitude.

Mackenzie King had been in Britain, a guest at the wedding of Prince Philip and the Princess Elizabeth, when the import and currency restrictions were imposed. That was why Doug Abbott had to impose "taxation by radio" instead of submitting his program to an immediate session of Parliament, the normal constitutional practice. (Of course Parliament could have met in the Prime Minister's absence, but Mackenzie King didn't want that either. He wanted to make an occasion of what might—and did— turn out to be his last appearance as Prime Minister at the opening of a session.)

This delay in calling Parliament, the defiance of constitutional procedure to meet a Prime Minister's personal convenience, was obviously the point on which the Government was most vulnerable. The second point of grave weakness, related but not identical, was the restriction program itself—not only its dubious legality but the austerity it imposed. With consummate gamesmanship Mackenzie King contrived that both these points were ignored when Parliament finally met.

While King purred quietly to himself on the Government's front bench, Opposition Leader John Bracken argued at great length that the so-called emergency legislation was not really urgent at all. Much more urgent, in Bracken's opinion, was "the perilous state into which Government policies have brought the basic industry of this country, the industry of agriculture." The farmers, he said, were very angry indeed. Since this is a farmer's normal mood toward any government in Ottawa, and since Bracken had delivered the same warning from time to time for several years, the Government was not unduly disturbed. All of the first day and half of the second, in what might have been a critical debate with the Government's survival in doubt, were frittered away in a wrangle over procedure. When the House finally got to the subject of emergency measures, a week or so later, all the steam had gone out of the debate and the average citizen had gone back to the sports pages.

What really saved the Liberals from public wrath, though, was nothing that happened in Parliament. It was the short life of the austerity program itself, shorter than the wildest optimist would have predicted in the summer of 1947.

The London *Economist*, when restrictions were first imposed in November, called the Canadian ministers "naïvely optimistic" about the possibility of an early removal of controls. In fact they turned out to be pessimists.

Even before the control program came before Parliament for ratification, the exchange crisis had begun to ease. The low point of Canadian reserves in mid-December was $461 million not $400 million as had been expected. By the end of January 1948 it was back to $514 million, to $742 million by June, over a billion by the spring of 1949.

No doubt some of this improvement was due to the program of exchange control. Austerity really did work in that winter of 1947–48—travel to the U.S. became difficult, cabbage was the only fresh green vegetable available, even semi-luxury goods were hard to get. The last of the restrictions on imports were not removed until 1951.

But the real cause of the upturn was quite different. It was positive, not negative. For reasons that the Government economists of 1947 had almost entirely overlooked, the great Canadian investment boom had begun, the boom that remained in full spate for ten years.

Partly its basis was oil in western Canada. Partly it was another, slower but even more solid development on the other side of the continent—the vast heritage of iron and other ores in northern Quebec and Labrador.

VII

Legacy in Chancery:
The Riches of Ungava-Labrador

MOST OF Canada's mineral wealth has been "discovered" three or four times, in the course of three centuries.

The rich gold deposits around Yellowknife, North West Territories, were first discovered in 1898 by a prospector who had failed in the Klondike; on his way home he noted, and staked, promising claims on the north shore of Great Slave Lake. Nothing came of a find so remote from any means of transport—the same difficulty that held up development until 1964 of the fabulous mineral wealth of Pine Point, on the southern shore of the same lake.

Yellowknife was "discovered" again just after World War I, by a prospector who so totally failed to interest anyone else in his new-found El Dorado that he died of a broken heart. Again the rich veins were "discovered" in 1927, by a man who did succeed in raising enough money to sink one shaft. His project ended abruptly when he lost a bargeload of machinery and his life in the Athabaska Rapids. Nobody survived to carry on his plans.

The effective discovery, by no coincidence, came in 1930 after the aircraft had made northern transportation, at least for light weights, relatively easy. It was the same with the silver deposits around Cobalt, Ontario, first discovered in the mid-nineteenth century when the nearest railhead was hundreds of miles away, abandoned by the creditors of the first companies formed to exploit them, then rediscovered in the early nineteen hundreds when the railway had become accessible. As for the colossal deposits around Sudbury, they had been known for at least a hundred years before they were ever exploited. What made them useless in earlier years was that the deposits of copper and other useful minerals were hopelessly mixed up with the ore of a shiny but then useless substance called nickel.

Around Thunder Bay at the western end of Lake Superior, pits thirty-five feet deep and the traces of old smelting fires may still be discerned. The North American Indians are commonly, and on the whole correctly, described as Stone Age people, but they did know about the copper of Thunder Bay long before the white man came to take away their lands, and they had some awareness of how to use it.

Knowledge of this Indian lore led Alexander Henry the elder, one of the great Canadian explorers and traders of the eighteenth century, to set up Canada's first mining company shortly after the defeat of the French on the Plains of Abraham in 1759. With the backing of the Duke of Gloucester, Henry was able to raise enough money to build a six-ton sloop to carry his copper ore from Thunder Bay to Sault Ste. Marie, the narrow rapids that separate Lake Superior from Lake Huron. But Henry's company went bankrupt, probably because there would not be a canal around the rapids of Sault Ste. Marie for another century or so. This lack of a canal remained decisive for all the base metals of eastern Canada, including especially the iron of Quebec and Labrador.

Iron is nothing new in Quebec—bog iron was mined there as early as 1732. It was also known, or suspected, that vastly greater quantities were available farther north. Quite possibly the fantastic tales of gold in the "Kingdom of the Saguenay," which intrigued and deceived Jacques Cartier in the 1530s, may have been based on observations of "fool's gold" (iron pyrites).

The first precise description of the iron resources in Ungava-Labrador was given in the Canadian Geological Survey report of 1894, by a remarkable man named Albert Peter Low. Low was the kind of man around whom legends cluster. On one of his numerous trips into the wilds of arctic Quebec he had an alterca-

tion with his companion about who was in charge of the expedition. To get the question settled, Low put on his snowshoes
at Christmastime and set off to walk to Ottawa, some four hundred
miles away. He arrived in February, got his own authority confirmed in writing, walked back to camp in the Lake Mistassini
region in good time for the spring breakup and the start of the
geological survey season.

Low's iron ore discoveries of 1893–94 were made in the course
of a 5500-mile journey by canoe, dog-sled and showshoe that
took him over vast areas of the Ungava peninsula. He brought
back samples of ore that ran as high as fifty-four per cent pure
metal, and reported "an almost inexhaustible supply of high-
grade ore," which, he added, "may at some future time be of
economic importance."

Low's appraisals were confirmed and pinpointed by two ex-
peditions of McGill University geologists, in 1929 and 1933. In
1936 something called the Labrador Mining and Exploration Company got a concession from the colony of Newfoundland (not yet
a part of Canada) for twenty thousand square miles in Labrador.
The company located six of the ore bodies that are now being
exploited, but had to give up for the same reason as Alexander
Henry a century and a half before—no transport. To get the
rich ore out to tidewater would require at least three hundred
and fifty miles of railway through formidably difficult terrain.

Labrador Mining and Exploration sold its rights to the Hollinger
Mining Company in 1942. At the same time Hollinger acquired
exploration rights to about four thousand square miles in northern
Quebec, just the other side of the Labrador border. By 1945
they had definitely located twelve deposits totaling at least one
hundred and sixty million tons.

What made this hoard of iron so persistently tempting, in spite
of its inaccessibility, was the dwindling reserves of the great
Mesabi Range in northeastern Minnesota. The greatest steel complex in the world was dependent on Mesabi for cheap, easily
accessible, high-grade ore, and the experience of two world wars
had given special importance to accessibility—sea-borne supplies

would always be vulnerable. If Mesabi was running out (something which had been predicted for decades, but now at last was coming true), then the resources of Ungava-Labrador took on a new value.

But in 1946 and 1947 it was still hard to find men with enough foresight to perceive this opportunity, and also enough money to seize it. Jules Timmins of the Hollinger interests tried repeatedly, and for a long time in vain, to interest Canadian capital in the venture. Something like $10 million had already been spent in exploration and survey work—a great sum it seemed in those times, even after World War II had got men accustomed to think in large sums—and not a cent of return was yet in sight. To the canny Canadian investor it seemed too long a shot to play.

Timmins never did find enough Canadian money to get his project started. It took six United States companies, including especially the Hanna steel interests, to put up the hundreds of millions that would be needed if the scheme were ever to pay. The railway alone would cost a quarter of a billion.

Faith triumphed in the end, though. By 1950 some four hundred million tons had been located, fifteen thousand square miles of wilderness had been mapped, two hundred thousand feet of drilling completed and—the final, decisive detail—the first equipment for building a railway and a townsite, a seaport and a mine was unloaded at the tiny Gulf of St. Lawrence outport of Sept Iles.

It was not altogether coincidence that, the following year, Canada announced her intention of going ahead alone on a project which had been waiting twenty years for American collaboration. The St. Lawrence Seaway, the deepwater ship canal that has made ocean ports of Toronto and Fort William, Duluth and Chicago, had been authorized first by treaty and then by agreement as an international undertaking since 1932. Every American President since Herbert Hoover had been in favor of it, but every American Congress had refused first to ratify the treaty, then to vote the funds to implement the agreement. Root of the opposition was the American railroads and the American Atlantic ports, all of which feared the competition of a seaway from the ocean to Lake Superior.

Canada's new determination was partly an effect of Canada's new self-confidence. Proud of her record in World War II, proud of having been able to build half a million new homes and a new industrial structure, proud of the new wealth that was beginning to make itself felt throughout the country, Canadians thought themselves capable of efforts they would not have dared to try before the war. One such effort was the seaway.

Lionel Chevrier, then Canadian Minister of Transport and later the first president of the St. Lawrence Seaway Authority, persuaded his colleagues to accept the go-it-alone idea—he didn't find it difficult, for all Canada was in a daring mood then, including her politicians. In the autumn of 1951, while the builders of the new Sept Iles were completing their first full season of construction, Prime Minister St. Laurent went to Washington to tell President Truman that Canada had decided to build the seaway without waiting any longer for American help.

The reaction in Washington, as Chevrier recalls it, was one of incredulous dismay. It had not occurred to U.S. congressmen, apparently, that their veto on the project was anything less than absolute. But Canada was not bluffing. Within weeks, the two bills setting up the St. Lawrence Seaway Authority had been passed unanimously by the Canadian Parliament, with the leaders of all parties speaking in support of them.

This caused a rapid change of mood in Washington. To prevent the seaway was one thing, to see one built that was beyond U.S. control was quite another. In the spring of 1952, President Truman sent letters to the committees of the U. S. Senate and House of Representatives, urging them to make the seaway a joint effort—and one under joint control—before it was too late. Before the end of that year American legislation to this effect was in the works.

The news brought more disappointment than joy in Ottawa. Canadians had been exhilarated at the thought of tackling singlehanded this vast enterprise that had deterred them for so long; they were far from delighted to learn that the U.S. was about to end its policy of stalling and come in too. But the canal would in fact be international, even if its every inch were to be dug in Canadian soil with Canadian money. To refuse American co-operation would not only have been churlish, it would have been silly. When the work finally began in the summer of 1954, it was a two-nation project.

But the sudden collapse of the American opposition, which had been so effective for so long, was not solely an effect of Canada's threat to do the job alone. It was partly the abrupt conversion of states like Ohio and Illinois, which had previously fought the seaway as a dangerous competitor for railroads, and which now became supporters almost overnight.

They realized, apparently, that it was their steel plants that would be feeding on the ore of Labrador and Quebec, and that this ore would only be cheap if it had cheap means of transport from the Gulf of St. Lawrence to Buffalo and Cleveland and Chicago. When the late Senator Robert A. Taft of Ohio, "Mr. Republican" and a long-time foe of the seaway project, became a supporter instead it made a lot of difference in the United States Senate.

Meanwhile, though, the mining job itself was rolling ahead— probably the biggest and most difficult job ever attempted in a region where all jobs are difficult. It was Jacques Cartier who first called Labrador "the land God gave to Cain." Many a later comment has been stronger; few have been kind.

The end of the rail line was a tiny Indian shack town called Burnt Creek, with a population of two hundred and fifteen. That was the townsite originally chosen; it had to be changed when drillers discovered that the village was sitting on ten million tons of high-grade ore, but the new site was not far away. It was called Schefferville after Monsignor Lionel Scheffer, OMI, Bishop of Labrador, and by 1961 Schefferville had a population of just over three thousand.

Sept Iles, the terminus at tidewater, was an outport village of eighteen hundred. By 1961 it was a town of fourteen thousand, clustered around a modern complex of highly mechanized docks. And between Sept Iles and Schefferville ran three hundred and fifty-eight miles of the most fantastically difficult railway any Canadian had built since the CPR went through the Kicking Horse Pass. In its brief length it has seventeen bridges and two tunnels, and it goes from sea level to a height of 2053 feet at the height of land, through country where the average winter snowfall is one hundred and fifty inches. Fifteen aircraft carried in the gear and the seven thousand men to build the road—"the only railroad ever built by air," the men used to say at the time. The last spike was driven in February 1954.

A great Canadian achievement, unquestionably, and a great new Canadian asset. By the early 1960s the area was producing some twelve million tons of ore a year, worth about $125 million in precious foreign exchange, and new facilities went into production in 1965 that were expected to produce another five and a half million tons.

This is the barest minimum appraisal of what the Ungava-Labrador development meant to the Canadian economy. By the fillip it gave to Canadian self-confidence, Canadian enterprise, and Canada as an attractive field for investment, it played a role in the Great Canadian Boom far beyond the intrinsic value of the goods actually produced. Labrador iron no less than Alberta oil changed the identity of Canada, the Canadian's image of himself and his country.

But—and this is the fly in that rich ointment—it also changed the balance of control in the Canadian economy. Not only in themselves but in the notice they attracted and the example they set, oil and iron brought American ownership and control into Canada on a scale never equaled before.

By 1966, Walter Gordon, the Liberal firebrand who was Minister of Finance from 1963 to late 1965, was able to write in his highly controversial book *A Choice for Canada:* "Non-residents control sixty-nine per cent of the value of investment in petroleum and natural gas, fifty-nine per cent in mining and smelting,

fifty-nine per cent in manufacturing. . . . There are approximately
five hundred corporations in Canada with taxable incomes in
excess of $1 million. These five hundred corporations accumulated
more than half the total corporate savings (in 1964). More than
half of these companies are controlled by foreigners; more than
one-third of them are wholly-owned subsidiaries in which Canadians have no financial interest whatever." And he went on to
list fifty-three Canadian companies taken over by American buyers
in the six years 1959–65.

To Gordon this represents a real and present danger, to Canada's identity and indeed to Canada's survival. He thinks drastic
action should be taken to stop the trend, and although he failed
dramatically in a first attempt (in his Budget of 1963) he has
not given up the intention. How many Canadians agree with
him is not clear, but at least there are enough to create a profound
and unsettled controversy.

But nobody thought of these things—or anyway not many—in
those heady days of the late 1940s and early 1950s when the
Great Canadian Boom was still gathering way. Never before had
Canadians felt so sure of themselves, so conscious of youth and
strength, so secure in their national identity. They had other
reasons than the economic, and deeper.

VIII

Middle Power Abroad:
From San Francisco to SHAPE

WHEN Prime Minister Mackenzie King got back from the royal wedding in December 1947, he discovered to his horror that Canada had undertaken a new international commitment in his absence.

Acting Prime Minister Louis St. Laurent and J. L. Ilsley, the Minister of Justice who headed Canada's delegation that year to the United Nations General Assembly, had allowed Canada to be nominated to a new United Nations Temporary Commission for Korea. UNTCK, to give it the elegant acronym by which it became known, had been created by a United States resolution put before the General Assembly by General George C. Marshall, the U. S. Secretary of State who was later to give his name to the Marshall Plan for the rescue of postwar Europe. General Marshall explained that UNTCK was needed so that "the urgent and rightful claims of the Korean people to independence" should not be further delayed by "inability of two powers [the U.S. and the U.S.S.R.] to reach agreement" on the holding of free elections and the establishment of a free and independent government of all Korea.

St. Laurent and Ilsley had been somewhat reluctant to accept nomination to this nine-nation commission. As an official document later explained, "the Canadian Government had grave doubts about the utility of this commission, because of its conviction that the Soviet boycott would extend to an actual refusal to allow the commission to operate in North Korea [a zone of Soviet occupation]. Also, Canada did not wish to endorse the use of the commission by the United States as part of an aggressive policy toward the Soviet Union."

Events soon showed these misgivings to be well founded. However, since Canada had voted in favor of General Marshall's resolution, St. Laurent and Ilsley felt they had no honorable reason for refusing to serve on the commission they had thus helped to establish. And so, without enthusiasm, they accepted.

They were not prepared for Prime Minister King's reaction to this decision. He was more than merely disturbed, he was appalled. With a violence that seemed, to colleagues and officials, out of all proportion to the occasion, he demanded that the decision be reversed, the acceptance rescinded, and the Canadian policy toward Korea revert to one of non-involvement.

Colleagues might have been less astonished had they known then what they learned later: that Mackenzie King used his frequent visits to London as opportunities to commune with the spirit world. The medium Geraldine Cummins revealed after King's death that in at least one such séance he was warned by the ghost of President Franklin D. Roosevelt to beware of the Far East. It was there, said Roosevelt's ghost, that the next war would break out.

Mackenzie King himself used this phrase, in talking to several people in Ottawa about the urgency of getting off the Korea commission. Officials vividly remember an evening when he invited St. Laurent to dine alone with him at Laurier House, and there gave him persuasion that amounted to instruction to reverse his recent decision. St. Laurent refused. He thought since Ilsley had acted on the instruction of the competent authority, the Acting Prime Minister, the Government was obliged to support and act upon his decision.

If any official record of that conversation exists, it has not yet been published. However, officials who were close to both men at the time say it marked a major watershed in Canadian history. Mackenzie King's wishes had never before been successfully defied by men who remained in his Cabinet. This time, defiance was effective. Not only Ilsley but the whole Cabinet backed St. Laurent's refusal to repudiate the acceptance of membership in UNTCK, and a Canadian delegate (Dr. George Patterson, interim head of the Canadian Liaison Mission in Tokyo) was dispatched to Seoul for the first meeting of the commission on January 12, 1948.

Nevertheless, even without any warnings from beyond the grave, other Canadian ministers shared Mackenzie King's misgivings to some extent. Canada remained an unenthusiastic and reluctant member. It was Canada's attitude, according to the official summary above quoted, "that if no truly national elections under the commission's supervision could be arranged, the commission should disband. . . . The Canadian representative maintained that the commission had no mandate to operate only in South Korea." The Canadian delegation therefore suggested to the UN that the commission "be asked to take no further action." Only Australia supported this motion, and Canada remained on the commission for another few months. But no regret was felt by anybody when, on December 12, 1948, the Assembly adopted a United States resolution setting up a new UN commission on Korea with Canada and the Ukraine deleted from the list of members.

The whole incident—both the halfhearted participation and the wholehearted withdrawal—illustrated a psychological split that has been typical of Canadian policy for a hundred years. The search for Canadian identity has an inner consistency of its own, but outwardly it is often expressed in contradictory ways, and this has been particularly true in the field of foreign policy.

On the one hand, there has always been a streak of isolationism —not limited to French Canadians, as some English Canadians think, but shared by every Canadian prime minister, including John A. Macdonald. (Sir John's best-known utterance on imperial affairs is the campaign slogan of 1891: "A British subject I was born, a British subject I will die." Not so well known, but more characteristic, was his reply in 1885 to a British request for Canadian help in the Sudan: "The Suez Canal is nothing to us. Our men and money would merely be sacrificed to get Gladstone and Co. out of the hole they have plunged themselves into by

their own imbecility." Thirty-seven years later Mackenzie King
gave a similar brush-off to a similar request when, during the
Chanak crisis of 1922, Lloyd George and Winston Churchill made
a public and rather peremptory appeal for contributions to an
"imperial" show of force against the Turks. Characteristically,
King answered neither yes nor no, but merely evaded the request
until the crisis was over.)

Side by side with the isolationism, however, has always been
a desire to get into the active business of international affairs
and play an independent role there. This sentiment, too, goes all
the way back to John A. Macdonald and has been shown by
every prime minister since. It is not as contradictory to the sentiment of isolation as it seems to be. Both spring from the same
root—a distrust of other people's competence, or good faith, in
handling affairs that affect Canada.

John A. Macdonald acquired this distrust in negotiation of a
fisheries treaty with Washington in 1870. The British Ambassador
to Washington led the negotiating team, since Canada was not
yet deemed to have any independent existence outside her own
borders, but the Canadian Prime Minister was graciously permitted
to form part of the British delegation. He came away bitterly
disappointed and convinced that Canadian interests had been badly
let down by the British, either through ignorance or for their
own interest or both.

Wilfrid Laurier had the same feeling, with even more reason,
when Britain named the third man to the commission that decided
Canada's dispute with the United States over the Alaska boundary,
at the turn of the century. President Theodore Roosevelt had been
uttering threats of what he would do if the commission failed
to come down on the American side of the argument. Rightly
or wrongly, Canadians believed (and still believe) that Britain
put her own friendly relations with the U.S. ahead of the interests
of Canada.

This suspicion, or others like it, underlay Sir Robert Borden's
attitude during World War I, and the famous or notorious Resolution Nine that Borden sponsored at the Imperial War Confer-

ence of 1917—the resolution that the dominions should be consulted in the formulation of imperial war policy. And the only difference of view between Borden and Mackenzie King would have been that King rejected the very idea of an "imperial" policy. He thought Canada should follow a *Canadian* foreign policy, and that the "single voice of Empire" so cherished in London did not and should not exist.

It was the desire for independence, as well as the desire to stay out of European quarrels, that prompted King's policy of "no commitments" in the interval between the wars. Yet 1939 had proved again that, when a major crisis comes, Canada cannot stay out of it but is propelled, by a mixture of emotional and rational considerations, into the thick of it. And once this fact of life was accepted, the problem was how to make the best of it.

For a time during World War II, Mackenzie King thought this problem had solved itself. Britain was at war while a sympathetic United States was neutral—and not only neutral but bound by a Neutrality Act whereby a wary and isolationist U. S. Senate had deliberately frustrated any urge the White House might feel to become involved in other people's wars. So Canada became a channel of communication between belligerent Britain and neutral America, and sometimes assisted in certain patriotic evasions of the American neutrality law.

Looking back now, we may doubt that Canada was ever as important in this role as Mackenzie King thought it was. One of the proudest moments of King's life, as he freely admitted, was when he was invited to Ogdensburg, New York, in August 1940, to spend the night on President Roosevelt's private car. He has recorded in his diary how the Permanent Joint Defense Board, an innocuous body which for some reason is still in existence, was concocted as a plausible cover for what Roosevelt and King were really discussing, which was the swap of British bases in North America for fifty over-age American destroyers.

It's not easy to see just why Mackenzie King was so urgently needed as a messenger in this matter, between two men who were already exchanging long personal cables every day. More likely, President Roosevelt's real purpose was to soothe Mackenzie King's own sensibilities and make sure he would not be upset by Britain giving the U.S. a base in Newfoundland—a step which did, in fact, cause a number of complications when Newfoundland became part of Canada in 1949.

But there can be no doubt whatever that King *thought* his role as a channel of communication was important, nor that he enjoyed it immensely. His pride in this office reached a climax, no doubt, on his first wartime visit to Britain a year later, when Winston Churchill coined the phrase that has since become one of the Great Canadian Clichés. Speaking at a Lord Mayor's luncheon at the Guildhall on September 4, 1941, Churchill referred to Canada as "the linch-pin of the English-speaking world."

King heard more to the same effect when he visited Britain just before D-Day, in May 1944. At a small dinner at Chequers, the country home of British prime ministers, at which Mackenzie King was guest of honor, Churchill said: "We all look to you as the link with America. That fraternal association must be kept up, and we look to you above all to keep the two together. Canada is the interpreter."

It's easy to imagine how King must have glowed, as any Canadian would, at such flattering words. And therefore it is even easier to imagine what a shock it must have been when King learned, the very next day, what Churchill had really meant by them. It was not at all what King thought he meant.

Churchill was explaining at the luncheon table the plans he and President Roosevelt had made for organization of the United Nations after the war. There would be a central council of four great powers (China had been thrown in to please the United States, Churchill said contemptuously; there was of course no mention of France). Then there would be regional councils in various parts of the world, and "on the regional council in the Americas, we in Britain hope that Canada would represent Britain."

Between the lines of the rather terse entries in King's diary for that day, one can discern that this was one of the major shocks of his whole life. He had supposed that during five years of war, in one of which Canada had been Britain's only strong ally, a sense of true partnership had developed—a partnership not quite perhaps between equals, but at least between "autonomous communities equal in status, in no way subordinate one to the other," to quote the Balfour Declaration of 1926, the nearest thing the modern Commonwealth has to a Declaration of Independence, in which King himself had played a strong hand eighteen years before. Now it turned out that this was all illusion. His supposed partners, of whom Churchill was the most eminent spokesman, were still rooted in the same old attitude, the same old determination to restore the "single voice of Empire" and have it spoken from Whitehall, that King had been fighting all his life.

King was very much taken aback, but he did not lose his presence of mind. He spoke up at once, to challenge both of the assumptions that underlay the Roosevelt-Churchill plan. First, he said, there should not be any monopoly of control by the great powers, be they four or three or any other small number. Second and even more important, Canada would certainly not consider herself the representative of any other country, nor would she want any other country to represent her. Canada intended to speak for herself.

He made the same point even more explicitly a few days later, at the luncheon preceding his speech to both Houses of Parliament in St. Stephen's Hall, Westminster. "We would wish," said King, "our own right of representation, if not as one of the Big Three or Four, at least as one of the middle powers, medium powers that should be brought into the world organization in some way that would recognize that power and responsibility go together."

It was perhaps an appropriate footnote to that disheartening day that when King went to make his speech to both Houses in St. Stephen's Hall, the Speaker of the House of Commons in introducing him used a cant phrase that he obviously meant to be flattering, but that must have had an ironic ring in King's ears. The Speaker described Canada as a nation of "twelve million Britishers"

—exactly what King had spent his life trying to show that they were not!

But if King was disappointed and disillusioned by his 1944 trip to Britain, he was far from being disabled. He came back to Canada with a new resolve to pursue the old objective—Canadian independence—in the new context of postwar organization.

The problem was to find a middle role for middle powers like Canada. King would have agreed with Churchill, Roosevelt, and Stalin that the truly petty nations of the world—the Costa Ricas of that time, the Upper Voltas of today—should not be endowed with imaginary power by the United Nations Charter. But he was equally determined that the smaller nations with real strength, like Canada or Australia (or, in the situation of 1945, France), should not merely be lumped in with the powerless rabble in a General Assembly that would be nothing but a talk shop.

Hence King developed the concept of "functional responsibility." Its motto might have been: "Let those who can, do." It was the theme of Canadian discourse all through the last year of the war, at the preparatory conference at Dumbarton Oaks, and at the founding conference of the United Nations itself in San Francisco. And it was (though it was not always acknowledged to be) the exact opposite of the "linch-pin" concept. Canada was trying to get in between the great powers, all right, but not to mediate. The object was to make sure that the great powers did not dispose of our affairs to suit their convenience.

Canada wanted to play an active role, Canada wanted to be recognized and respected in international affairs. But at the same time Canada still retained more than a shred of the old isolationism, the fear of becoming involved in foreign quarrels. The Korean assignment was one illustration of this; another was the occupation of Germany.

The subject came up in the Canadian House of Commons when, in the winter of 1946–47, it began to appear that the great powers had no intention of inviting small (or even "middle") powers to the peace conference with, or rather upon, Germany.

Canada had been acutely dissatisfied with the conference in Paris in the summer and autumn of 1946, where it seemed that the great powers had in fact made all the decisions on the treaties with the Axis satellites and the smaller belligerents were called in merely to rubber-stamp them. However, at least the smaller countries were there. Preliminary indications were that, in the case of the German treaty, not even this privilege would be granted.

From the standpoint of twenty years later it seems a minor grievance, since in fact the conference has never taken place at all, but in 1947 it caused a spontaneous and unanimous burst of indignation. All parties in Canada, and not least the Liberal Party then in power, were furious—the Opposition had fewer inhibitions about saying so in public, but the Government was probably even more angry.

In the course of an emotional debate on the question, Opposition spokesmen brought up a related but different topic. Why had not Canada been included, as an active participant in the conquest of Germany, in the postwar occupation of the defeated Reich?

Louis St. Laurent, Minister of External Affairs, gave a reply that became instantly famous and is still unforgotten: "The reason why we have no occupying troops in Germany is that we were kicked out."

That's at least what MPs and parliamentary reporters thought they heard him say. When the printed Hansard came up next day, though, the words appeared not as "kicked out" but as "left out." Either we had all misheard him, or the Minister had committed the sin of altering the substance of Hansard.

If he did change Hansard, though, he had this much valid justification: it was the amended version, "left out," that was factually correct. Canada had not needed to be kicked out, because Canada made no effort or request to be included among the occupying powers, and had no intention of doing so. Canadian troops wanted home, not more years of exile in a war-torn Europe.

Brooke Claxton, Minister of National Defense, made that clear in the same debate: "There is no proof that the return to their homeland of Canadians, many of whom had been absent for six years, had any effect whatever on our position abroad, or in the making of the peace." The Netherlands, he went on, *had* contributed troops to the occupation but had no more influence with the Big Four on that account. And he turned directly to Gordon Graydon, the Opposition foreign affairs critic, with this challenge: "What's your idea of the size of the force Canada must have in Germany in order to have some weight? Would we need to have five thousand, or ten thousand, or fifteen thousand Canadians kept from their homes?"

Both sides evidently agreed upon the major object of Canadian foreign policy in those early postwar years. It was "to have some weight"—to be taken seriously, and to be effectively consulted when the big decisions were faced. But within weeks of that heated debate in March 1947, Canada had started work on a quite different kind of project—a joint effort for peace in which Canada took the initiative.

The whole world was living in a state of chronic alarm in those days, with Andrei Vishinsky at the United Nations giving a virtually constant display of Josef Stalin's implacable hostility toward the capitalist world, but no nation was more keenly aware of this than Canada. It was in Canada, after all, that Igor Gouzenko had so dramatically revealed the existence of a Cold War which had never stopped even at the height of the hot war with Nazi Germany. At the Paris Peace Conference of 1946, Molotov and the other Soviet delegates walked out when Mackenzie King made his speech. Small wonder that Canada was rather particularly conscious of the rising tension between the Societ bloc and the West, and the demonstrated incapacity of the United Nations to cope with it.

When the five-power Treaty of Brussels (Britain, France, and the Benelux countries) was signed on March 17, 1947, St. Laurent's words of approval had a prophetic ring. This was, he said, "a long step toward closer political and cultural unity."

Events soon showed that he was already thinking of expanding that unity across the Atlantic.

Senior officials of the External Affairs Department, including Under Secretary Lester B. Pearson, flew cautious kites during the summer, testing public reaction to the suggestion of some smaller but stronger instrument of collective security. Then, in his speech to the United Nations General Assembly on September 18, St. Laurent spelled it out.

Nations "in search of peace and cooperation" could not and would not, he said, wait forever for action from a Security Council "frozen in futility and divided by dissension." Instead, "if forced, they may seek greater safety in an association of democratic and peace-loving states, willing to accept specific international obligations in return for a greater measure of national security." This did not mean, as he explained in later speeches, any abandonment of the United Nations or repudiation of its Charter; such an association could be formed under Article 51, which explicitly authorizes regional groupings for mutual security. But in truth the North Atlantic Treaty Organization, for which these were the first formal proposals, has seldom been confused with the United Nations.

The treaty was signed in Washington on April 4, 1949, when St. Laurent had become Prime Minister of Canada and L. B. Pearson had taken his place at External Affairs. It was by no means universally popular in Canada, though it got unanimous approval in the House of Commons. This new overseas commitment was the occasion, in fact, for almost the last flare-up of specifically French-Canadian isolationism. French-language newspapers in Montreal and Quebec City saw it as "appeasement of the imperialists" in the Liberal Party, and attacked St. Laurent as a mere "half-French-Canadian" (which, literally speaking, he was).

But by this time too many things had happened to let anyone bask in the old illusion of isolation. The Czech coup in February 1948, the Berlin blockade and the response of the Allied airlift in the autumn (a response which could have become at any

moment the start of World War III, if Russian fighters had
started knocking down American or British aircraft)—these, plus
the daily exchanges of harsh words at the United Nations, made
it difficult for anyone to suppose that a country like Canada,
lying between the U.S. and the U.S.S.R., could sit out a major
war.

It was perhaps a concession to this traditional feeling, though,
that Canada insisted on the inclusion in the North Atlantic
Treaty of Article II, the article that provides for economic as well
as military cooperation. It turned out in practice, of course, to be
a completely dead letter. NATO is not an economic organization
and was never really intended to be one. But Article II was needed
so that St. Laurent, Pearson, and others (no doubt for their own
reassurance as well as the nation's) could insist that NATO was
"more than a mere military alliance."

In fact, of course, it wasn't. When L. B. Pearson was made one
of a committee of "three wise men" in the summer of 1956, to
make a final desperate effort to discover or to contrive some non-
military purpose for NATO, he and his two colleagues had to
report failure. Article II was never more than a monument to
Canada's repugnance for purely military involvements abroad, for
sending Canadians overseas on solely military missions.

Serving abroad still seemed in 1948, with the memory of 1939–
45 so fresh, to be a tremendous sacrifice on the part of the soldiers
assigned to this duty. It would have seemed very odd, almost sub-
versive, had anyone prophesied that within a few years Canadian
soldiers and airmen, their wives and their children would be
looking forward to their European assignments with excitement,
and looking back on them with a nostalgia that many more
years would not entirely cure.

IX

An End and a Beginning:
Mackenzie King to St. Laurent

OLD MEN hate to let go. It took Mackenzie King a full year to
bring himself to retire from the leadership of the Liberal Party.
Then it took him three more months, and a breakdown in health,
to give up the office of Prime Minister.

Of the breakdown in health, he seems to have had plenty of
warning. When he came back in December 1947 from the fairly
protracted European tour that followed his attendance at the
royal wedding, King was already feeling far from well.

"An old dog is bad enough, but a sick dog is worse," he told
his Minister of Finance, Douglas Abbott, "and I'm a sick old
dog these days."

Even before leaving he had talked to his colleagues about retirement. As he recalled later in a public speech of somewhat
premature farewell, he had been thinking of it since the previous
summer and had taken it up with the Cabinet in September.
But when he finally decided to make the announcement, to the
National Liberal Federation on January 20, 1948, he was careful
to lard it with qualifications.

"As you well know," he said not quite truthfully, "I have not
concealed my desire to be allowed to retire from active politics
just as soon as the party's interests, and the country's, would seem
to justify that step. . . .

"The one thing I would dislike more than anything else, after
the years I have had of party leadership and of office, is that I
should ever be accused of having held on to the position of leadership to what might be termed the last moment—and then, what-

ever the circumstances might be, to have it said that I let the party down, so to speak, because of not having let the party know sufficiently in advance of any fears I might have entertained of finding myself unequal to the task of leadership in a national campaign."

And so he formally requested that the party call a convention, the first since 1919, in August. But what was the convention to do?

The Prime Minister's words were ambiguous: "I cannot forget that a man's allotted time is three score years and ten, and that I am now in my seventy-fourth year. It seems to me, therefore, that the party should have *at least the opportunity* [my italics] to consider what in its own best interest would be for the best, and that as its leader I should not be responsible for longer withholding that opportunity."

The audience gave him a standing ovation, but its members were puzzled. Some thought—rightly, as it turned out—that this was a swan song, and were moved almost to tears. Others thought, perhaps not altogether wrongly, that the old man was leaving a whole array of back doors open so that *if* he should feel better by August, and *if* the party should choose to urge him to stay, then he might after all carry on at least to the thirtieth, and not just to the twenty-ninth, anniversary of his accession to the Liberal leadership on August 7, 1919. Mackenzie King had a fondness for round figures, especially in celebrating anniversaries.

The doubt was widespread enough that when, several months later, King made another and more definite retirement speech at the Press Gallery dinner, he brought on an unprecedented incident. Gallery dinner speeches are traditionally, and very strictly, off the record. But King's retirement speech was deemed to be such hot news even then, that the Canadian Press rang him up next morning, asked if he had any objection to the speech being published, and on being told he hadn't, dispatched a complete report of it to Monday morning's newspapers. The competing agency, British United Press, and the large platoon of special correspondents, who had taken it for granted that the off-record

rule would be binding, were furious at having been thus scooped
on a speech that everyone had heard, and the bitterness persisted for a long time.

But if King had mental reservations, the Cabinet didn't. The
ministers knew that the Old Man was going to retire in August,
and most of them—all but one—knew who would succeed him.
The one who didn't know was the Right Honorable James Gar-
field Gardiner, Minister of Agriculture, Liberal sachem of Saskatchewan, and a man who had long nursed the honorable ambition to be Primo Minister. Right up to the moment that the
results of the ballot were announced, Jimmy Gardiner thought he
was going to win. At Canadian political conventions the delegates are not obliged, as they should be, to stand up and be
counted—they vote by secret ballot and so can avoid the embarrassment of telling any candidate they intend to vote against him.
Enough moral cowards had lied to Jimmy Gardiner to keep him
in a false optimism to the very end.

But the Cabinet choice was not Gardiner, shrewd and able
politician as he was. The choice fell on a man who only seven
years before had had no notion of ever entering politics—the
quiet, courteous, rather self-effacing corporation lawyer from Quebec City who, when no one of anything like equal stature could
be found to enter Mackenzie King's wartime Cabinet and stay
in it through two conscription crises, had calmly put his reputation on the line.

Louis Stephen St. Laurent did almost no campaigning or
lobbying to win the Liberal leadership—so little, in fact, that his
followers were somewhat disturbed. His nomination speech was
delivered without a text, from notes he had jotted down on a
work bench of the convention hall an hour or two before. He
acted as if he didn't really want the job, which was probably
quite true.

Indeed, he hadn't wanted to stay in politics at all, once his
war job was done. He wanted to go back to his law practice in
Quebec, and his wife was more anxious to go than he was.

At the Paris Peace Conference two years before, Mackenzie

King had offered Brooke Claxton the portfolio of External Affairs which, until then, had always been held by the Prime Minister. External Affairs would have been the summit of Claxton's ambition at the time, but he advised Mackenzie King to choose someone else.

"If you offer it to St. Laurent," said Claxton, "I think he would accept."

"Out of the question," King replied. "I've spoken to him several times about staying on, but he's determined to go back to Quebec City."

"I suggest you try it anyway," Claxton said. "He might be tempted—and if we could get him to stay on, it would be a great thing for Canada."

Claxton's hunch was right. St. Laurent did change his mind when offered the tempting post of External Affairs; Claxton himself got the onerous, thankless job of National Defense, and two years later had the ultimate disappointment of seeing another man, L. B. Pearson, get the coveted job that he himself, out of loyalty to the party and the Government, had turned down.

Once St. Laurent yielded to the persuasion to remain in federal politics, the succession to Mackenzie King became a foregone conclusion. Already the great majority of his colleagues had decided he was the one, from among their own number, under whom they'd prefer to serve.

This called for an act of renunciation by several younger men, and by their respective organizations. Brooke Claxton, Doug Abbott, Stuart Garson, the Premier of Manitoba, Angus L. Macdonald of Nova Scotia had all been mentioned for the top job from time to time, and some of them took it seriously. So had, and did, the then Minister of Health and Welfare, Paul Martin of Windsor, Ontario.

They all knew, of course, that none of them could win against St. Laurent in 1948. That wasn't the point. Except for Angus Macdonald, they were all young enough to be eligible for the *next* Liberal convention—St. Laurent, after all, was only eight

years younger than Mackenzie King, and might decide to retire
after one more Parliament.

But if all of them were to run, there was just an outside chance
that they might divert enough votes from St. Laurent to make
Jimmy Gardiner a first-ballot leader, and after that anything
might happen. So the young men got together before the convention opened, and agreed among themselves not to let their names
go forward.

As the delegates began to assemble, though, an odd thing
happened. Something called the "Draft Paul Martin Movement"
circulated an open invitation among the arriving delegates:

"Come to Room 152, Château Laurier, tonight between eight
and nine for an important talk about making Paul Martin leader
of the Liberal Party. Bring everyone who believes that Martin's
The Man."

Pondering this missive, the other young contenders decided
to change their strategy. Instead of ordering their men not to
put their names in nomination, they sent out word to do the
opposite—nominate everybody. Even C. D. Howe's name was
thrown in for good measure, to his apparent embarrassment next
day. The plan was that each man should be nominated, then
formally refuse to stand and ask his backers to vote for St. Laurent
instead. They figured, correctly as it turned out, that this would
help Paul Martin resist any temptation he might feel to yield to
a "spontaneous" nomination from the floor. The plan worked.
With audible reluctance, but firmly, Martin too declined to let
his name go forward "at this time." (His overenthusiastic backers
had already upset him by marching into the convention hall,
waving placards and led by a pipers' band, in the middle of
Mackenzie King's farewell speech.)

That parade of withdrawals left the field virtually undivided.
(C. G. Power, the unreconstructed, old-style Liberal who had resigned from the King Cabinet on the conscription issue in 1944,
was a candidate in name only—he wanted to give a rallying point
to any Liberals who might happen to agree with the point of view
he had been urging on the party, but he knew perfectly well he'd

get only a handful of votes, and he did.) The real contestants were St. Laurent and Gardiner, and even between them it was hardly a contest. St. Laurent won on the first ballot by a crushing majority.

But now began a curious interlude. St. Laurent was Liberal Party leader, but Mackenzie King was still Prime Minister. It was King (though with St. Laurent's full approval) who persuaded the brilliant Canadian diplomat Lester B. Pearson, whose position as Under Secretary of State for External Affairs meant permanent head of the Canadian foreign service, to leave the safe haven of the civil service for the uncharted and uncertain seas of politics.

Pearson was sworn in as Secretary of State for External Affairs—St. Laurent's post—on September 10, 1948. His once and future leader, Louis St. Laurent, was not sworn as Prime Minister until November 15, and then only because Mackenzie King had collapsed shortly after his arrival at the Commonwealth Prime Ministers Conference in London, and St. Laurent had to fly over to take his place.

So for two months and five days St. Laurent was kept waiting in the wings, a party leader without a post in the Government of which he was Prime Minister-elect, because King couldn't bring himself to face the awful reality of not being Prime Minister any more. *Saturday Night* published a witty and withering cartoon showing King on hands and knees, playing with an electric train, while St. Laurent in the garb of a small boy stood wistful and empty-handed beside a Christmas tree.

Obviously this couldn't have gone on very long, but it did in fact go on until King was felled by the illness from which he never fully recovered. In the two years of life that remained to him he never summoned strength enough for any real work, not even the memoirs for which he had been keeping his famous, massive diary all these years.

To call King's retirement the end of an era is an understatement. His career had spanned not one era but three, not one

reign but five, not one government but seven, of which three
were his own—or eight, if you count the St. Laurent Government
which he arranged (however reluctantly) and under which he sat
for six months as a private MP. He had been sworn as a deputy
minister under Queen Victoria, as a minister under Edward VII,
as a Prime Minister under George V, Edward VIII and George
VI. He had been a guest at the wedding of Elizabeth II when she
was still the Princess Elizabeth, and he sent personal congratulations to her on the birth of Prince Charles. King George VI called
on him in his sickroom in the Dorchester Hotel, during the illness
that brought his active career to an end.

Because of that illness he never got to a single meeting of the
Commonwealth Conference on which he had set such store that
he had clung to office in order to attend it for one last time.
Yet his journey to London that year was not wasted. Some people
thought at the time, indeed, that it was a fitting climax to his
whole career, a last and greatest service to the modern Commonwealth he had helped to create twenty-two years before.

The 1948 conference was the one that formally admitted India
and Pakistan to membership in the Commonwealth as free and
independent nations. Pandit Jawaharlal Nehru, Prime Minister
of India, had grave scruples about coming in. How could he, who
had spent eight and a half years in His Britannic Majesty's
prisons, now hold high office in a Commonwealth of which the
British King was the head?

Nehru talked about his scruples, when he called upon the ailing
Canadian stateman in his hotel sickroom. King's rejoinder was
to tell about his grandfather William Lyon Mackenzie, the rebel
of 1837 who had fled to the United States with a price on his
head. King told of the proclamation, issued in Queen Victoria's
name under signature of Sir John Colborne, and offering a thousand pounds' reward for the capture of William Lyon Mackenzie
dead or alive, which now hung in the hallway outside King's
study in Laurier House, Ottawa. Beside it hung the parchment
that proclaimed the rebel's grandson a member of the Order of
Merit, a royal order of rare distinction which is limited to twenty-

four persons. King used to say often, and must have said again on this occasion: "My chief reason for accepting the Order of Merit was to hang it beside that proclamation of the price on my grandfather's head."

Nehru was impressed. He called again next day and left a gift of jade, which King valued highly for the rest of his life. Indian as well as Canadian officials have told me that this interview weighed heavily in Nehru's final decision to enter the Commonwealth, prison record and all.

But whatever King himself may have thought of that incident, there was no doubt what he himself regarded as the greatest achievement of his career. He answered that question at one of his last press conferences as Prime Minister: "Keeping Canada united during the war."

It's rather ironic to reflect that Mackenzie King could not hope to be chosen Liberal leader today because he spoke no French, not even the bare minimum that Pearson and Diefenbaker are able to display. His formal obeisances to bilingualism, at campaign meetings in Quebec in the 1940s, never ran longer than a sentence or two in an execrable accent. Yet his concern for the unity of French and English Canada was perhaps the most consistent theme of his whole half century in public life. And despite the rather ungraceful reluctance and delay of his last few months in office, this theme was maintained in the succession that King played a major part in arranging.

St. Laurent, too, would give the same sort of answer to the question. The marriage of French and English in Canada, from which he himself had so literally sprung, was for him, too, the primary concern of statesmanship.

Yet by the quietly revolutionary standards of the 1960s, he would not have been thought either typical or adequate as a spokesman of *la belle province*. He cared little for the cults of biculturalism. Having himself learned both languages in infancy, he thought it natural for other French Canadians to do so—that English Canadians should be unilingual he took for granted.

As for the "special status" of Quebec which is now demanded

and more or less conceded, St. Laurent would have none of it.
It was he, not some Ontario Orangeman, who said that "Quebec
is a province like the others." Maurice Duplessis, the arch-apostle
of "autonomy" for Quebec, was probably the only man in
Canada whom St. Laurent regarded, and who in return regarded
him, as an enemy.

St. Laurent's service to the Canadian identity was not to advance the cause of Quebec or French Canada as such, but to
present to all Canada the image of grace, courtesy, and culture
as the image of French Canada. For his staff, his Cabinet and
the Members of Parliament he proved to be as easy to work for
as Mackenzie King had been difficult. Opposition parties found
him an almost impossible man to attack. (They relieved their
frustration by attacking his ministers, especially Claxton and
Howe, who gave as good, or as bad, as they got.)

These qualities quickly endeared him to the English-speaking
voters. The French-speaking, who also appreciated them, had not
yet discovered his indifference to Quebec's special claims—or if
they had, they didn't care. It was enough that one of *les nôtres*
should be Prime Minister of Canada.

So when he called a general election six months after taking
office, Prime Minister St. Laurent came back with what was then
the greatest electoral triumph in Canadian history. He won one
hundred and ninety-four seats, counting four independents who
voted with the Government. George Drew, who had replaced
John Bracken as Conservative leader about the same time St.
Laurent replaced Mackenzie King, went crashing down from sixty-
seven seats to forty-one.

It seemed a magnificent beginning to a new day. Not for
several years did anyone realize that it was, instead, the beginning
of a long twilight.

X

The Reluctant Dragon Killer: Canada in Korea

IT WAS A COINCIDENCE, but an appropriate one, that the decision to send Canadian ground troops to the Korean War was reached on the train that brought the St. Laurent Cabinet back to Ottawa from the funeral of Mackenzie King.

In spite of (or, in part, because of) the fact that he had headed the Government of Canada throughout World War II, Mackenzie King was far more a symbol of Canadian isolation than of Canadian involvement overseas. He had been chief author of Canada's interwar foreign policy: "No commitments." His war leadership was remembered by more people, friend and foe, for his resistance to the clamor for all-out conscription than for any of his uninspiring calls to arms. And in the specific case of Korea, King was the man who had tried—unsuccessfully, but not entirely without effect—to keep Canada from becoming involved in any way.

When the Korean War broke out on Sunday, June 25, 1950, the Canadian reaction showed that Mackenzie King was still alive in spirit as well as in body.

During Sunday and Monday the Cabinet evidently assumed that nobody was going to do much of anything about the North Korean invasion of South Korea. After all Dean Acheson, U. S. Secretary of State, had made a public statement in January that the outer perimeter of American interest and American security was a line that ran *between* Japan and the Korean peninsula. The last American troops had withdrawn from Korea a full year before—June 29, 1949. When the Canadian Minister of External

Affairs, L. B. Pearson, went through Tokyo on his way home
from the Colombo conference in February, American generals
had given him exhaustive and emphatic briefings on the utter
uselessness of Korea, North or South, as a military base for
Western forces. He believed them.

The UN Security Council met in New York on the Sunday and
was able, thanks to the absence of the Soviet delegate (who had
been boycotting the Council for several months), to pass a strongly
worded resolution against the North Korean aggression. In the
Commons next day Pearson sounded a note of cautious optimism,
or what passed for optimism at the time: "As a result of this
intervention by the United Nations, some effective action may be
possible."

He didn't really think any action would be taken. At an off-
record press conference the same evening, his answers to questions
were obviously based on this assumption. He tried to persuade the
reporters (and perhaps himself) that the expected failure of
Western nations to intervene in Korea would *not* mean the failure of collective security in principle. Korea was a special case.
As the Toronto *Globe and Mail* correspondent said in a front-
page dispatch the next morning:

"While the situation is explosive and *likely to remain so for
some days* [my italics] it is rather different from what would
already have developed had the Korean incident taken place in
the area of the North Atlantic."

Pearson went home from the press conference just in time to
get a telephone call from the Canadian Embassy in Washington.
The early edition of the New York *Times* was already on the
street with President Truman's announcement that the United
States would fight in Korea against the Communist attack.

By Wednesday four countries announced the dispatch of naval
forces to Korea—Britain, Australia, New Zealand, and the Netherlands. Canada followed suit on Friday. Two destroyers, later
increased to three, were ordered to proceed westward from Esqui-
malt to be ready if called upon by the United Nations. Meanwhile South Korean defenses had already crumpled under the

Communist assault, the United States had flown in troops from Japan, and those troops were already in battle.

During the next two weeks they fared badly. The North Korean invaders seemed to be carrying all before them—overran the South Korean capital of Seoul, pushed southward until they were only about a hundred miles from Pusan, the southernmost port of Korea, which was the indispensable beachhead for the landing of United Nations reinforcements and supplies. So far, to call the Korean operation a "United Nations" affair was sheer flattery to the organization, since in fact all the foreign troops there were Americans, but this was far from American intentions. They wanted help, urgently, and they asked for it.

On Friday, July 14, UN Secretary-General Trygve Lie issued an open appeal to all fifty-two nations then members of the UN asking them to send ground troops to reinforce the Americans in Korea. In Ottawa at least, such a public exhortation by a man who was, after all, an international civil servant was regarded as shocking bad form. "Unthinkable," one Canadian official called it. The idea of embarrassing member nations by asking them out loud to do something, without first ascertaining privately whether or not they were willing to do it, struck him as sheer heresy.

Reporters found it difficult to get any quick reaction from the Canadian government. Prime Minister St. Laurent was away fishing. So was the Minister of National Defense, Brooke Claxton. (His department said later he hadn't really been merely fishing, he'd been in Newfoundland for important talks with U.S. commanders at the American bases there, but anyway he was away.) L. B. Pearson was off on a speaking tour. In one of his speeches, delivered on the evening of the day Trygve Lie issued his appeal for troops, Pearson warned his audience that Canada would have to be careful not to overdo aid to Korea, since trouble might break out elsewhere in a troubled world.

The danger that Canada might overdo her aid to Korea seemed to be extremely slight. When an Ottawa reporter got a telephone call through to Prime Minister St. Laurent at his summer home in St. Patrice on the Lower St. Lawrence, and asked him for comment on Trygve Lie's appeal, he said "I wish you newspapermen wouldn't bother me when I'm on holiday," and hung up. Later his office let it be known that, although he hadn't originally intended to do so, in view of the international situation the Prime Minister would return to Ottawa for the *regular* weekly meeting of the Cabinet on Wednesday.

He did. The Cabinet met at 11 A.M., adjourned for lunch, met again at 3 P.M., rose in time for the Prime Minister and other vacationists to catch the afternoon train out of town. While he waited for the car to take him to the station, Prime Minister St. Laurent said to the reporters who were waiting in the corridor:

"Well, gentlemen, I hope to be out fishing again by the day after tomorrow."

After he left, his office handed out an authorized statement. It said the Cabinet had decided not to send any ground troops to Korea, but instead to send an RCAF transport squadron to Washington State to ferry American troops and supplies across the Pacific.

Americans did not feel any great surge of gratitude for this kind of assistance. They had no serious shortage of transport planes or of small naval vessels. In one of his speeches the previous weekend, L. B. Pearson had remarked that Canada's dispatch of three destroyers had been "no mere token." At the U. S. Embassy in Ottawa, a senior official remarked sourly: "Okay, let's call it three tokens."

It did not enhance Canada's prestige that, on July 26, Britain, Australia, and New Zealand announced that they were sending troops to Korea immediately.

It was the next day, Thursday, July 27, that the Canadian Cabinet held its historic meeting on the train coming back from Mackenzie King's funeral in Toronto.

Sentiment within the Cabinet had not, from the very first, been as unanimously calm and collected as it appeared to the outside world. L. B. Pearson, in particular, believed and argued very strongly that Canada should do more and do it faster. As a lifelong advocate of collective security, as one of the major architects of the North Atlantic Alliance, as one who had played an active role in the United Nations and was destined to play a still more active one in future, he felt deeply humiliated at the lackluster light in which Canada was appearing.

On the trip back from the funeral, Pearson put his case more eloquently, more cogently than he had ever been able to put it before. As one of its members remarked later, this was the first time since the Korean crisis began that the ministers had been together for a period of hours without the tyranny of an agenda, free to talk the subject out. Before they reached Ottawa, Pearson had carried his point.

Ten more days went by, though, before the decision was made formal and final. Not until August 7 did Prime Minister St. Laurent go on the CBC national networks, in English and French, to announce that a special expeditionary force of one brigade would be *recruited*, not dispatched at once, for Korea. He explained the procedure thus:

"Having in mind other obligations for the employment of the Canadian armed forces, and the uncertainty of the whole world situation, we reached the conclusion that the dispatch, at this stage, of existing first-line elements of the Canadian army to Korea would be unwarranted. That remains the view of the Government. We have developed an airborne brigade group, highly trained for operations in the north, and designed to *share* [my italics] in the immediate defense of this continent. But at this time we have no expeditionary force in being."

It sounded terribly lame. The notion that five thousand fully trained professional soldiers had to be kept in Canada to repel the Red Army, in case the Soviet Union should decide to attack across the Arctic, was preposterous enough in any case—Canada's own Exercise Musk-ox, a large-scale experiment in winter and summer operations in the north, had already demonstrated that such an attack would be so difficult as to be unlikely. What made the thesis even more absurd was the fact that, although these professional soldiers would not be *sent* to Korea in their units as already constituted, any or all of them would be free to *volunteer* for Korea as members of the special force. And, of course, thousands did—about half the required number of five thousand men had volunteered by the end of the first day of recruiting, August 9. Not five thousand but eight thousand had been enrolled by August 26.

The authorities still seemed to be in no hurry to get them off. It was an unhappy but not unjust coincidence that, during the week that recruiting for Korea began, the army's public relations department put out a press release announcing "Exercise Shoofly," an experiment in mosquito combat north of tree line. The United Nations set up something called UNCACK—the UN Civilian Assistance Command, Korea—to which the United States donated $395 million worth of food and other supplies. Canada's contribution was 2800 tons of salt cod, worth $750,000.

By November 7, three months after Prime Minister St. Laurent had announced the special force, an advance party of three hundred and forty-five men reached Pusan to make the housekeeping arrangements for arrival of the brigade. The Princess Patricia's Canadian Light Infantry, Second Battalion, sailed from Seattle November 27 and reached Pusan December 18. Their time at sea covered the peak period of the Chinese attack, which drove the American, British, Australian, and South Korean forces back from just south of the Yalu River to forty miles south of Seoul. The P.P.C.L.I. was able to join the rest of the Commonwealth Brigade in the front line by February 1951, but the other two battalions of the Canadian Brigade—the Royal Canadian Regiment and the Royal Twenty-second—did not leave Seattle until April 19 and reached Pusan only on May 4. They saw action for the first time on May 17, 1951, just seven weeks before the beginning of the protracted armistice talks at Kaesong, later switched to Panmunjom, which reduced the combat in Korea to near zero and brought hostilities to a formal end two years later.

Late as they were in arriving, the Canadians gave a good account of themselves once they got there. The Princess Pats received a U. S. Presidential Citation for their conduct in battle at Kapyong on April 24, 1951. Altogether the Canadian special force lost 309 killed, 1101 wounded. Except for the South Koreans themselves and the Americans, the only contributors to the United Nations force to suffer more casualties than the Canadians were the British and perhaps the Turks (Turkish casualty figures are somewhat inexact).

This is not an effort that any army need be ashamed of. Yet the glacier pace of the Canadian government, in getting the effort launched in the first place, leached most of the glory out of it. Why were they so slow, so reluctant?

Many people guessed at the time that it was for the usual reason—fear of the political effects in French Canada. There was some documentation for this conventional view. *Le Devoir* of Montreal, when the special force was announced, complained bitterly: "What are we doing in all this? Merely proving that we are becoming more and more a satellite of Washington." And even *Le Soleil* of Quebec, which proclaimed itself "A Liberal Organ" on its own masthead in those days, said: "The best way to avoid war is not to meddle in the affairs of foreigners."

But although this reluctance was genuine enough, it was not confined to French Canada. Brooke Claxton, the decorated (D.C.M.) sergeant-major of World War I, was just as strongly against a precipitate involvement in Korea as any of his French-speaking colleagues. So was James Gardiner of Saskatchewan, if not more so. Their reasons for hesitation were many and complex.

One was distrust of American competence. It was true, after all, that Dean Acheson had said (quite unnecessarily, in the view of his Canadian critics) that American interests did not extend as far as Korea—thus leading the Communists to conclude that, if they did invade, the U.S. would not intervene. It was true that American generals, including General MacArthur, had assured L. B. Pearson that Korea was of no military use to either side, and not worth fighting for.

Much more important, though, was the fact that the appeals to Canada for help came only in the midst of military disasters which Canadian forces would have been powerless to avert, but in which they would have been hopelessly involved had they got there in time. Canada had had recent experience of that sort of appeal.

On two occasions a month apart, Canadian forces narrowly escaped being engulfed to no purpose in the military disasters of 1940. A force of battalion size was ordered to Norway in April, with the consent of the Canadian commander, General Andrew McNaughton, but without the knowledge of the Canadian government; luckily the British War Office changed its mind before this expedition to oblivion actually embarked, but the incident aroused grave misgivings in Ottawa. Then in May a Canadian Brigade group was ordered to France, just before the Dunkirk evacuation and after Allied resistance had already dissolved in chaos. This time McNaughton himself went over on a journey of reconnaissance, found the situation hopeless, and so reported to the British chiefs of staff, who called off the whole enterprise.

A year later, against its own better judgment but in deference to the wishes of Winston Churchill, Canada agreed to help "reinforce" Hong Kong. Churchill wanted no more than a token force, which indeed any force in Hong Kong would be against a Japanese attack if one came. So Canada sent two half-trained, half-armed, half-equipped battalions—the Royal Rifles of Quebec and the Winnipeg Grenadiers—to Hong Kong just in time for them to be engulfed in the Japanese explosion of conquest that followed Pearl Harbor.

Both lessons were pertinent in the Korean situation. In all three cases a small Canadian force was, or would have been, added to a much larger force under foreign command which was, in fact, retreating in disorder. In no case would the Canadian force have been large enough to make a decisive difference—it could only have shared in either victory or defeat, it could not have achieved the one or averted the other.

Deeper than these common-sense fears was the reluctance, based on much experience, to put Canadians under non-Canadian command without making sure that they would retain some freedom of choice and of initiative. On that point, at least, English- and French-speaking Canadians saw eye to eye.

So, from the standpoint of Canadian identity, the Canadian experience in Korea probably did more good as it was than as it might have been with more enthusiasm in Ottawa. French-speaking soldiers were as prominent and as active there as English—the first Canadian officer ashore in Korea was Major Roy Bourgeois, of the Royal Twenty-second, commanding the advance party of Canadians; one of the commanders of the Canadian Brigade was Brigadier Jean Allard, later commander of the Fourth Division, British Army of the Rhine, and in 1966 appointed (by now a full general) to be chief of the Canadian Defense Staff.

Long before this, all argument about the Korean War had ceased at home between the two major ethnic groups. True, not much interest was shown in it by either of them—at one point the Vancouver *Sun* ran the same Korean War story on its front page for three days running, then gleefully announced that not a single reader had noticed this fact.

But when all the cynical remarks have been made and all qualifications noted, it is still a fact that for the first time in history Canada had conducted a substantial military venture abroad without putting any visible or audible strain on the relations between French and English. As the French say, *c'est déjà quelque chose.*

XI

The Great Canadian Cultural Revolution:
Stratford and All That

CANADA'S CULTURAL REVOLUTION began in characteristic Canadian fashion, with a Government Order in Council appointing a Royal Commission.

Not that the St. Laurent Government had anything revolutionary in mind when on April 8, 1949, it set up the Royal Commission on National Development in the Arts, Letters and Sciences. Chairman was the Right Honorable Vincent Massey, soon to become the first Canadian-born Governor-General. Members were a university president, two senior professors, and an ultra-respectable engineer. Altogether it looked like a working model of the cultural Establishment, and moreover it behaved like one. It worked for two years, traveled ten thousand miles, held 224 meetings, patiently received 462 briefs and 1200 live witnesses from 13 federal Government agencies, 7 provincial Governments, 87 national and 297 local organizations that considered themselves organs of culture, including 35 private radio stations. Its report, published in the summer of 1951, was irreproachably bland.

Yet this sober document turned out to be a cultural bombshell in the upper megaton range. Its recommendations, the most important of which were implemented in due course, led to state support on an unheard-of scale for scholarship, arts, and letters. But perhaps of even greater impact in the short run were the twenty-eight "critical studies" the Commission had ordered from a platoon of eminent Canadians, and published along with its report. These provided official documentation, for the first time, for that familiar but disputed cliché: "Canada is a cultural waste-land."

One of the few Canadian novelists to win national recognition in the first half of the twentieth century was Frederick Philip Grove. A Briton born in Russia of parents who lived in Sweden, Grove was already a highly educated and sophisticated young man when he first came to Canada in 1892. While he was here his father died, unexpectedly bankrupt. The son was left stranded and penniless in a strange land, which eventually he adopted as truly his own.

It could hardly be said that Canada returned the compliment. For the first twenty years of his working life, Grove was an itinerant farm hand on the prairies, and for another twenty years thereafter he was an ill-paid rural schoolteacher. Somehow he managed to write a dozen novels during this time (in longhand, on both sides of the paper) but got none published until 1922 when he had been trying to write for thirty years.

Toward the end of his unhappy life, in an article quoted at some length in the Commission's "critical studies," Grove wrote:

"The Canadian public is ignorant, cowardly and snobbish; it is mortally afraid of ideas, and considers the discussion of first principles as a betrayal of bad manners.

"Unless they are very sure it is socially disgraceful not to own a given book, they refuse to buy it. If it is imperative socially that they are able to talk about it, they borrow it. . . . More appallingly, Canadians are at bottom not interested in their own country; I honestly believe they prefer to read about lords and dukes, or about the Civil War in the United States."

For Canadian critics, Grove had even more virulent words:

"I know of hardly one book-reviewer in Canada who, in judging a book not previously heralded by discussion in Great Britain or the United States, does not hopelessly flounder. The best that can be expected is a brief 'I like this' or 'I dislike it,' and almost invariably the reviewer likes what he should dislike and dislikes what he should like."

Actually, "reading about lords and dukes" was already somewhat out of fashion, but Lister Sinclair had some acid remarks (also quoted in the Commission study) for the self-conscious "Canadianism" that was taking its place:

"Some of us merely take care to talk about Saskatchewan and Toronto, moose and trilliums, which we may take to be the penny plain equivalent of the twopence colored Mountie. Similarly, we adjust our poetic imagery so that it keeps nudging in the right direction. . . .

"In this way we can take a story that might be located in New York or Berlin or, better still, one which it is really impossible to think of as taking place anywhere at all, and turn it into a regular piece of Canadian literature. The only trouble is that local color (as we call it) tends to make a good deal of Canadian writing haunted by geography and wild life."

Morley Callaghan, then, as now, one of Canada's best-known novelists, was quoted in a biting description of Canadian publishers:

"The Canadian publisher operates under special conditions because he can remain in business as a distributor of fiction and never publish a work of fiction by a Canadian writer. . . . Of course, fiction by Canadians has been published in this country, but the chances are that it was published in some other country first."

Some of these strictures were already out of date. Callaghan himself by then had had many novels published over a period of twenty-odd years, and knew from experience the commonsense reason for having them published abroad—a book printed in New York or London would have access to the big American or British market, and still be sold in Canada as a matter of course. The converse was not, and in most cases is not yet, true.

But in the main the reproaches were just. Callaghan, a mature novelist with a dozen books to his credit, was probably better known in Canada as chairman of a radio panel show than as a writer. Hugh MacLennan's novel *Two Solitudes* assumed the stature of a Canadian classic almost from the morrow of its publication in 1945, but to finish writing it—even though he was already the author of a successful first novel—MacLennan had to get a fellowship from the Guggenheim Foundation in the United States. Not until he sold a book to Hollywood could he have lived comfortably on the earnings of his novels.

On the other hand, there was equal justice in the counter-reproach gently phrased by the author of this "critical study," Professor Edward McCourt of the University of Saskatchewan:

"Since the fall of Quebec, much of English-speaking Canada has been populated—if somewhat thinly—by a highly literate people, drawn in part from the educated classes of the Old Country, yet in its two hundred years of existence it has produced few good books and not a single great one. What is true of literature is true of all the creative arts. When all possible allowance has been made for the difficulties under which the creative artist in Canada works, it seems strange indeed that no one of outstanding talent has spoken in a voice to catch the ear of the world."

In the performing arts it seemed rather less strange, at least in the Canada of the 1940s. Robertson Davies, one of the two or three Canadian playwrights whose work has ever had professional (albeit unsuccessful) production outside Canada, wrote the Commission's "critical study" on the theater. Davies' essay, which incidentally was the only one of twenty-eight papers to show a gleam of humor of its own, was cast in the form of a dialogue between a Mr. Lovewit and a Mr. Trueman—characters who, as Davies recalled in a prefatory note, had conducted a dialogue on the state of the English theater in a pamphlet in 1699. Some excerpts:

> TRUEMAN: I know a needy, pragmatical fellow who, for a trifle of money, will supply us with a rare show of statistics to prove anything we choose to say, and these shall provide us with appendices to drag at the tail of our memorandum, and give it weight.
>
> LOVEWIT: And I know an astrologer who has forsworn the casting of horoscopes and now gives all his time to making pie-charts for business houses.

TRUEMAN: O rare! The press agent, the pedant and the astrologer shall give our memorandum the modish air of a modern state paper. But if it is to have any sense in it, Lovewit, we must provide it. . . . I suppose, for a beginning, we must answer those who question whether the theatre exists at all in Canada, in any form which deserves careful consideration. . . .

LOVEWIT: Have you ever asked a group of Canadian schoolteachers, professionally engaged in teaching Shakespeare, how many Shakespearean plays they have seen on the stage?

TRUEMAN: I confess I have shrunk from such depressing investigation.

LOVEWIT: Their answers would sadden your heart and chill your blood, I promise you. What can they know about Shakespearean drama if they have never experienced it in its proper form? Who attempts to explain the works of Beethoven if he has never heard an orchestra play them?

TRUEMAN: You need not confine your pity to schoolteachers alone. I think it very likely that a majority of Canadians of good education—as education goes here—and good financial estate, have never seen a Shakespearean play performed.

However true this may have been in 1951, it ceased to be true—at least for the teachers of central Canada—within a very few years thereafter. Whether or not the Massey Report acted as a stimulus, an event did take place in Stratford, Ontario, between 1952 and 1953 that ranks as a minor miracle.

The wizard who wrought it was a Stratford businessman named Tom Patterson—a slim, unassuming, prematurely bald young man who had never had any other connection with the theater than as a member of the audience, and scarcely even that until his wartime service took him to London and to Europe. Patterson decided that Stratford, Ontario, like Stratford, England, should have its own Shakespearean Festival.

It seemed an improbable notion. Stratford, Ontario, had no other theater than a small local movie house, and had never entertained any ambition to have one. True, the town was modeled in many ways on its English namesake—its little river was also called the Avon (though pronounced to rhyme with "spavin" instead of "haven") and a long-dead city father had somehow contrived to save the center of town from commercial development and make of it a beautiful park. But in all other respects it was a typical, prosaic, Ontario small town with no more pretensions to culture than any other in its rich, flat, farming region.

Somehow Tom Patterson persisted. Somehow he got enough other people interested and enough money scraped together to invite the well-known British director Tyrone Guthrie to fly over from London and discuss the project. Guthie arrived in July 1952.

His analysis of the plan and his advice were candid to the point of brutality. Open-air production would not do; some kind of theater was a necessity. But a permanent theater would be too expensive, so a tent theater must be used—in a town where summer temperatures run into the high nineties. Effective presentation of Shakespeare would be expensive, but to try to do it cheaply would guarantee failure. Moreover it would not be enough to produce just one play, a reasonable repertory would be needed. Stars could be imported, indeed they would have to be in order to draw the necessary crowds, but most of the actors should be Canadian. And the imports, whoever they might be, would have to be stars of international fame and reliable competence. A failure in the first season would be more than a mere disaster, it would be a catastrophe.

To Guthrie's astonishment, the Stratford committee listened to all this, agreed with it, and decided to go ahead anyway. So when Tom Patterson went to London a few months later and asked Guthie to come out as the Stratford Festival's first director, he agreed. He also persuaded Alec Guinness to come too, as the Festival's first and glowing star.

By Christmas 1952 the project was well advanced. Tanya Moiseiwitch agreed to come as designer. Guthrie and Guinness decided on the two plays for the first season, *Richard III* and a modern-dress *All's Well That Ends Well*. Guthrie paid a five-day visit to Canada during which he interviewed 317 would-be Shakespearean actors, winnowed them down to about 60 "probables," and took a kind of informal option on the services of these latter. A site was found, for which the provincial Government gave the land. A tent was ordered from Chicago.

It was at this point that the financial magnitude of the scheme began to be clearly apparent, and it staggered many who up to then had been stouthearted. As Guthrie recalled the period, in a book that he and Robertson Davies wrote about the Stratford adventure:

"It was about now that the Jeremiahs began to have a good time, the Headshakers, the Fingerwaggers, all the vast majority of mankind who derive almost their keenest pleasure from the words 'I told you so.' It is at about this period that one must admire and respect the guts of the committee. It was still just not too late to withdraw."

The decision was to carry on, but it was not reached without stress. Some committee members resigned, washing their hands of the irresponsible harebrained scheme. Even those who voted to continue did so with some uncertainty now—the original confidence had been shaken.

The real crisis did not come until May when, strictly speaking, it *was* too late to withdraw, but for a while it looked as if no other option was open. The Chicago tent manufacturer stopped work and refused to go on until he had received a down payment which the committee did not have. Great amounts of money had been committed to other things—properties, costumes, contracts with actors at home and in Britain—before the actual cash had been collected. But a last desperate effort, a large donation from one anonymous supporter, and loyal confidence from some at least of the Festival's creditors overcame the obstacles and the show went on.

Incredibly, it was a success—artistic, financial, every other sort. Not that it made money, of course. The deficits were substantial and remained so for years. But they were at least manageable—all bills were paid, and another season confidently planned on the strength of that first magnificent season. When the second and the third seasons turned out to be equally triumphant, Canadians began at last to believe that the impossible had happened.

Canada had produced—albeit with a lot of British help, but no matter—an artistic achievement that was unchallengeably first class.

Until then, the only art in which any Canadian even dreamed of being thus classified was painting. First class or not by any international standard, Canadian painters had managed at least to satisfy their own countrymen. Painting was accepted as respectable.

Not without a struggle, though. Canadian painters had the same kind of uphill climb as all other Canadian artists. They merely had it one generation sooner.

Emily Carr, who was already famous in her own land when she died in 1945 and whose paintings of her beloved British Columbia forests are the treasures of the Vancouver Art Gallery, kept a diary intermittently at various periods of her life. Excerpts from it were published in the autumn of 1966—a plain informal narrative, a book "just to jot me down in, unvarnished me, old at 58," she wrote in 1930. Of her first trip east in 1927, and her first meeting with the already famous Group of Seven Canadian painters, Emily Carr said:

"These men are interesting and big and inspiring, so different from the foolish little artists filled with conceit that one usually meets. They have arrested the art world." And looking at an A. Y. Jackson canvas, she reflected: "His Indian pictures have something mine lack—rhythm, poetry. Mine are so downright! But perhaps his haven't got quite the love in them, of the people and the country, that mine have. How could they? He is not a westerner—and I took no liberties! I worked for history and cold fact."

But a few days later, after the failure of an exhibition on which she and the Group of Seven had all counted rather heavily, she wailed: "Canada and her sons cry out for a hearing but the people are blind and deaf. Their souls are dead. Dominated by dead England and English traditions, they are decorating their tombstones while living things clamor to be fed."

Before she went home one of her new friends recommended some books to her. "I'll get these if it costs my last penny," she confided to her diary. But when she went to another show in Toronto, a less unsuccessful one at which several Group of Seven paintings were hung, she could only stare wistfully:

"Three of them were for sale—$65, $75 and $85. How I'd love to have bought one."

Any Group of Seven painting, even by those survivors who are still painting in their eighties, would fetch thousands today.

For this and for other evidences of cultural growth there is no way of discerning all the causes. Certainly the Massey Report was one, even though its direct effects were not to be felt for several years more. Certainly the Canadian Broadcasting Corporation played a role, especially in the field of music—almost totally unknown to Canadians of a generation before, and now flourishing with local support in half a dozen cities.

There was another tremendous stimulus in the decade that followed World War II—the rush to Canada, for a variety of reasons and from an even greater variety of countries, of several million new citizens whose cultural backgrounds were richer and deeper than ours, and who changed our way of life in more ways than most of us realize.

XII

Third Force: The Postwar Immigration Boom

WHEN L. B. Pearson was in Europe for the now forgotten Peace Conference of 1946, he went over from Paris to Geneva for a few days in August to attend the final, winding-up meeting of UNRRA—the United Nations Relief and Rehabilitation Agency. UNRRA was the forerunner of the greatest international aid program ever known, a series of projects soon to write a chapter unique in all human history, but it then seemed about to go out of business with its work less than half done.

Pearson had just been appointed head of the Canadian foreign service, an unwanted promotion from his job as ambassador to Washington, and UNRRA was no longer one of his prime concerns. But he had been at the founding conference in Atlantic City three years before, had seen this infant institution through its pre- and postnatal struggles, and he wanted to be present at its deathbed too.

In Geneva he met men and women from all over Europe who were dedicated to postwar relief work and appalled at the apparent possibility that their work might be allowed to cease unfinished. One of these was C. M. Drury, later one of Pearson's Cabinet ministers but then a Canadian brigadier still in uniform, and seconded to rehabilitation work in Poland and neighboring countries. Drury and others persuaded Pearson to take a brief trip after the UNRRA conference ended, through the Displaced Persons camps in northern Europe that housed some fifty thousand exiles from the Baltic countries. These were refugees who had fled not the Nazis but the Red Army, after Stalin in 1940 had gobbled up the small republics of Latvia, Estonia, and Lithuania.

Pearson was charmed by what he saw in the Baltic camps. Unlike some other Displaced Persons, the Balts had never abdicated responsibility for their own welfare. Their camps were run like self-governing small towns. Schools for the children, vocational and other classes for adults, theater groups, orchestras, choirs—every imaginable way of keeping people cheerfully busy at no expense, the Balts had somehow managed to bring into operation.

Pearson went back to Paris, and soon afterward to Ottawa, convinced that as many as possible of these admirable folk should as soon as possible be brought to Canada. He thought they would make just the kind of citizens his country wanted and needed, and he resolved to do everything he could to bring them in.

That may seem a commonplace thought now, but in 1946 it was almost revolutionary. Ever since the beginning of the Great Depression the doors of Canadian immigration had been shut tight. There were plenty of immigrants in Canada—a slightly higher percentage, in fact, than there were in 1966—but most of them were elderly folk who had been in Canada not less than fifteen years and more commonly for thirty or forty. In the whole decade of the 1930s, fewer people were admitted to Canada than have often come in a single year since 1948. An Order in Council of March 21, 1931, barred all immigrants except British or American citizens with sufficient means to maintain themselves until they found employment (which meant, in those days, only the relatively rich), their wives or fiancées and unmarried children under eighteen, and—the only non-Anglo-Saxon category—farmers with sufficient means to set up independent, self-employed farming.

Moreover all politicians thought, and had good reason to think, that immigration was unpopular with the voters. The fear of unemployment was so deep-seated as to be almost obsessive—especially since most people, including many eminent economists, expected the postwar boom to be followed very quickly by a postwar depression. Even in 1954, when mass immigration had been resumed for six years, a Gallup Poll showed less than a majority in favor of it—and a solid majority *against* it in French-speaking Quebec.

There was more ground than mere prejudice for this hostility. An incident in the spring of 1947 showed that not all who wanted to restore Canadian immigration were moved by altruistic motives.

J. Ludger Dionne, a Liberal MP and a rich millowner from the rural Quebec county of Beauce, besought the Mackenzie King Government to give him special dispensation to bring in about a hundred girls from Poland, or rather Polish girls from the Displaced Persons camps of Europe, to work in his textile factory. He was refreshingly candid about his reasons for wanting this reinforcement of his staff. His mill employed a total of four hundred and thirty-five persons, yet its annual labor turnover exceeded five hundred. Ludger Dionne knew why.

"The trouble seems to be," he said in his letter to the Cabinet, "that people have too much money to spend."

They certainly had too much money to be interested in the wages that Dionne was used to paying. Even in Quebec, where the pay especially of female workers had never been the highest in Canada, women were averaging fifty-four cents an hour in the textile factories for an average forty-four-hour week. Dionne proposed to pay his Polish girls twenty-five cents an hour to start, and later to raise them to thirty cents. In return for bringing them out he would bind them to two-year contracts at these wages. Originally he intended to deduct, from the girls' weekly pay, an amount that in two years would equal the cost of their ocean fares, but apparently he dropped that in the end—possibly realizing that an indentured labor force bound to work two years at half the prevailing wage rate was worth a modest investment on his part.

Dionne got his special permission, an Order in Council of April 1, 1947. He had brought his hundred girls to Canada and put them to work on their two-year contracts before his project attracted any public notice. But when it did come up in the House of Commons it came up with a loud bang.

On June 2, M. J. Coldwell, national leader of the socialist CCF Party, demanded and got an emergency debate on "a question of urgent public importance," namely "the traditional policy of Parliament that indentured labor shall be completely prohibited." He quoted a newspaper interview with one of the Polish girls, who said, "We signed a contract to work for Mr. Dionne for two years; we're not allowed to leave or to get married during that time." (Dionne later denied that the contracts forbade the girls to get married. However, as one of his managers explained to reporters, "Down here it's considered a disgrace for a married woman to work, no matter how great her need." And since the girls were certainly bound to work for two years, perhaps they thought the pledge of celibacy was implied.)

Opposition parties had a field day. Labor Minister Humphrey Mitchell, a onetime trade unionist long since converted to management's point of view, had already defended the Dionne dispensation when he answered a question in the House: "There's no secret about it. Like any other employer of labor Mr. Dionne has been given permission, in view of the shortage of labor in his area, to recruit if possible a hundred workers for his textile mill in Beauce." The wages to be paid, said Mitchell, would be "the prevailing rates in the district." Speakers for all Opposition parties had a lot of fun with that statement before the special debate was over.

There was more than a touch of hypocrisy in their indignation. Because a farmer's vote in those days was worth at least two urban votes and usually more (many rural ridings were little better than rotten boroughs, in which a handful of farm voters returned a Member of Parliament) no party ever liked to say anything to which a farmer would object. Therefore none had uttered a peep about the arrival of another indentured labor force the year before.

Four thousand five hundred Polish ex-soldiers, men of General

Anders' force who for a considerable period of World War II had actually formed part of the First (and only) Canadian Army, were admitted to Canada as farm hands. They all undertook to work for two years at an alleged "prevailing rate" of forty-five dollars *a month*—this at a time when wages in Canadian industry averaged substantially more than forty-five dollars a *week*, and were going up rapidly. It was hard to prove what the "prevailing rate" for farm labor was, because in fact most farmers couldn't get help at any wage they were able or willing to pay, but it was certain that forty-five dollars a month had not "prevailed" since before the war. (The amount was paid in addition, of course, to room and board, but even at that it was ludicrously low.)

Domestic help was also hard to get, in those days of full employment. Housewives considered themselves lucky to get unskilled maids for seventy-five to a hundred dollars a month, with everything found. But when Displaced Persons were brought in for domestic service, as some fifteen thousand of them were between 1947 and 1953, the "prevailing rate" was officially stated to be thirty-five dollars a month. Nobody made any fuss about that, either.

Actually the so-called "indentured labor" contracts were not as bad as they sound. For one thing, they weren't enforced. Most of them were observed, as gentlemen's agreements, but many were ignored, and there is no record of any legal sanction being invoked for breach of them.

Also, the Displaced Persons enjoyed a lot more protection than the ordinary immigrant got, or gets now. If any fell ill —as many did, in spite of strict medical screenings on the other side of the Atlantic—they could be sent to hospital at the Government's expense. (One girl spent a full year recovering from tuberculosis, which did not develop until she had been a full year in the country; she paid nothing.) Their ocean fares were paid by the International Refugee Organization, and their fares from the Canadian port of entry to their place of employment were paid either by their prospective employers or by the Canadian government. They were housed and fed on arrival in Government hostels, one at St. Paul l'Hermite near Montreal and another at Ajax near Toronto. For people in a strange land who did not speak the language, and who moreover had been accustomed for several years to a barrack-type life in which all their fundamental needs were provided but little else, the period of semi-tutelage and special protection was probably not unwelcome.

More important than its effect on the individual Displaced Person, though, was the effect of this program on the Canadian attitude toward immigration. In an astonishingly short time, half a lifetime of rigidly exclusionist policy and prejudice had given way to an almost open door. And this door was not slammed shut even against former enemies.

Here again, the motives were not all altruistic. The labor supply in the DP camps soon began to dry up, while the demand for labor remained insatiable. Even in years of relatively high unemployment, native Canadians showed no interest in the more unpleasant jobs—stoop labor in the fields or in the mines, or lonely work in the bush. The Immigration Department's annual report for 1950–51 says: "Because the International Refugee Organization had difficulty providing enough Displaced Persons for underground work in the metal mines and for work in the bush, arrangements were made for group movements of eight hundred and twenty German nationals for a metal mine, and one thousand German nationals for work in the bush."

It was a trickle that soon became a flood. For the decade 1953–63 the ex-enemies, Germans and Italians, roughly equaled the British among immigrants to Canada. In most years since 1958, the Italians have outnumbered the British arrivals by several thousands.

But when all the cynical remarks have been made, it remains true that Canada has a good record in postwar immigration, and especially in the treatment of refugees. No fewer than a quarter of a million of these homeless exiles came to Canada in the first two decades after World War II (and they are still coming, almost unnoticed, at the rate of a couple of thousand a year from refugee camps in Austria, Italy, and other places at this side of the Iron

Curtain). Displaced Persons moving to Canada in organized groups totaled 165,697 between 1947 and 1952, when the organized movement ceased. At the time of the Hungarian rebellion in 1956, Canada took in 37,566 men, women, and children who had fled Hungary—more than the United States even in absolute figures, and twenty times as many proportionately. (The Eisenhower-Dulles Administration talked of admitting one hundred thousand Hungarians at the time, but Congress never got round to passing the necessary legislation.)

Important as these mercy projects were, in changing Canada's attitude toward immigration, they represented only a small fraction of the postwar immigration flow. Refugees of all kinds were no more than ten per cent of all immigration between 1946 and 1966. And the two and a half million newcomers constitute an even more substantial bloc of present-day Canadians than their mere numbers indicate.

More than half of them went straight into the labor force, of which they make up about one fifth. Some of course are not yet able to vote, for reasons of citizenship, but immigrants of voting age are almost one quarter of the electorate. They are particularly strong in the professional and highly skilled occupations—a third of all architects and engineers in Canada, a quarter of all doctors and research scientists, were born and educated abroad.

The result has been a radical change in the make-up of the Canadian people, not entirely in a mere twenty years but certainly in one lifetime.

English Canadians who are not yet old were taught, in school, to sing *Rule Britannia* as a patriotic song, along with *O Canada* and (equally if not more sacred) *The Maple Leaf Forever:*

> *In days of yore, from* Britain's *shore,*
> *Wolfe the dauntless hero came*
> *And planted firm* Britannia's *flag*
> *On* Canada's *fair domain . . .*

Neither Canadian song was taught as a national anthem, of course. The national anthem was *God Save the King.*

By the mid-1960s this Canada had, if not quite vanished, at least faded into quaintness and old age. The new Canada was a nation in which those of British origin were outnumbered almost three to two—forty-four per cent in the 1961 census and dropping, proportionately, every year. Of the normal flow of immigrants each year, less than one third are British.

Because of the natural tendency of ethnic and language groups to congregate, these newcomers have become a political force out of all proportion to their numbers. In at least twenty-five ridings across Canada the ethnic vote is decisive—and in several the ethnic vote is Chinese, who until 1947 could not vote at all.

This new third force has brought new complications to the problem of Canadian identity. New Canadians who are neither British nor French by origin resent any references to "the two founding races." They object, far more strenuously than English Canadians, to any preference for French over other "foreign" languages, and the fact that the French were here first has less than no weight with them. Had they known it was such a great advantage to come first, they say, they themselves would not have come last.

French Canadians, on their side, have not lost their old distrust and hostility toward immigrants. They have always suspected that immigration was merely a sinister device by the English to perpetuate their own majority position and frustrate French Canada's *revanche des berceaux*. Lately, though, the old "revenge of the cradles" has ceased to be effective anyway. Birth rates have proved to be more a matter of environment, rural or urban, than of religion or ethnic origin, and Quebec no longer has the highest natural increase rate in Canada—it is now fourth instead of first among the ten provinces.

Partly for this reason, partly because the "Quiet Revolution" of the early 1960s reopened Quebec's eyes to the world in general and to modern France in particular, Quebec is now planning to set up its own immigration service—as Ontario did in London just after World War II, and thereby stimulated the federal Government to hasten its reforms. France has never been a rich source of

Canadian immigrants, even in the days when Canada was French territory, and recently the flow of settlers from France has been only about two thousand a year. Quebec is now hoping to change that, and match the "Anglophone" reinforcements with a larger flow of French-speaking.

To the extent that this effort succeeds it will hasten, not impede, the pace of change in French Canada. Already there are enough French-speaking Jews and French-speaking Protestants, not to mention French-speaking agnostics who may have been brought up as Catholics, to rouse a steady and rising protest against the "confessional" school system in Quebec. (English-language schools, nominally Protestant, are actually non-sectarian and are attended by Jews and other non-Christians, but all French-language public schools and most of the private ones are strongly and uncompromisingly Roman Catholic. Non-Catholics would not be happy sending their children to be taught there.)

So it may turn out in the end that Fortress Quebec, once breached, will be even more affected by its own New Canadians than English Canada has been already. Up to now, the Canadian cultural "mosaic" has been as much a myth as the contrasting "melting pot" of the United States. In practice the schools of the nine English-speaking provinces have been turning out English-speaking North Americans who, if not precisely alike, are at any rate no more different from each other than New Yorkers are from Texans; the French-language schools, archaic in their curricula, have concentrated on preserving a type of French culture which in France itself disappeared with the Revolution of 1789.

All this has changed. Quebec is now resolved to make its culture, if not truly French, at least truly international and internationally respected. Canadians of other origins have been stimulated thereby into a new interest in their cultural heritage, and a new reluctance to accept the disadvantages of foreignness. The result will certainly be a new Canada.

XIII

A Cloud Like a Man's Hand

ON THE St. Laurent election campaign train in June 1957, as it lay overnight at a siding in Truro, Nova Scotia, a Liberal Cabinet minister was having a nightcap with the press in the club car. We were all fresh from a political meeting which had gone rather well, and the minister was in an expansive mood.

"If the Conservatives had any sense," he said, "they would stop trying to compete with us in welfare promises. There's room in this country for a true conservative party, one that adopts a real conservative position. But the Tories keep trying to squeeze in to the left of us, and there just isn't any room there. Anybody who is left of us is a socialist."

Liberal complacency has seldom been better expressed. Even at the time it sounded not quite plausible, and the traveling reporters jeered their distinguished guest a little, but it didn't then sound too preposterous. It seemed natural to any Liberal, and not unnatural to political journalists sealed into the atmosphere of Ottawa, to think the Liberal pace of progress was the inevitably right pace, and Liberal power eternal.

For eight of the nine years that the St. Laurent Government had held office, the view from Ottawa had been one of almost undisturbed calm. Movement there was, but it was like the quiet sweep of a great river—on the surface all seemed motionless and permanent, as it was in the beginning, is now and ever shall be, world without end.

It began with the completion of Confederation, the addition of Newfoundland as Canada's tenth province. Strictly speaking, this was an achivement of Mackenzie King, since the terms of union had been negotiated and the two-ballot referendum held before Mackenzie King's retirement. But all senior St. Laurent ministers had been King ministers too, and several including St. Laurent had a lot to do with bringing Newfoundland in. None had done more than Jack Pickersgill, nominally only Minister of Immigration but then as always the Prime Minister's right-hand man.

Indeed, Pickersgill used to say jokingly that he had brought in Newfoundland singlehanded. Mackenzie King was never an unqualified enthusiast about the Newfoundland project. He didn't want a halfhearted Canadian province, and he'd always said that he would accept nothing less than "a substantial majority" in the referendum on Confederation.

In fact, the first of the two ballots in 1948 (which offered Newfoundlanders three choices for their constitutional future) failed to bring a clear majority. Even the second, run-off ballot approved Confederation by only fifty-two per cent to forty-eight. Question: Would Mackenzie King regard this slim four-point margin as "substantial"?

Pickersgill foresaw this query and prepared for it. On the morning after the second Newfoundland ballot the Prime Minister asked him in a sour tone: "Well, what did you think of the referendum?"

"Wonderful, sir," said Pickersgill. "A magnificent victory. Do you realize that the majority for Confederation was larger than your party has ever won in any Canadian election?"

In a very different tone, King said: "Is that so?" It was. The size of the Newfoundland majority was never mentioned again.

Certainly one factor in the Newfoundlanders' decision, and almost certainly the decisive one, was the opportunity to share Canada's family allowances, old-age pensions for the needy, and similar social benefits. These were well established when St. Laurent took over, but they continued to be expanded.

Old-age pensions had been paid to the destitute of age seventy and over since 1927, with the federal Government paying a steadily increasing and the provinces a shrinking share. The pension, originally twenty dollars a month maximum, had risen by 1949 to forty dollars. But it was the St. Laurent Government, conservative as it seemed in its senior membership, that introduced universal old-age pensions in January 1952. The Prime Minister himself became an old-age pensioner the following month, when he celebrated his seventieth birthday. So did James G. Gardiner, the Minister of Agriculture and defeated contender for Liberal leadership, who reached seventy in 1953. And so in 1956 did C. D. Howe, the dynamic executive who had done as much as any single Canadian toward winning World War II, with his remarkable work in munitions and supply, but who was also a millionaire and generally regarded as the spokesman and symbol of Big Business in the Cabinet. Pension universality could hardly have gone further, though the actual sum paid out each month remained forty dollars.

Hospital insurance was still in the future, but it was foreseen. Grants were being paid to the provinces each year for the construction of new hospitals, expansion of medical training facilities, and similar preparations, all necessary but taken at a leisurely pace. The rate of progress was in fact like that of a glacier, not quite visible to the naked eye, but the Liberals assured any inquirer that it was the right rate in the circumstances.

Other things were happening quietly in fields not related to welfare. The British North America Act (Canada's Constitution) was amended in 1949 to permit the Parliament of Canada, not Britain, to make any further amendments in matters that concerned the federal power alone; it was hardly noticed at the time that Maurice Duplessis of Quebec opposed this change, or that there was no definition of the "federal matters" on which Ottawa was to have sole jurisdiction.

It seemed even more eccentric of Duplessis to object to the abolition, the same year, of judicial appeals to the Privy Council in London. After all, wasn't Quebec supposed to be the anti-imperialist province, always accusing *les anglais* of being docile colonials? And wasn't the abolition of Privy Council appeals another step toward total Canadian independence? Few English Canadians even noticed, let alone understood, that Quebec's real objection was to vesting final authority on all constitutional issues in a Supreme Court of Canada which was appointed solely by the Ottawa government, and on which French Canadians would always be a minority.

These reservations and hesitations were almost inaudible in the superconfident bustle of Canada in the early 1950s. Everything was moving ahead with such deliberate speed. The Massey Royal Commission reported on the state of Canadian culture, and on its advice the Government set up the Canada Council. One hundred million dollars (a lucky windfall from the taxes on two vast estates of multimillionaires who had just died, I. C. Killam and Sir James Dunn) gave the Canada Council its working capital. Half of that sum was to be doled out in capital grants for university construction; the rest was to be invested, and the income used to give scholarships in arts and letters, or grants to worthy causes like local orchestras, theater groups, ballet companies, and the newborn Stratford, Ontario, Shakespearean Festival.

The first Canadian-born Governor-General, Right Honorable Vincent Massey, had been appointed in 1952; he was an instant and continuing success, to the amazement of many who had viewed this innovation with alarm. L. B. Pearson became president of the United Nations General Assembly for a year. Television arrived in Canada, somewhat belatedly but no less welcome for that.

Meanwhile the economy continued the boom that Canadians had begun to take for granted. The gross national product, five and a half billion in 1939, hit seventeen billion by 1950 and thirty-two billion by 1957. (It crossed the fifty-billion mark in 1965.) As Ministers of Finance, Douglas Abbott and his successor Walter Harris were embarrassed by the inadvertent surpluses they piled up year after year. Abbott's ran between $132 million and $670 million. Harris was less acutely "embarrassed"—he had a deficit of $152 million in 1955. But his cure for the mild slump was to cut taxes and stimulate the economy, and it seemed to work. The next year's accounts were almost back to a break-even position, and by 1957 he was again reporting the customary surplus, $282 million.

Amid all this prosperity, this eternity of fine weather, it was hardly surprising that the Liberals did not notice the few signs of impending difficulty—clouds no larger than a man's hand, like that which presaged the rain for the prophet Elijah.

One was the fact that people were bored with them and by them. They should have remembered the fate of Aristides, who was finally ostracized by his fellow Athenians because they were so tired of hearing him called Aristides the Just. In a magazine article written during the 1953 election campaign (which the Liberals, of course, won as usual) the novelist Hugh MacLennan began with these words: "I wish I didn't have to vote for the Liberals—those cautious, inhibited trustees."

Another cloud, equally unnoticed, was the fact that their leaders were growing old.

In February 1954, just as he turned seventy-two, Prime Minister St. Laurent set off on a trip round the world. With a daughter as his companion (his wife did not wish to go) and a small party of officials he made a triumphal tour that began in London and ended in Tokyo, with a side trip to the quiet front line in Korea.

Everyone remarked how tireless he seemed. The young men in his retinue took pleasure in confessing how he ran them ragged, how after a day that left them exhausted he would appear bright and early next morning, the picture of relaxed good health. He was still in that form when he got back to Ottawa and faced, beaming, the microphones and television cameras that awaited him at the airport.

Within a month the accumulated fatigue of the journey struck him like a virus. Not exactly ill, suffering no infection and no easily definable symptoms, he was nevertheless in a state approaching collapse. In addition to physical malaise he was depressed, and he began to talk seriously—though privately—of retiring from public life.

His colleagues were horrified. "Uncle Louis" was a legendary figure (indeed, about three parts myth) but he was their sure guarantee of victory, the very symbol of Liberal eternity. With urgent sincerity they begged him to stay on, dismiss all thought of retiring, continue to lead them forever and ever. He consented.

From time to time in the next three years, some of the younger ministers wondered if they had done the right thing in so persuading him. St. Laurent and Howe in 1954 were at the peak of power and fame, with a record of unbroken success in peace and war, crisis and calm. Had they retired then, this record would have gone into the history books unqualified. As it was, things began to take small but frequent turns for the worse.

The first public evidence of this came in the summer of 1955. The occasion seems trivial enough in retrospect—a small amendment, no more than three lines long, to the Defense Production Act of 1951. But what it produced was a successful filibuster in the House of Commons, the first time since 1935 that the Opposition had managed in a major debate to force the lordly Liberals into a change of policy.

As adopted in 1951 during the Korean emergency, the Defense Production Act armed the minister, C. D. Howe, with extraordinary powers. He could renegotiate contracts, commandeer plants if necessary, generally do whatever he might deem best for the security of Canada. Absolute authority of this kind had been commonplace during World War II—it saved the taxpayers hundreds of millions by allowing revision of contracts, and it prevented any such mushroom crop of war millionaires as had disgraced the country in World War I. Its readoption for the duration of the Korean crisis roused no serious objection, especially since the act itself declared its own expiry date, July 31, 1956.

But a temporary act meant a temporary department, and Howe was finding it difficult to hire and retain good men in jobs that might, under the letter of the law, disappear overnight. He wanted the act and the department made permanent. So he introduced a one-clause amendment saying merely that "Section 41 of the act is repealed"—Section 41 being the one that set an expiry date.

Without Section 41, the Defense Production Act would remain in effect forever unless formally repealed.

In the debate on introduction of the bill in March 1955, Donald Fleming led off for the Conservative Opposition by questioning the wisdom of making the emergency powers permanent. "These powers are absolute," he said, "with scarcely any limitation." Howe replied: "The situation now is no different from what it was in 1951. Every one of these powers has been used, and used many times." But he did add a sentence often quoted against him later: "I quite agree that not all of these powers should be continued permanently."

To the suggestion that the expiry date should merely be put forward three years instead of abolished, however, Howe had already made a brusque reply: "That would mean coming back to Parliament every three years, and I've more to do than spend my time amusing Parliament."

But it was in this very first stage of the debate, on March 14, that Howard Green for the Conservatives made the suggestion that was finally adopted four tempestuous months later: "Why is it not possible to word the bill in such a way that the *department* is made permanent but these *powers* are made temporary and subject to review?"

Why indeed? It was a question many Liberals asked themselves in the weary weeks ahead, and there was only one answer: because C. D. Howe, who in twenty years of public life had never been seriously thwarted before, flatly refused to be thwarted now.

This exhibition of stubbornness was not unprovoked, though the provocation was not then known to the general public. Howe had just come through a battle in Cabinet on an entirely different matter, and for the first time in his life had been defeated. The subject of this struggle behind the scenes was one that was to become notorious a year later—the building of a trans-Canada pipeline.

The builders of this three-thousand-mile pipeline, which now carries natural gas from Alberta to the industries of eastern Canada, wanted the Government to guarantee them against loss by underwriting eighty million dollars' worth of their securities. Howe agreed. Having given his word, he took it for granted that the Government of which he was the senior member would back him up. As it turned out, he was mistaken. A group of younger ministers, notably the new Finance Minister, Walter Harris, could see no reason why the taxpayers should guarantee a group of private enterprisers against loss while leaving them complete enjoyment of any ensuing profits. After a fight in Cabinet that lasted for weeks, Howe had to accept the humiliation of defeat and the greater humiliation, for one of his temperament, of having to go back on his word to the pipeline builders. He was very bitter about it.

This is why the Liberal Cabinet did not accept Howard Green's suggestion in March instead of July. They had been so totally pre-occupied with the pipeline fight that the Defense Production Act amendment went through Cabinet almost unexamined. Months later, one of the younger ministers said privately:

"We realized as soon as Howard Green spoke that he was right, that this was the easy way to amend the bill and satisfy everyone. But old C.D. was still so furious that nobody wanted to start another fight with him."

So the opportunity passed for a quiet acquiescence that would have meant no loss of face for anyone. Colleagues sat silent when, as the debate on second reading began June 7, C. D. Howe defiantly announced that the Government was not "prepared to amend the Defense Production Act in any manner whatsoever," except simple deletion of its time limit.

When Donald Fleming taunted him by saying, "Everybody knows the Cabinet has been divided on this question," Howe responded with fury: "That's an absolute falsehood." But it wasn't. With every day that the Conservative filibuster went on, the Liberals became more and more unhappily aware that they were in an untenable position.

Finally they gave way. Howe left on a Thursday night to keep a series of speaking engagements; the Prime Minister rose on the Monday to say, in Howe's absence but with his reluctant con-

sent, that the act would be amended in exactly the fashion Howard Green had suggested four months before.

Few members of the general public realized at the time what
a historic watershed had been crossed. It was the sort of thing
editorial writers brood about; the ordinary voter isn't much interested. Even Members of Parliament, especially on the Liberal
side, were only half aware that anything important had happened.
Many Liberal backbenchers thought it rather a good thing that
the great C. D. Howe had been taken down a peg.

As for the Conservatives, they of course were simply delighted.
After twenty years of unbroken discouragement they had actually
fought and won. Their small numbers—a mere fifty-one against
the Liberal phalanx of a hundred and seventy—had been enough
to triumph in a righteous cause. They felt like Gideon's army, and
the still complacent Liberals didn't blame them. It was good, they
said indulgently, for the Opposition to get a little encourage-
ment once in a while.

But in retrospect it's obvious that the Liberal defeat was both
massive and ominous. A fabric that already had been quietly
rotting for a year or more had finally torn. As it turned out, the
tear was never mended. Within a year it became visible to the
whole population, in that strange parliamentary debacle, the pipeline debate.

XIV

C. D. Howe:
The Canadian Giant from Massachusetts

IN A BIOGRAPHY of Clarence Decatur Howe published in 1957, Leslie Roberts quoted Lord Beaverbrook: "C. D. Howe is one of the handful of men of whom it can be said 'But for them, the war would have been lost.'"

There may have been some hyperbole in that statement. Beaverbrook liked a sweeping phrase, and as an ex-Canadian he liked to see Canada's war effort get all the emphasis it could take. But it would have been no exaggeration to say, at least, that Howe did as much as any other man *in Canada* toward winning the war, and perhaps more than any other.

It was Howe who organized the building of the 126 airfields, who first found, and later built, the training aircraft that made possible the British Commonwealth Air Training Plan, probably Canada's greatest single contribution toward victory. It was Howe who created an aircraft industry out of nothing, a shipbuilding industry out of next to nothing, a massive arsenal in a country that until then had comprised only agriculture, primary extractive industries, and a negligible, branch-plant manufacturing in its economic structure. First for war and then in peace, Howe changed the very structure of the Canadian economy.

What escaped most people's attention in the earlier stages of this process, and what Howe himself never quite understood to his dying day, was that the qualities wherewith he achieved these triumphs were not the qualities of a democratic politician. In emergencies they were invaluable, but in peace they became intolerable.

For example, three months of negotiation with the British, Australians, and New Zealanders were required to establish the British Commonwealth Air Training Plan. Vitally important issues, on which there was no agreement and in some cases violent disagreement, had to be ironed out—some involved the status, and almost the very existence, of the Royal Canadian Air Force.

Senator C. G. Power, who was then Minister of Defense for Air, says in his memoirs: "At one time, on the last day of the negotiations, the whole plan almost fell through. There were cables to and from Great Britain, excursions to the Governor-General, hurried, despairing, last-hope conferences and interviews." When the agreement was finally signed on December 15, 1939, its negotiators felt they had reached harbor after a stormy and dubious passage.

C. D. Howe had paid absolutely no attention to all this fuss. When the first communication came from Britain about the air training plan on September 26, he assumed the arrangements would be completed somehow. As Minister of Munitions and Supply, he immediately dispatched survey teams across Canada to line up suitable sites. Before the negotiators had even set pen to paper he had the land chosen, and in some cases even purchased, for the 96 airfields in the original plan (the increase to 126 came later).

At the time it seemed, and it was, an admirable use of foresight and disdain for diplomatic red tape. Thanks to Howe, it was possible to start construction as soon as the snow was off the ground in 1940 (despite the fact that a national general election had taken place in the meantime). But seventeen years later this same foresight, and the same willingness to short-circuit formal procedures and anticipate predictable decisions, had become the "contempt for Parliament" and "disregard of democracy" that Howe's critics so earnestly deplored.

Why did it take so long for Canadian voters to discover that the great organizer of their war effort, the man who made Canada an industrial nation, was also the "dictator" they finally believed him to be? The answer can be found in the accidents of Canadian history and the varied developments of Howe's own life.

Born in Waltham, Massachusetts, in 1886, he became a Canadian by sheer accident—literally on the toss of a coin. Howe was a part-time lecturer at the Massachusetts Institute of Technology, where he had graduated in 1907, when a job at Dalhousie University, Halifax, opened up for the following year. He and another young faculty member were equally qualified and equally anxious for the Dalhousie professorship, which paid two thousand dollars a year. They tossed for it, and Howe won.

He liked Canada. A natural-born builder, he liked the challenge of a raw young country where so much was still to be built. After five years at Dalhousie, as professor of civil engineering, he was offered the job of chief engineer for the federal Board of Grain Commissioners in Ottawa. Most of his work consisted of supervising the construction of grain elevators. After three years of this, Howe resigned from the Government service and started to build the grain elevators himself. In the next twenty years he worked in every part of Canada, gaining an intimate knowledge of communities which became the basis for many of his famous "snap judgments" in wartime and after.

This experience, and his austere New England upbringing, gave Howe a rather stern code of personal responsibility. The code was severely tested on the very first contract he got as an independent builder—a large grain elevator at the Lakehead, which was destroyed by a hurricane when it was half built. Howe's equipment was mostly destroyed with it, and he was left virtually bankrupt. But he managed to get another bank loan, started the building job again from scratch, got it finished by the date specified in his contract. Leslie Roberts tells what happened next:

"When he turned the elevator over to the Saskatchewan Co-operative Grain Growers' Association its chairman, knowing of the storm damage, asked Howe how he had fared on the contract. In typically laconic language he answered 'I lost my shirt.' But he asked for no adjustment. What had happened was his

personal problem. When the next meeting of the Grain Growers'
board voted money to make up his loss, he was surprised as he
was pleased to be solvent again. His feelings for prairie wheat
men have been warm ever since."

Howe used to say that he "got all the worrying of a lifetime
out of his system" on that first contract. His calm under pressure
amazed the younger men who worked with him during the war.
One of them once told me:

"I've seen Mr. Howe worried only once. That was when the
ship on which his son Bill was an officer was torpedoed in the
Indian Ocean, and for five days nobody knew what had happened
to the ship's company."

But his calm was a product of his self-assurance, his own acceptance of personal responsibility and of the powers needed to
discharge it.

"When I was a young engineer," he told Roberts, "my seniors
gave me jobs to do and I carried them out according to instruc-
tions. When I went into business for myself, *I* gave the orders,
and I expected them to be obeyed because the responsibility was
mine."

Natural enough in a business executive, these sentiments are
unusual among politicians, whose language has many synonyms
for words like "compromise" and "consensus." But by a series of
historical coincidences, Howe was able to carry his executive's
habits of mind and temperament through twenty years of politics without serious impairment.

The early years presented no problem. Howe was forty-nine and
a self-made millionaire when Mackenzie King and his Liberals,
bursting with confidence in their ability to overturn the collaps-
ing Government of R. B. Bennett, asked Howe to run in his
home town of Port Arthur. He accepted and won, and then became a Cabinet minister before ever taking his seat in Parliament,
but his own code of conduct ("new boys should be seen and
not heard") kept him from overasserting himself at the outset.
He got specific jobs to do—setting up the National Harbors
Board, creating Trans-Canada Airlines out of nothing—and he

did them with efficiency and dispatch. When challenged in Parliament he defended himself competently, but showed little promise of being either a great parliamentarian or Parliament's *bête noire*.

In 1938 came an incident in which Howe was not involved directly, but which had great effect upon his career—the Bren gun affair, considered in its time to be a major scandal, though by modern standards it was tame enough.

It was started by an article in *Maclean's Magazine* by Colonel George Drew, later national leader of the Conservative Party, then provincial Leader of the Opposition in Ontario. Drew called in question the contracts given to the John Inglis Company, Toronto, for the manufacture under license of the Bren gun (soon to be the basic weapon of Canadian infantry battalions). His charges led to the appointment of a Royal Commission, and to acrimonious debates in Parliament during which many wild charges were voiced. Howe intervened to answer some of them; his speech attracted much attention because he had taken the revolutionary step—the only MP to do so, apparently—of actually going to inspect the Inglis plant to see whether the things being said about it were true.

The Royal Commission report on the Bren gun scandal was well illustrated by a cartoon in the Toronto weekly *Saturday Night*—the Commission was shown carrying a placard to Parliament Hill which said, on one side, "The Boys Didn't Do Anything Wrong," and on the other side "But Don't Do It Again." If not the honesty, at least the efficiency of the Defense Department's procurement was seriously impugned. This led to the setting up of a Defense Purchasing Board, which in turn was replaced as soon as war broke out by a separate Department of Munitions and Supply. C. D. Howe was the natural choice as minister of that department, and thus the stage was set for the period of his greatest service to his adopted country.

He performed superbly. He gathered around him in Ottawa the ablest executives in the country—sometimes the president of the appropriate company, sometimes the hitherto anonymous young

man at the third or fourth level who had really been doing the
work for his more prestigious elders. Working closely with the
Wartime Prices and Trade Board run by another Titan of World
War II, Donald Gordon, Howe and his team took over the management of the Canadian economy, and managed it well.

Naturally, their powers were immense. Nobody questioned this
—not in the English language, anyway. Except in Quebec (where
so many complained that the war effort was "excessive") the bay-
ing of critics was for more exercise of authority, not less. They
were thinking primarily of conscription, of course, but the general approval for authority and efficiency gave Howe and his men
a good press.

His own war service was not without danger. In December
1940 he went to Britain, with a small group of senior aides, to
straighten out various problems of production and procurement.
Their ship, the *Western Prince*, was torpedoed in mid-Atlantic.
Her captain and two officers went down with the ship, but had
managed to get their civilian passengers and the rest of the crew
off in lifeboats. One of the lifeboats capsized, however, with
the loss of several lives. Gordon Scott of Montreal, one of Howe's
senior advisers and close friends, was killed in the course of
abandoning ship, crushed between the tossing boat and the ship's
side. Howe and the others were adrift for eight hours of darkness
before they were picked up, and landed in England with nothing
more than the salt-stained clothes they were wearing.

This narrow escape augmented the prestige that Howe had already won by his executive talent. It remained unimpaired, and
almost unimpugned, throughout the war.

The end of hostilities did not mean an immediate end of
Howe's dictatorial authority. "Orderly decontrol" was the watch-
word of the day, as opposed to the chaos that followed demobilization after World War I. And in Canada, "orderly" meant "controlled by C. D. Howe." Again, nobody minded. It seemed
quite natural.

Howe became Minister of Reconstruction, responsible for a
new agency called Central Mortgage and Housing, set up to help

clear up the colossal backlog of demand for dwellings. Howe oversaw the winding up of wartime contracts, the disposal of Crown assets that were assets no longer with the coming of peace.

Before these tasks had been completed, along came the foreign exchange crisis of October 1947. Again, extraordinary powers were required to keep the economy under strict control. Capital imports had to be restricted to necessities, and even the necessities had to be rationed by some rule of thumb. Only one man had the know-how, the intimate acquaintance with the economic structure of Canada, and that man was Howe.

Said a Government economist at the time: "I would class C. D. among the top half dozen economists in Canada, though he would be insulted if I told him so. He thinks economists are half-baked theorists, and that he is a hardheaded businessman with no time for theories. But whether he knows it or not he *has* theories, and his quick decisions are based on them. That's why so many of his 'snap' judgments turn out to be right."

Even in wartime Howe had had no more authority than he wielded in 1947–48 and, unlike wartime, this was a period when Canadians (or anyway their editorial writers) worried aloud and a lot about the infringement of personal liberty. Much misgiving was expressed about the assumption of despotic power by the Mackenzie King Government. But even then it seemed natural that, if such authority were to exist, C. D. Howe should exercise it.

He himself, speaking in Parliament in the debate on the 1947 control legislation, said: "During the past eight years I have had unusual powers for making decisions that affected business and industry. I had no desire to spend a further period carrying out a program of that kind. But I felt that if business had to deal with Government, to obtain decisions that might be considered arbitrary, business would rather deal with the devil they know than with the devil they don't know."

Apparently he was right. All through that crisis period, businessmen from all over Canada poured into Ottawa to talk to C. D. Howe, if they could get in to see him, and find out where they stood—whether or not they would be allowed to import the steel or the cement or what not for the projects they had in mind.

Howe managed to see about fifteen or twenty a day, besides carrying on the enormous work burden of his department. The antechamber of his office was always full. His reception clerk, Tony Pelletier, was offered bribes of up to fifty dollars to slip someone in without an appointment, or to promote him to the head of the queue.

Once in, the visitor would find himself in a large bright office with a large untidy desk, behind which sat the minister—a broad-shouldered, gray-haired man of middle height, with a year-round tan, a quick smile, and a manner that was brisk but not brusque. He had a gift for bringing people quickly to the point, without seeming to hustle or harass them. Once the problem was stated, he could usually give a quick answer:

"Yes, I think we can let you have that"; or "Sorry, I'm afraid that will have to wait until we're out of this jam."

Sometimes he was wrong, of course, and he never minded admitting this if he himself was persuaded it was so. But oftener than not, his quick decisions were sound.

Even at the height of his power, Howe exercised no more than the authority that any corporation's chief executive takes for granted—true, he exercised it over a wider area, but the difference was one of degree. History made it possible for him to spend twenty years in politics acting like the business executive he had always been. The foreign exchange crisis was no sooner over than the Stalinist threat became acute, with the Berlin airlift, the beginnings of NATO and rearmament, the Korean War.

It was hardly surprising that by 1955, when the Defense Production Act came up for renewal, Howe had grown to take this acceptance of his authority for granted. The reverse of 1955 was the first he had ever experienced, and he took it rather badly. This was unfortunate, for worse was to come.

XV

Pipelines and Parliaments:
The Twilight of an Era

IT IS ALMOST IMPOSSIBLE to explain, and difficult now even to remember, just why the great pipeline debate of 1956 was the crisis in Canadian parliamentary history that in fact it was.

Explicably or not, it was in many ways a major turning point. As the first clear outward sign of decay in the Liberal Government, it marked the beginning of the end of an era. As an exercise in emotional journalism it was the first demonstration, and a disquieting one, of the unique impact of television on the electorate. As an unprecedented breakdown of decorum in the House of Commons, and of respect for the authority of the Chair, it started a new and nasty tradition of parliamentary behavior which repeatedly, in the course of the next ten years, seemed to hover on the brink of anarchy.

Yet in actual substance, viewed in perspective a decade later, the whole affair seems oddly trivial. The project itself had general approval—an all-Canadian pipeline, the longest ever built, was to bring natural gas from the oilfields of Alberta to the industrial markets of eastern Canada, incidentally supplying cheap fuel to all the smaller communities along the route.

George Drew, Leader of the Opposition, said on the very first day of the protracted debate: "All Canadians want this line built." He and his party wanted it built by an all-Canadian company, though they were a little vague about which all-Canadian company could raise the $375 million that the project would cost. The socialist CCF wanted it built under public ownership. Both parties objected to the Government's proposal that public money, or at least public credit, should be pledged to guarantee the private builders (mainly American-owned companies) against loss.

But there was not, then or since, any financial scandal connected with the project. Later exposures of the handout of shares to politicians, at low prices or for no price at all, involved different companies and different politicians—these were provincial and municipal deals, and had nothing to do with the original trans-Canada pipeline. In that vast multimillion-dollar scheme no one was ever accused of financial impropriety, except for a brief flare-up, eight months after the debate itself, about the issuance of stock options as part of the compensation of two senior executives. This caused some embarrassment to the Government, but it was in fact a routine business practice.

Altogether, in the light of events, it is hard to recall just why the pipeline was supposed to be such a lethal threat to Canada's welfare, sovereignty, and independence. On the other hand it is equally hard to remember why the Government was so implacably determined, at all costs, to ram the legislation through Parliament and get the job started in 1956. As things turned out it was not done in 1956 anyway; a strike in the United States steel industry delayed delivery of the pipe, and the Government's suicidal efforts to meet the builders' deadline were all in vain.

C. D. Howe, Minister of Trade and Commerce and sponsor of the pipeline bill, was a man who liked to get things done. In spite of his twenty-one years in public life he still thought, felt, and acted like a business executive. He made no secret of his contempt for Parliament, which he regarded as a talk shop whose principal function was to waste his time.

He saw the trans-Canada pipeline as a great national project comparable to the building of the Canadian Pacific Railway in the 1880s. Like the CPR, it was to give Canada a massive infusion of economic lifeblood while at the same time relieving an "intolerable" situation in Alberta where gas was being wastefully flared at the oil refineries for lack of industrial customers to use it.

"Why are we pressing on with this?" Howe asked one day, at a point midway through the tumultuous debate. "I don't know—perhaps I get overenthusiastic about a project."

Overenthusiastic or not, he had no patience with the faint-hearts who doubted that the project would succeed. Therefore he felt no hesitation in pledging the Government's credit to protect them against loss. He believed firmly (and rightly, as it turned out) that there never would be any loss, and that his guarantee would not cost the taxpayer a penny.

But these things alone would not have accounted for the depth of Howe's determination to force the pipeline bill through. He had already been frustrated in his first attempt to give the scheme a Government guarantee (as related in Chapter XIII). That failure still rankled. All through the autumn of 1955 and the winter of 1956 he fought in Cabinet to get a suitable replacement for the original, simple guarantee of pipeline company bonds which his colleagues had refused him the year before.

A compromise emerged. The federal Government, in partnership with the provincial Government of Ontario, would itself build the 675-mile stretch through the empty wilderness between the Manitoba border and Kapuskasing, Ontario. The cost would be $118 million, of which Ontario would contribute $35 million and Ottawa the balance. When the line was finished it would be leased, and eventually sold, to Trans-Canada Pipe Lines Limited. The deal would be self-liquidating—lease and sale would return all the money advanced by the public treasury, with interest—but it would make possible an earlier start than the private company was able to finance unaided.

This was the project announced in the Speech from the Throne as Parliament opened on January 10, 1956. A resolution to introduce the bill was moved in the House of Commons by C. D. Howe on March 14. Even this measure met strong opposition—Conservatives and CCF had already promised, in speeches outside the House, a filibuster against it that would make last year's fight against the Defense Production Act "look like a picnic." The CCF signaled its intention by opposing, and requiring a recorded vote upon, the formal motion to go into committee to consider the resolution.

It's doubtful, though, that they could have succeeded. The measure was not particularly controversial. Strong provincial Governments in Alberta and Ontario, the latter a Conservative regime, were heartily in favor of it. With the debate starting in March, Parliament would have had three full months to deal with it before the deadline for commencement of construction in 1956, which was about the end of the first week of June. But all this became academic in the light of a new development.

Trans-Canada Pipe Lines' promoters came to Howe with bad news. Not only were they unable to raise money to build the unprofitable stretch of 675 miles through the wilderness, they were even $80 million short of the sum they needed to build the western section, as far as Winnipeg. Unless the Government were willing to put up this $80 million, they could not start building before 1957—by which time some of their essential permits, franchises, and sales contracts would have expired.

Howe went back into battle with his colleagues in Cabinet. To him it still seemed a relatively small matter. What was $80 million more or less—a mere loan, which he was certain would be recovered in full with interest—in a project of this magnitude and national importance? But aside from all rational considerations, it's fair to say that by this time the pipeline scheme had become an obsession with him.

It was more than a great national project now, it was a test of his authority—even, as he saw it, of his integrity. He, C. D. Howe, had given his word a year ago and had been forced to go back on it, for the first time in his long life, by the failure of his perfidious colleagues to back him up. This time he had given his word again, and had taken care to exact the consent, however reluctant, of the colleagues who had refused to back him the last time. He was determined to get this bill through Parliament if it was the last thing he did—as, politically, it nearly turned out to be.

By the time Howe had heard and digested the bad news from

Trans-Canada, and had fought and won his fight in Cabinet to get authority to lend the required $80 million, it was May. Instead of three months the Government had little more than three weeks to get the legislation through all stages. The one-day debate in March became worthless, because a new resolution had to be drafted—which appeared on the Parliamentary Order Paper along with the previous one, and thus gave pretext for many an argument on procedure as the debate wore on.

Three weeks is long enough for Parliament to debate most bills, but not long enough to exhaust a filibuster. Obviously, if the deadline were to be met, strenuous measures would be needed. The Government decided to proceed by imposing closure at each stage of the legislative process.

Again, it's hard to explain why this decision should have appeared to be so flagrantly outrageous. In the British House of Commons it would have been commonplace—routine procedure. Even in Canada the rules have since been changed to make such an allocation of time quite legal, even if not quite ordinary. But in the Canadian Parliament of 1956 it seemed, to everybody except the Liberals and secretly to many of them, a scandalous abuse of majority rule.

Howe served notice of closure in the very speech that opened debate on the resolution: "It's obvious," he said, "that some honorable members prefer to obstruct this motion rather than debate it. Therefore I beg to give notice that at the next sitting I shall move that further consideration of this resolution shall be the first order of business and shall not be further postponed."

Tumult broke out immediately. Stanley Knowles, the CCF's expert on House rules, shouted: "The guillotine." Other members bellowed, "Dictatorship." Some talked as if closure had never been applied before in Canada, though in fact it had been used on seven previous occasions between 1912 and 1932.

What was truly new—and, in the circumstances, truly outrageous even in retrospect—was the application of closure before debate had even begun. The use of majority power to terminate debate, and force a vote to its foregone conclusion, had always been considered a kind of ultimate weapon to be used only when a subject had been fully discussed, all its details known, and further argument nothing but mere obstruction. None of these qualifications applied in the pipeline debate. The bill had new and unexpected details which, a few weeks before, had not been known even to the Cabinet and were still not fully known to many Liberal MPs. It had not in its present form been discussed at all, in public. Obstruction had indeed been threatened by Opposition parties, but they'd had no time to carry out the threat. It was true, as the Opposition alleged, that the Government planned to use its steamroller majority to meet a deadline of its own choosing, and in the process to bend the rules of Parliament as they had never been bent before.

The pipeline debate lasted fifteen sitting days from its beginning on May 14 to final passage of the bill at 3:20 A.M. June 6. Closure was imposed four times, not counting a series of postponement motions in committee, which had somewhat the same effect. Fifty-three divisions of the House were required, some mere head-countings in committee but most of them formal recorded votes, each of which, in the Canadian Parliament, takes about three quarters of an hour to complete. Donald Fleming, a Conservative frontbencher who later became Minister of Finance and then Minister of Justice, was expelled from the chamber for defying an order from Mr. Speaker to resume his seat. (His colleagues, who apparently anticipated that somebody would be expelled that day, had thoughtfully brought in a large Canadian Red Ensign with which they decorated Fleming's empty chair.) On each of the closure motions the rules required that the final vote be taken at 1 A.M., but in fact—what with interminable points of order, questions of privilege, motions to adjourn the House and similar procedural rear-guard actions—the closure motions kept the House in session most of the night on each occasion. The first time, adjournment came at a quarter to five in the morning, and the earliest of the four late sittings went on until a quarter to two. Exhaustion sent one elderly Conservative to hospital and probably caused the death, a week later, of a popular Liberal MP, Jack McDougall of Vancouver, who dropped dead in his office of a heart attack.

The pipeline debate also caused another personal tragedy, of a different order but hardly less sad. It ruined, and terminated, the political career of a man who until then had been deemed one of the most promising in public life—René Beaudoin, Speaker of the House of Commons.

Beaudoin was then forty-four, a bright young Montreal lawyer who had already been in Parliament for seven years. Disappointed in his hopes for a Cabinet post, he had originally accepted the Speakership rather grudgingly, and on the understanding (well founded or not) that he would join the Cabinet later as several predecessors had done. But as he settled into the job of presiding over the House he began to find it fascinating. He also brought a new grace and *panache* to the social side of the office—he and his handsome wife entertained Members of Parliament and senior officials on a scale, and with a Gallic verve, to which no previous Speaker had ever aspired. Then as now, there was much talk of taking the Speakership out of politics and appointing a permanent Speaker who would thereafter be elected by acclamation. When the pipeline debate began, just a week after his forty-fourth birthday, René Beaudoin was everybody's choice for this important post.

For the first two weeks of the pipeline debate he did amazingly well. Bombarded every day with points of order, the fruit of much research in musty reference books upon rules that had seldom if ever been invoked before, Beaudoin kept his temper and somehow managed, in a House that grew daily more chaotic, to maintain both his own dignity and a respect for the authority of the Chair. Some Liberals thought he was too permissive, listening *ad nauseam* to cooked-up points of order, but it didn't really matter —the closure motions would cut off debate at a certain preordained time, whether the intervening hours were spent debating the bill itself or not.

Beaudoin's personal breakdown came on Thursday, May 31, when the debate itself was nearing its climax. Prime Minister St.

Laurent had risen at the outset to move the closure motion of which notice had been given the day before, and which would dispose of the committee stage for all seven clauses of the bill. Toward the end of the afternoon, for the umpteenth time since the bill reached the committee stage, Mr. Speaker was called back to the chair to hear an appeal from a ruling by the committee chairman.

All he had to do was give his own ruling in support of the chairman, and wait while it in turn was appealed and sustained by the usual majority vote. Parliament would then have gone on with the debate until, at one in the morning, the final votes would have been called in accordance with the closure rule.

Instead, Beaudoin let himself be trapped into hearing first a frivolous point of order, then a so-called question of privilege, trumped up by Colin Cameron, the elderly Puck who was, and still is, Socialist MP for Nanaimo, British Columbia.

Cameron admitted later that he never expected to be allowed even to finish his own speech, let alone go on discussing the "question of privilege" until 10 P.M., adjournment time. He was drawing Mr. Speaker's attention to letters in the Ottawa *Journal* which, he said with a straight face, were insulting to Mr. Speaker and therefore to the whole House of Commons. Cameron may have hoped, since Beaudoin was a man of considerable personal vanity, that he would be more inclined to listen to a defense of his own dignity than to any other irrelevant topic. But Cameron's wildest hopes could not have gone so far as the actual event.

For two hours and forty-five minutes Parliament debated this outlandish digression. Then came ten o'clock. "Pursuant to standing order, without question put," the House adjourned. The closure motion, which had decreed that the House should sit until 1 A.M. and then take its final vote on the clauses of the pipeline bill, was somehow forgotten.

The Government was livid with exasperation. Only a week remained before the deadline of June 7 would be upon them. If the legislation had not been passed, and the $80 million made available, by that time the builders would not be able to start work in the 1956 season. And if they had to give a new notice and then a new motion of closure they would fall two full days behind schedule and miss their deadline by the same length of time.

Exactly what took place that night and the following morning, what representations were made to Mr. Speaker by whom, has never been officially revealed. But for whatever reason, René Beaudoin rose in the House of Commons next day to make an unprecedented admission.

"I consider," he said, "that I made a serious mistake yesterday in allowing the point of order and other dilatory motions." And he therefore suggested that everything that had happened since five-fifteen the previous afternoon should be deleted, or expunged, and that Parliament revert to the point it had reached at that time. Thus the closure motion would once more be in effect, the final vote would take place that night instead of the night before, and the Government (though he of course did not say this) would be able to meet its June 7 deadline after all.

Bedlam broke loose. Opposition members left their desks, shouting, and swarmed onto the green carpet in front of Mr. Speaker's chair. Even M. J. Coldwell, the saintly and mild-mannered leader of the socialist CCF, was shaking his fist at the Speaker of the House. This was the day that has been known in Ottawa ever since as Black Friday.

When he could make himself heard George Drew rose to move an unprecedented motion: "That in view of the unprecedented action of Mr. Speaker in reversing his own ruling . . . this House resolves that it no longer has any confidence in its presiding officer."

With an outward appearance of calm, Mr. Speaker pointed out that this motion required forty-eight hours' notice. He then went on to deal implacably with other motions before the House—a motion to adjourn was voted down 143 to 51, and then a vote was called on no motion at all but to answer the question: "Shall the course suggested by Mr. Speaker [to revert to the status of the previous day] be followed?" The Opposition refused to vote, saying the whole procedure was monstrously irregular—as indeed it was. So the Liberals and their Social Credit allies voted endorsement of Mr. Speaker's strange suggestion by 142 to 0. The debate proceeded under the closure rule, and ended with a series of votes beginning at 1 A.M. The House adjourned in a mood of unprecedented bitterness at a quarter to two.

On Monday, June 4, George Drew opened proceedings by repeating his motion of censure against Mr. Speaker Beaudoin. He made a long speech, followed by M. J. Coldwell (who said, among other things, there was now "no other way than to dissolve this House and go to the country, so that a new Parliament, with all this sort of thing wiped out, may be assembled within a few months.") Prime Minister St. Laurent then moved "that this debate be now adjourned," and his motion carried 134 to 57.

Back to the pipeline bill. C. D. Howe moved third reading. Prime Minister St. Laurent gave notice he would move closure the following day. Debate continued, with a bitterness that by now had become habitual, until the last of the fifty-three divisions was completed on C. D. Howe's motion "that this bill be now passed," at 3:20 A.M. Wednesday, June 6.

Less than twelve hours later debate resumed on the motion of censure against Mr. Speaker. It was suddenly adjourned within minutes of its commencement, as word reached the chamber of the death of Jack McDougall, and the House rose in an atmosphere of sobriety that it had not known for many weeks. But the censure debate continued next day, with each opposition speaker professing his high *personal* regard for René Beaudoin but going on to arraign him nonetheless.

Beaudoin never recovered. He continued as Speaker until the end of that Parliament, was re-elected, and sat in opposition for one more term, but his career as a rising young politician was over and nobody knew it better than he. Within two years he had disappeared completely from the public eye.

But with all the excitement and tension inside the Commons chamber, the Liberals were unperturbed—at the outset, at least—by any concern about public reaction. They believed, rightly, that the average voter would never understand all the complexities of the pipeline issue, or work up much interest in the constitutional niceties of parliamentary procedure. They therefore concluded, quite wrongly as it turned out, that the pipeline debate would not become a matter of much public interest.

This complacency began to dissolve as the debate went into its second week. First to their amazement, then to their mounting horror the Liberals saw massive queues of indignant citizens waiting, day after day and night after night, to crowd into the public galleries of the House of Commons. As one of the all-night sessions broke up, C. D. Howe, then seventy years old and accustomed to the deference his age and eminence deserved, was almost physically mobbed by a group of shouting young men at the main door of Parliament. Howe was a man of courage, and he certainly showed no fear of this angry crowd, but he was visibly taken aback. He really did not understand why they were so angry, or why their anger focused on him, and the realization of it disconcerted him.

There were two main reasons for this unprecedented public concern with what seemed to be an abstract issue.

One was television. The Canadian Broadcasting Corporation had not then established its corps of staff reporters in the Parliamentary Press Gallery. Instead the CBC relied, as it had done for years, on a panel of correspondents employed by various newspapers or other news media, and chosen by the CBC with the intention of maintaining a fair balance of views and prejudices.

In the pipeline debate this careful balance broke down completely. Normal differences of opinion among reporters disappeared. Rightly or wrongly, the Press Gallery was unanimous in the view that the Government's behavior was outrageous, and reports to every newspaper in Canada glowed with indignation—even in the papers which, editorially, were supporting the Government's stand.

But the effect of printed reports was nothing compared to the breathless broadcasts, delivered on the steps of Parliament from handwritten notes by reporters fresh from the horrors within. The CBC showed great courage in resisting the pressure, which mounted as rapidly as did public indignation, from Government sources to choke off this barrage of unfavorable publicity. One result was that the CBC, which until then had been popular on balance with the Liberals though hated by the Conservatives, became hated and feared by three of the four political parties in Canada. (Social Credit had always regarded the CBC as an infamous organization of godless intellectuals.) In the particular case of the pipeline debate the Conservatives reaped the benefit of the CBC's news policy, but they were not converted to admiration—rather, their former suspicions were strengthened and confirmed, as they noted what lethal damage a hostile broadcast could do to a government and a political party.

In fact they somewhat overestimated the broadcasters' strength. Potent as they were, these hostile reports would not have had the effect they did had they not borne out an opinion the Canadian public had already formed—the opinion that the Liberal Establishment was corrupted by the arrogance of long-continued and seemingly unchallengeable power.

It's not easy now to recall the mood of those days. After ten years in which every party in turn has been racked with self-doubt and subjected to public humiliation, it is almost incredible that only a decade ago the Liberals were regarded, not only by themselves but even by their enemies, as eternal. The very voters who disliked them most despaired of getting rid of them.

Hence the pipeline debate became a symbol of the pattern of behavior that the Government had established, more or less unconsciously, in all fields. For better and for worse, the powers that be were accepted as ordained of God. The men in office sometimes asked themselves whether they really deserved to be God's chosen instruments in molding Canada's destiny, but that they were so chosen they never doubted for an instant.

Or if they did, the doubts were fleeing—a mere symptom of a passing mood.

In December 1957, six months after the Liberal defeat, I had a conversation with C. D. Howe in the quiet study of his Rockcliffe Park home which had then become his principal place of business. I had gone to see him on business, late one afternoon, but when we finished that, C.D. poured a drink apiece and began to talk politics. Naturally, he was pretty sharply critical of the new Diefenbaker Government—so much so that I felt moved to say: "I think I should tell you, Mr. Howe, that I was one of those who thought your Government should be turned out last June, and I still think so."

"Of course we should have been turned out," said Howe. "We were too old. *I* was too old. I didn't have the patience any more that it takes to deal with Parliament."

He took a sip of his drink and then went on: "You know, over a year ago I went to the Prime Minister [St. Laurent] and suggested that he and I ought to retire. He wouldn't hear of it—I guess he'd decided he was going to live forever, and everything was to go on as it was going. So he said nonsense, we must both stay. So we did—and look what happened."

XVI

Suez: The Thankless Task of Mediation

AT THE PRESENTATION of the Nobel Peace Prize in Stockholm in late 1957 Gunnar Jahn, chairman of the Nobel Committee, said: "The Suez crisis was a victory for the United Nations and for the man who contributed more than anyone else to save the world at that time. That man was Lester Pearson."

But it was an ironic coincidence, if indeed it was a coincidence at all, that in the year since the Suez crisis Lester Pearson had been voted out of the office that made possible his services to peace in 1956. The former Secretary of State for External Affairs, former chairman of the United Nations General Assembly, former draftsman of the North Atlantic Alliance and the Colombo Plan for Commonwealth mutual aid, former diplomat of international fame was now a private member of the Canadian House of Commons, not yet (though soon to become) even Leader of the Opposition. For this sudden transformation there were many reasons, but one of them undoubtedly was the Suez crisis and the behavior therein of the St. Laurent Government and its foreign secretary, Lester B. Pearson.

Pearson's sin, in the eyes of his Canadian critics, was his failure to stand at the side of Britain, France, and Israel as Australia and New Zealand had done, and make a minority of six instead of five against the overwhelmingly adverse votes the UN General Assembly had given against the Anglo-French adventure in Suez. Earl Rowe, who as the party's senior MP and only privy councilor was Acting Leader of the Conservative Opposition, found it "shocking" that a Canadian Prime Minister had "repudiated the

British in public, for taking action which has now been generally justified and has meant perhaps the saving for the time being of the Middle East." Howard Green, a staunch British Empire man who in 1959 became Minister of External Affairs in the Diefenbaker Cabinet, was even more bitter in his attack:

"It's high time Canada had a Government that will not knife Canada's two best friends in the back."

John Diefenbaker, who was to become Leader of the Opposition a few days later (George Drew had resigned because of illness), was more moderate in his language but he did use several times a phrase he was to reiterate all through the 1957 election campaign: St. Laurent and Pearson, by their policies, had "put Britain and France in the same bag with Soviet Russia" as aggressors.

Exactly the opposite was the case, but this was not easy to explain in the foggy days of November 1956. Canada's Parliament was not the only one in which confusion reigned, and to which honest men were making contradictory statements with passionate conviction. Pearson was one of the very few statesmen in the entire world to form a clear and accurate appraisal of the Suez affair from the outset, and to retain it through all the twisting and turning, the chaos and calamity that ensued.

President Nasser of Egypt seized the Suez Canal, literally at gun point, on July 26, his retaliation for the refusal of U. S. Secretary of State John Foster Dulles to lend Egypt the money to build the high dam at Aswan. Reaction in Britain and France was immediate and indignant. The Suez Canal was operated by a private company, whose shareholders were mainly French and included citizens of many nations, but the canal itself was traditionally regarded as "Britain's life line," and in truth it was the channel for all Europe's oil supply. British troops had occupied the canal as recently as 1953, and the fact that Sir Anthony Eden (then Foreign Secretary) had arranged the terms of their departure with Nasser made him all the more furious at Nasser's breach of their understanding. He and French Prime Minister Guy Mollet determined on a joint reoccupation of the canal zone.

Had they been able to carry out that intention immediately, with little or no bloodshed, the Suez crisis might never have become a crisis at all. Even Egyptians did not expect Britain and France to take this affront lying down. "We wouldn't really have blamed them for taking action at the time," a leading citizen of Cairo said to me six months later. Blockage of the canal was recognized as a threat to the vital interests of western Europe, and nobody—not even Nasser himself—was sure on July 26 that the Egyptians would be able to keep the canal open without the help of the highly paid, and supposedly highly skilled, European pilots whom the Suez Canal Company employed.

Military unreadiness made prompt intervention impossible. It turned out, despite the huge amounts of money that the armed services consumed in both countries, that the French could not land forces in less than a month and the British would need at least six weeks. That left plenty of time for international consultations, which were called at once, and a series of plans for peaceful settlement of the Suez "issue," which in abstract legal terms was a very complex issue indeed. Even Britain and France admitted the right of a sovereign nation to expropriate a private company within its borders, and Nasser, once the coup was complete, made very conciliatory noises about negotiating compensation in one form or another. Most important of all, the canal was not in fact blocked. Ships continued to pass through as usual.

But Lester Pearson, for one, was not reassured by the seeming calm of August. In a memorandum written August 6, and quoted at length in Terence Robertson's book *Crisis*, he said: "Our main worry is that the United Kingdom and France have gone too far in committing themselves to the use of force if the forthcoming conference [of Suez Canal users] does not produce a result satisfactory to them. . . . I hope I am wrong, but if not, where do we go then? . . .

"It is clear that every possible effort must be made to prevent a chain of developments which would result in Anglo-French military force being exerted against Egypt in a way which would split the Commonwealth, weaken the Anglo-American alliance, and have general consequences that would benefit nobody but Moscow."

What was written as a political analysis turned out to be a chillingly accurate prophecy. But meanwhile, so far as outsiders could see, things began to shake down into the customary calm. The maritime nations met and set up a Suez Canal Users Association (SCUA) which was to negotiate with the Egyptian government on the operation and maintenance of the canal. The Egyptian authorities did not stop those ships which, on the instruction of their owners or their governments, had paid their tolls in Paris to the Suez Canal Company. The withdrawal in September of the European pilots did not, as predicted, lead to instant blockage of the canal. (This was a surprise to the British and the French but not to the Norwegians, who had taken the trouble to question their own sea captains and learned that any competent seaman could take his ship through this narrow stretch of flat water with no pilot at all, if necessary.)

Pearson was still apprehensive. He had been appointed to a three-man committee of NATO that summer, to examine and report on any non-military functions that the North Atlantic Alliance might assume, and in that capacity made a quick tour of Europe in August. He came back very worried. "The British and the French haven't cooled down in the least," he said in a conversation just after his return. "The way they talk about Suez is enough to make your hair stand on end." But as September and then October went by with no serious incidents, and as negotiations with the Egyptians proceeded with ever increasing calm, he too began to hope that the critical period was over.

It was merely approaching. Without a hint to any of their allies the French, British, and Israeli governments were planning a joint campaign for late October and early November. It was hardly surprising that Prime Minister Eden did not inform his friends in Washington or in the Commonwealth, since he was keeping his own foreign service and even some of his own Cabinet equally in the dark, but the secrecy aggravated the feelings of outrage in Washington and in Ottawa when the Israeli invasion of Sinai began on October 29, and the Royal Air Force supported it by knocking out the Cairo airport and the bombers Egypt had got from the Soviet Union.

Pearson was not as upset by this as St. Laurent was. "After all," he said reasonably, "they couldn't have told us or the Americans what they were going to do, or we'd have stopped them." But to Prime Minister St. Laurent, who regarded candid consultation as a fundamental of the relations among friendly countries, Eden's secrecy was a major betrayal which he never quite forgave.

Thousands of ordinary Canadian voters, and dozens of Canadian editorial writers, felt the same. There was heavy pressure on Pearson, when he left Ottawa for New York to attend the emergency session of the United Nations Assembly, to join the United States in open denunciation of the Anglo-French adventure.

But there was also heavy pressure in the opposite direction. Thousands more believed Britain must be right, and Canada's duty was to support her—"Ready, aye ready"—in this hour of trial. These were the folk, some but by no means all of them British-born, who felt and still feel that Pearson "let the Commonwealth down" by abstaining on some votes, voting with the majority on others, and generally leaving it to Australia and New Zealand to stand alone beside the Mother Country of her ill-starred associates.

Pearson resisted both pressures, and was duly criticized for being halfhearted, wishy-washy and not knowing his own mind. He knew his mind very well. His objective was not to pass judgment or apportion blame but to find a basis on which the unity of the Commonwealth and the Western Alliance could be restored. To do this he had first to avert a formal denunciation of Britain, France, and Israel as aggressors, and the imposition of sanctions against them. Second and much more difficult, he had to find some face-saving device whereby Britain and France could retreat, without too much loss of dignity, from a position which had become patently untenable.

There was no serious doubt on this latter point—the position was untenable, all right. The Soviet Union had offered to back the Egyptians with "volunteers" and even with nuclear weapons if necessary. The United States had pointedly refrained from promising any support against such Soviet action, provided it took place outside NATO territory. Militarily, Britain and France were hopelessly vulnerable.

Politically, their posture was even worse. The official British doctrine was that their forces were deployed to "prevent the spread of war" and to "separate the combatants" while protecting that vital avenue of European supply, the Suez Canal. But the Israeli-Arab war was already over, a UN cease-fire resolution adopted and accepted by both the combatants (albeit somewhat reluctantly on Israel's part), fully thirty-six hours *before* British infantry landed at Port Said behind a curtain of naval shellfire and French paratroops dropped on the other side of the canal's northern entrance. As for the protection of the canal as an international facility, it had not been closed for a single hour until the British attacked to "keep it open." It then was closed by the sinking of Egyptian blockships, and remained closed for months.

Pearson knew all this when he suggested, and got the UN Assembly to accept by a vote of 57–0, the United Nations Emergency Force which, in the event, patrolled the Israeli-Egyptian frontier in the Gaza strip for ten and a half years. As a concept it was anything but new. UN police forces had been proposed repeatedly since 1945 at every official and unofficial level, notably by John Diefenbaker in the Canadian House of Commons the previous January. The merit of Pearson's initiative was not its originality as an idea but its timeliness at a critical moment— that, plus the diplomatic skill by which he managed to get it accepted by all concerned.

This was a considerable achievement, as the Nobel Committee decided the following year, but it made strangely little impact at home. The Canadians who went to the Middle East at the time, too late for the five-day war in Sinai but in plenty of time for the long painful aftermath, had good reason to feel proud of their country. It was generally conceded, not only by Arabs and

Americans but even by the numerous Englishmen who were still there, that the Suez adventure had been an unmitigated disaster and that Canada had done a splendid job of picking up the pieces and minimizing the damage. Especially was it clear that the Canadian action had saved the Commonwealth from breaking in two along the color line.

So it was more than merely surprising, it was astounding to come home and discover a widespread and deeply rooted opinion in Canada that Lester Pearson had somehow "let the Commonwealth down" by his failure to vote with Britain and France on each and all occasions. Voices that had died away even in Westminster were still strident in Ottawa. And Hansard revealed that in the four-day special session of Canada's Parliament at the end of November, the Government's posture had been curiously defensive.

Partly this was due to a fuss that arose over Canada's contribution to the United Nations Emergency Force. Pearson at the outset had offered a Canadian contingent, and in the second week of November a battalion had started to move—the Queen's Own Rifles, then based in Calgary. The aircraft carrier *Magnificent* was called home from the coast of Scotland, and arrived in Halifax on November 13, the same day the Queen's Own began to arrive by air. Within five days the *Magnificent* was refitted as a troop carrier and floating military base, at an approximate cost of $50,000, and the Queen's Own was ready to sail.

But then disquieting word came from Cairo. President Nasser, it turned out, did not like the idea of a regiment called the Queen's Own—dressed in British-type uniforms and owing allegiance to the Queen of England—coming in to replace the British invaders who were withdrawing from the Canal Zone. The resolution itself had stipulated that the UN force should be set up "with the consent of the nations concerned," of whom Egypt was undeniably one. And although it had also been stated, in the intervening days, that neither Egypt nor any other nation was to have a veto power over the composition of the force, even the UN could see the point of Nasser's reluctance to accept a regiment called the Queen's Own. So it was tactfully conveyed to Canada, through a message from the Canadian General E. L. M. Burns, who was commander of the UN force, that the Canadian battalion was not really required at this time. Canadian technicians would be preferred, and 637 of these were sent to Egypt by air. The Queen's Own Regiment stayed home.

The whole incident was an acute embarrassment to the Government in Ottawa. Why, asked John Diefenbaker in his most accusing tone, should a "thug" like Nasser be allowed any say in which Canadian unit was sent to take over from the British in Suez? Not only in Parliament but among the public, the notion was widespread that the purpose of this expeditionary force was to punish Nasser, not protect him. (It was even shared by soldiers in the field. A Canadian private, gloomily raking leaves at the base camp at Abu Suweir in late November, said: "I thought we was coming here to clear them Egyptians out of the canal zone. And now, damned if they ain't treating us like prisoners of war.")

Another ground of accusation was a message sent by St. Laurent to Eden which, rumor said, had been couched in "blistering" terms. St. Laurent asked Eden's permission to make public the exchange of two messages between them, which of course had been sent on a mutually confidential basis. Eden refused. The text of the "blistering" message has never been officially published.

Terence Robertson, however, was able to obtain and print an extended paraphrase of it, including several direct quotations. From Robertson's account it appears that St. Laurent said no more than that he thought it "regrettable" for Britain to take military action when the Security Council was seized of the affair. What disappointed Eden most was nothing St. Laurent said, but something he did not say. He did not offer what Eden had specifically requested, some indication of "understanding and support" for the British action and policy.

Even this much, however, was not known during that heated debate in the last days of November 1956. The Government was of course sustained in Parliament, only the Conservatives voting for their own amendment to the Address in Reply to the Speech from the Throne; the two minor parties supported the Liberals. But the wound was deeper than it seemed, and did not quickly heal.

Two full years later, at the 1958 meeting of the UN General Assembly, a Canadian diplomat happened to mention Pearson's Nobel Prize to a Conservative MP who was on the Canadian delegation. The MP snorted with contempt. "Nobel Prize," he said scornfully. "That was just Pearson's reward for voting with the Russians."

XVII

The Diefenbaker Phenomenon

CONSTERNATION IS far too mild a word for the effect on the Progressive Conservative Party, and especially on its leadership group, of George Drew's sudden illness in August 1956.

Drew was then sixty-two years old, but he looked ten years younger—tall, ramrod-straight, with a ruddy complexion and a clear strong voice, he seemed the very picture of mature vigor. Yet he was far from well. He'd had an illness the previous winter which his party spokesmen minimized at the time, passing it off as no worse than a bout of flu. It was a type of meningitis from which, until then, nobody Drew's age had ever recovered. A new antibiotic saved his life but left him gravely weakened.

Because party leaders must always be presented as full of health and energy, Drew bravely cooperated in the pretense that he hadn't really been sick at all. As soon as he was able he got out of bed and reappeared in his office, looking and sounding far better than he really felt, and he never took time for a proper convalescence.

Then came the pipeline debate and the great Conservative filibuster. Because House rules allow the Opposition Leader unlimited time, Drew put on marathon performances at each stage of that long-drawn-out battle, often speaking for several hours at a time. Like everyone else, and with even more reason, he was exhausted when the session was over.

In August the accumulation of fatigue and the delayed reaction from his winter illness caught up with him. He went to hospital in a state of collapse not dissimilar to the one Prime Minister St.

Laurent had suffered two years before. Doctors were unable to find any identifiable infection, but it was obvious the patient was very ill. He was also deeply depressed. Like St. Laurent, he decided to retire and, unlike St. Laurent, he stuck to that decision.

This was shattering news to a party that was preening itself on its best year in more than two decades. The successful fight against the emergency powers of the Defense Production Act in 1955, the unsuccessful but no less glorious fight against the pipeline bill in 1956 had made George Drew's leadership more secure than it had ever been since he was chosen in 1948. The rumbles of discontent that followed his second electoral defeat in 1953 had died away. The party was on the march, and though nobody really expected to win the next election—to foes as well as friends, the myth of Liberal invincibility was still strong—there were high hopes for a near victory in 1957 and a clear win the next time around, when the unbeatable St. Laurent would have retired.

Thus far, the dismay was felt by all Conservatives. For the party's leadership group there were other, even more disconcerting reflections.

At the previous Conservative leadership convention in 1948, the runner-up to George Drew had been John Diefenbaker, MP for Prince Albert and favorite son of Saskatchewan. (He was in fact, and remained for nine more years, the only Conservative elected in that province.) Diefenbaker believed, and persuaded many others to believe, that he had been robbed of the leadership in 1948 by a sinister conspiracy of eastern politicians and rich men from Bay Street and St. James Street, who had captured the convention by bringing in droves of delegates from ridings in Quebec where no real Conservative organization had ever existed. This charge had never been proved, but it was widely enough accepted to make Diefenbaker a bit of a martyr. Since he was also, on other grounds, the favorite candidate of western delegates and of many a rural Conservative MP, he was from the start the strongest candidate to succeed George Drew.

By definition, therefore, the men who ran the party under Drew were not the men closest to John Diefenbaker. They were a mutually congenial group of true conservatives, in the dictionary as well as the political sense, and they regarded Diefenbaker quite rightly as an agrarian radical who was a Conservative only in name. Aside from this fundamental difference of philosophy there was also, after so many years of intraparty feuding, a large accumulation of mutual, personal dislike.

The last thing the Drew men wanted was to see Diefenbaker win the convention. The problem was, how to stop him?

Donald Fleming had been a candidate for the leadership in 1948, though not at that time a serious one. This time he was serious. He was highly regarded by Drew's inner circle, of which indeed he was a prominent member, but his friends had grave doubt that he could win. They cast about for someone else.

George Nowlan, the tall smiling Nova Scotian who was a pillar of the party's in-group at the time, was sent off to Toronto to see if he could persuade Sidney Smith, president of the University of Toronto, to stand for the leadership. Smith and Nowlan had lived in the same boardinghouse at Dalhousie University, when Nowlan was a law student and Smith a very young professor, and both were just back from World War I; they had been close friends ever since. In Toronto, Nowlan put up a persuasive case, and Smith was tempted. But after mulling it over and consulting his doctor, he decided to stay where he was.

By coincidence I happened to come back from Toronto on the same train with George Nowlan returning from his last, fruitless mission. We sat up all night in my compartment, with me listening and Nowlan canvassing and recanvassing, with ever deepening gloom, the probabilities at the party convention. He would of course support Don Fleming, and so now would all his friends, but he had even less hope than before of averting a Diefenbaker victory—which he regarded as an unmitigated disaster.

When the convention came in mid-December, John Diefenbaker won by a crushing majority on the first ballot. To his 774 votes Fleming had only 393, of which more than two hundred were from Quebec. Davie Fulton, the former Rhodes Scholar from Kamloops, British Columbia, got 117.

As the Diefenbaker victory was announced Leon Balcer, the leader of the party's Quebec group, turned on his heel and walked out of the hall—under the glaring eye of the television cameras. Whether he meant it or not, it looked like a public renunciation by French-Canadian Conservatives of the party's new leader.

Not, therefore, the most auspicious of beginnings to a new era in Conservative fortunes. Few would have suspected on that December evening that in six months' time John Diefenbaker would become the first Conservative Prime Minister of Canada since the defeat of Richard Bedford Bennett in 1935.

True, there were negative as well as positive reasons for thinking it might happen. The Liberals, weakened by the Defense Production Act and the pipeline debates, weakened further by the Suez crisis, were calmly continuing to do themselves no good.

Financial policy was under fierce debate in that winter of 1956–57, the months preceding Walter Harris' third Budget. The Bank of Canada and the Finance Department were convinced that inflation was still the major threat, and were arguing for a tight-money policy to combat it—high interest rates, credit restrictions, no tax cuts even though it was an election year. C. D. Howe's Department of Trade and Commerce, of which Mitchell Sharp was deputy minister, thought the economic weather signs pointed to recession. The department's analysis of the economy for the coming year, signed by Sharp as deputy minister but prepared by a team of economists under V. J. Macklin, predicted a slowdown of economic growth and a rise in unemployment, and argued therefore for a policy of expansion. (This confidential document, prepared as one side of a policy debate within the Government, was the famous "Hidden Report" with which Prime Minister Diefenbaker was to make so much hay a year later.)

The tight-money faction won the policy debate. In the spring of 1957 housing loans were hard to get, as indeed were loans of any kind. Even though Harris reported a surplus of $282 million, tax cuts were minimal. An old-age pension increase of ten dollars a month, from forty to fifty dollars, had been planned—but when Quebec Liberals demanded and got a rise in family allowances too, the Finance Department insisted that this amount should be taken out of the pension boost. So the old-age pension went up only six dollars a month, and "Six-Buck Harris" became the favorite target of the Diefenbaker campaign.

Meanwhile western farmers were unhappy. Unsold wheat had been piling up in Canada for several years, until every grain elevator in Canada was bulging. Farmers were storing surplus grain on their own land, but getting no money for it. They started a campaign for "cash advances on farm-stored grain"—to which the inflation-minded Liberals paid no heed. C. D. Howe said it would be administratively impossible, even if it were not economically unwise, to lend on such security.

Moreover, Howe didn't believe the farmers were in any real distress, and hadn't the slightest hesitation in saying so. At an election campaign meeting in Carman, Manitoba, a rather portly farmer was voicing the usual complaints. Howe poked him in the belly, and said: "It looks to me as if you've been eating well enough, under a Liberal Government." Nobody in his audience thought this funny. A similar incident took place in Morris, Manitoba. Howe said to a complainer: "When your party organizes a meeting, then you can have the platform and we can ask the questions." The heckler pushed his way forward and identified himself as the president of the local Liberal Association. Even the imperturbable C. D. Howe was a trifle abashed. Some of his colleagues began to realize for the first time that they were in serious trouble. (One such was that so-called political apprentice, L. B. Pearson. "Don't be so complacent!" he told a party audience in Kingston, Ontario. "If we don't work as hard as we can, we may lose this election.")

The incident that sticks in my own mind most vividly, as a symptom of Liberal decay in 1957, was minor and pathetic—an accident really, and perhaps therefore a symbol of how accident-prone the lordly Liberals had become.

It happened at the climactic Liberal rally in Toronto's Maple Leaf Gardens, in the final week of the campaign. The meeting had everything money could buy—lavish decorations, two-tone spotlighting, Lorne Greene flown in from Hollywood to intone a kind of Hymn to Canada as overture, written in the finest of advertising-agency prose and accompanied by background music composed for the occasion. From the serried ranks of Cabinet ministers and other dignitaries on the platform, a fortunate few stepped forward to make brief, punchy speeches. Finally "Uncle Louis" St. Laurent took the podium, warmed by the rapturous cheers of real affection that greeted him, and began to read a speech that went over, at the beginning, quite well.

In the middle of it a slight figure, carrying a placard with a large photo of St. Laurent, marched to the front of the great hall and mounted the steps to the platform. The Prime Minister hesitated, evidently thinking this must be a part of the program of which nobody had warned him. But once arrived in front of the speaker's stand, the boy took the photo of St. Laurent, tore it in four pieces, and threw the shreds at the Prime Minister's feet.

One of the Liberal vice-presidents in the front row, a chunky ex-athlete, charged forward like an angry bull. He hit the boy full in the chest and knocked him backward, a drop of seven or eight feet to the cement floor. Spectators crowded around. The boy was carried out, apparently unconscious.

As it turned out, he was not seriously hurt, and his unprompted gesture had been a shocking piece of rudeness. But it was hard to keep this in mind, watching his limp body carried out of the hall. He was a schoolboy, aged fifteen, who apparently had taken the pipeline-cum-Suez campaign speeches more seriously than they were intended to be.

The Prime Minister resumed his speech, but the spell was broken. Now he sounded like a tired, confused old man. His large platoon of supporters on the platform looked suddenly, and most unjustly, like a rather brutal and nasty gang. The previously enthusiastic audience turned cool, and the meeting broke up on a very low note of enthusiasm. Like the campaign.

Meanwhile, for John Diefenbaker the trend was exactly the opposite. From a slow start, when even he didn't seriously expect to win, he had been moving steadily upward toward a now unmistakable triumph—not, to be sure, toward anything like certain victory, but toward the certainty of such massive gains as would count as a moral victory anyway.

He himself said later that it was the meeting in Charlottetown, Prince Edward Island, early in the campaign, which first made him think he might really turn the Liberals out. Prince Edward Island in those days rated as Liberal territory. Of its four seats, one had been Liberal since 1904, two since 1935; the fourth and only Conservative seat was held by the immensely popular Angus MacLean, who was much stronger than his party. It was not unreasonable to think that if Diefenbaker could sweep Prince Edward Island he could win almost anywhere. The wild enthusiasm of that Charlottetown meeting convinced *him*, if nobody else, that he might do exactly that. As the campaign progressed, his confidence grew. Unlike St. Laurent, he loved campaigning, and he felt stronger day by day as he met ever larger and ever more enthusiastic crowds.

By Peter Newman's computation (in his book *Renegade in Power*), Diefenbaker traveled 20,845 miles and delivered 103 speeches to a total audience of 50,000 in 180 electoral constituencies. The size of the audiences mattered less than their mood. They were ecstatic. Diefenbaker was not, after all, a wholly unfamiliar figure in Canadian politics, having by then been an MP for seventeen years and a chronic loser in previous elections for approximately seventeen more. But in that miraculous year 1957, people greeted him as if he had just stepped out of a golden chariot from heaven. He made approximately the same speech to all of them, varying it in voltage rather than in substance according to his mood and theirs, speaking without notes and often without much coherence, but responding to the masses who were so audibly responding to him.

Election night was a triumph for him, a shambles for the St. Laurent Government.

Nova Scotia, the first province to be heard from, had elected only one Conservative in 1953, George Nowlan. In 1957, ten of the twelve Nova Scotia seats went Conservative, and one of the Liberals defeated was the Nova Scotia minister, Robert Winters. Newfoundland, Joey Smallwood's fief, had gone solidly Liberal in 1953; in 1957 the Conservatives took both the St. Johns seats. New Brunswick's three Tories became five. So it went across Canada. Only Quebec, loyal to their own Louis St. Laurent, sent back sixty-four Liberals from its seventy-five seats, and even there Conservative strength rose from four to nine.

Of Liberal defeats, the quality was almost as important as the quantity. Nine of the twenty Cabinet ministers went down, including Walter Harris, Stuart Garson the mainstay of Manitoba, Hugues Lapointe in Quebec, the son of the great Ernest, and even—most incredible of all—the great C. D. Howe himself, felled by a then unknown schoolteacher named Douglas Fisher of the CCF.

Howe's last words as an active politician were characteristic.

"I'm not conceding anything," he said rather grumpily, about half past ten on election night, "but I think I'll go round and congratulate my opponent, and then go to bed."

When the Liberal survivors gathered themselves together in Ottawa later in the week, their resignation was not inevitable. They had held 105 seats to the Conservatives' 112, but the CCF had twenty-five, a gain of two over their previous standing, and CCF leader M. J. Coldwell had always (except in the pipeline debate) tended to side with the Liberals rather than the Tories. Some ministers, notably Saskatchewan's Jimmy Gardiner (who himself had squeaked back with only 349 majority), urged St. Laurent to carry on, face the House of Commons in September and see whether he could win a vote of confidence.

St. Laurent wouldn't hear of it. So far as he was concerned, the people had spoken. They had voted no confidence in the Government, and he accepted their judgment. On June 21, 1957, just eleven days after the election—barely time to tidy things up for an unexpected departure—he presented his resignation to the Governor-General, Right Honorable Vincent Massey, who thereupon "sent for" John George Diefenbaker.

XVIII

Diefenbaker Years: The Rocket and the Stick

EXHILARATION WAS THE MOOD of practically all Canadians in the
latter half of June 1957. Most people, even Liberals, had been
heartily sick of the Liberal Government. Most people, even Conservatives, had nevertheless thought the Liberal Government invincible. The fact that we had managed to turn them out was a
triumph, and was felt as a triumph even by those who had voted
Liberal. The 2,702,573 men and women who *had* voted Liberal
(actually 129,647 more than had voted Conservative) seemed to
vanish overnight—they suddenly became as hard to find as those
who admit to having voted Social Credit in Calgary or Vancouver.

As the new Conservative Cabinet emerged from Rideau Hall
after being sworn in on the morning of June 23, Robert B. Bryce,
Cabinet secretary and clerk of the Privy Council, said: "Don't
forget there's a Cabinet meeting this afternoon." George Nowlan
said, with mock gravity: "Will there be someone to show us
where to go?" His colleagues laughed uproariously at the mild
joke. A trifle self-conscious in their morning coats and their newly
acquired dignities, they were nevertheless as happy and excited as
a group of children on Christmas morning.

All intraparty feuds seemed to have been dissolved in the
warm glow of victory, and all grudges forgotten. Donald Fleming, the stop-Diefenbaker candidate at the convention only six
months before, had become Minister of Finance, and George
Nowlan, Minister of National Revenue. Davie Fulton, the third-
place candidate for party leadership, had got the Justice Depart-

ment, which he wanted (as well as Immigration, which he didn't want), and even Leon Balcer, most implacable of all the anti-Diefenbaker men, had not been excluded altogether. He was Solicitor-General, a sort of parliamentary assistant to the Minister of Justice but at least a member of the Government. J. M. Macdonnell was disappointed, after his twelve years as financial critic, to be Minister without Portfolio instead of Minister of Finance, but he was seventy-three and not in the best of health; no one seriously suggested that he had been demoted for having opposed the chief.

Civil servants, too, were excited and pleased at the election result. True, the two Ottawa seats had gone Liberal as usual, but political color in the civil service was not as deep-dyed as some Conservatives thought. Mitchell Sharp, then Deputy Minister of Trade and Commerce (and six years later a Liberal minister of the same department), called his senior staff together on June 22 and gave them a pep talk on their duty to the new regime.

"This is a challenge to us and to our form of government," he said. "It's up to us to show that we can be just as loyal and just as capable with a different political party in office. They'll need our help. Let's make sure they get it."

The day after his Cabinet was sworn, Prime Minister Diefenbaker flew to London for his first Commonwealth conference. He took the rooms at the Dorchester Hotel that had been reserved for Louis St. Laurent, and the invitation to speak to the Canada Club July 1 that had previously been accepted by L. B. Pearson. Since he himself had taken the portfolio of External Affairs for the time being, he did not require the presence of any Cabinet colleague, but for old times' sake he took along his new Minister of Defense, George Pearkes, the venerable soldier and Victoria Cross winner who had nominated Diefenbaker for the Conservative leadership both in 1948 and in 1956.

Pearkes took the opportunity to go on to Paris to be briefed at NATO headquarters. On his return to London a few days later he had an informal press conference with the Canadian correspondents. Someone asked what changes he intended to make in defense policy. Pearkes said he didn't expect to make any. Rather surprised, the reporter reminded General Pearkes that he had, after all, been uttering rather sharp criticisms of defense policy for twelve years; how could he now continue it unchanged?

Pearkes's reply was disarming. "I have learned more about the defense situation in the last eight days," he said, "than I had been able to learn in the preceding twelve years. I now see that some of my criticisms were ill founded."

He couldn't have said anything that would have made a better impression. By implication he sounded a keynote that was never actually spoken out loud, but that was probably more effective for the Conservatives than any other in the months to come:

"Give us a chance."

Meanwhile Diefenbaker, at his level, was going over extremely well. This was the year Ghana entered the Commonwealth, the first trickle of the African flood, and some older members—notably the Australians—were putting out tentative feelers about the formation of a two-tier Commonwealth, the Old Dominions (who happened to be white) in one category and the New Dominions, brown shading to black, in another. Diefenbaker said nothing, but he made a publicized point of calling on Kwame Nkrumah, the coal-black President of Ghana.

For the Commonwealth as a whole, though, he had things to say so friendly, so enthusiastic that the British could hardly believe their ears. Ever since Mackenzie King's first days they had been used to hearing Canadians demand more autonomy, less imperial supervision, greater centrifugal force in this Commonwealth of Nations "equal in status, in no way subordinate one to another." Now, here was a Prime Minister of Canada talking as if the Statute of Westminster had never been drafted, as if Canadians were indeed (as a Speaker of the British House of Commons misguidedly called them in 1944) a nation of "sixteen million Britishers." And his talk about expanding Commonwealth trade was music in the ears of a nation already worried about its lagging exports and anemic balance of payments.

Only a few notes of dubiety were struck.

At the Canada Club dinner in the Savoy Hotel, before a capacity audience mainly composed of Englishmen with interests in Canada, Diefenbaker delivered a long, rambling speech on which he'd obviously had little time to work. At the end of it, the Englishman sitting beside me turned and asked: "Was that speech being broadcast directly to Canada?"

I said no, I didn't think so.

"Odd," my companion said. "It sounded to me more like a political speech for Canada than an address for this audience."

More quietly, at lunch a day or two later, a British civil servant said: "We're all delighted by the spirit of your Prime Minister's speeches, the friendly tone. But what does embarrass us a bit is the fact that your Prime Minister has not yet made himself clear. The impression has gone abroad that he has made some definite proposals [about expanding Commonwealth trade], but so far he hasn't."

This British expectancy was satisfied on the very day of Diefenbaker's return to Ottawa. He went straight from the airport to the Parliamentary Press Gallery, and there (in answer to a question) elaborated his view of what Canada should do about Commonwealth trade. About fifteen per cent of Canadian imports, he said, should be shifted from the United States to the United Kingdom.

The statement caused great excitement in Whitehall. The new British High Commissioner to Canada, Sir Saville Garner, was called home to discuss this Canadian "offer." Garner was new as head of mission (he'd arrived in the midst of the Suez crisis the previous autumn) but he had already served a term in Ottawa in the 1940s as deputy high commissioner, and he knew Canadian politicians quite well. He suggested, hesitantly and politely, that perhaps the Canadian "offer" had not been quite as specific as it sounded.

The suggestion was greeted with incredulity. Don't be silly, they said in effect; this was a statement by the Prime Minister of Canada, and prime ministers didn't make idle remarks off the top of their heads. It must, it simply must have been a serious offer.

What they did believe, though, was that a man so newly in office might not have realized the difficulty of extending or enlarging a trading preference without violating the terms of the Geneva Agreement on Tariffs and Trade. This was a complex technical problem which the British felt it was up to them, as the more experienced, to solve. They quickly saw one solution—a complete free trade agreement between the two countries, which GATT specifically permitted.

Derick Heathcoat Amory, then Harold Macmillan's Minister of Agriculture (and later, as Viscount Amory, British High Commissioner to Canada), came to Ottawa early in September to discuss the possibility of a free trade agreement. The suggestion (it never really developed into a formal proposal) was greeted with a horrified silence. Heathcoat Amory could see at once that Garner had been right—the new Government had no clear idea and no serious intention of changing the pattern of Canada's foreign trade, except by urging the British and everyone else to buy more Canadian goods. Free trade with Britain, even with the fifteen-year interval of adjustment which the British were suggesting, was politically unthinkable.

But the British government had a political problem of its own. Prime Minister Macmillan was just beginning his long campaign to take Britain into the European Common Market. Opponents of that policy, of whom Lord Beaverbrook and his *Daily Express* were the most vociferous, were continually pointing to "expansion of Commonwealth trade" as a preferable alternative, and the "new Canadian offer" had been grist to Beaverbrook's mill. It became important to the British to make it known that the "Canadian offer" had not meant anything.

While Commonwealth finance ministers were meeting at Mont Tremblant, Quebec, at the end of September, the story of the British free trade offer appeared in the *Financial Times* of London and in the Montreal *Star*. The *Star* reached Mont Tremblant just as Donald Fleming was about to hold a joint press conference with Peter Thorneycroft, British Chancellor of the Exchequer. Fleming, queried about the *Star* story, brusquely replied that he did not comment on such newspaper rumors. Then, to his visible horror, he listened while Thorneycroft, in answer to the same question, confirmed the story in every detail. For the rest of the press conference Fleming continued, in a stunned sort of way, to refer to "this press report," ignoring the fact that the man beside him had just confirmed it.

The revelation of the British offer caused great indignation among Canadian Conservatives. The Toronto *Globe and Mail*, then still a supporter of the Diefenbaker Government, said: "This is the sort of diplomacy we would expect from Moscow, not London." The general public in both countries, of course, quickly forgot the whole incident, but the two governments did not. This was the beginning of a mutual disenchantment which, four years later, became open and bitter.

But in the piping days of 1957 this, too, was no more than a cloud like a man's hand. In general the political barometer at home and abroad was "set fair" for the Diefenbaker Government. It had come into power with a long list of expensive promises, which the Liberals said could not be kept. Diefenbaker proceeded immediately to fulfill the most important, and most expensive, of them:

Western farmers got $150 million for cash advances on farm-stored grain, which the Liberals had called impossible.

Old-age pensioners got a second increase, from forty-six to fifty-five dollars a month, which the Liberals had considered improvident.

Income taxpayers got a cut of $178 million, which the Liberals had deemed inflationary—though in fact, despite budgetary deficits that totaled more than three billion in the Conservatives' six years of office, the cost-of-living index rose by less than two percentage points a year.

These were some of the factual grounds for Diefenbaker's claim, which became first a campaign slogan, then a catch phrase, and finally a bit of a joke: "They said it couldn't be done, but we did it."

In 1957 and 1958, at least, the public was willing to give the new Government full credit for these achievements. The Government was nominally in a minority, in the Parliament that met for the first time on October 14, but in fact it was in a position of impregnable strength. The CCF, not only from remembrance of the pipeline affair but also from the fact that it shared the general feeling of benignity toward the new regime, was not disposed to join in any ganging up of the Opposition. Neither was Social Credit. As for the Liberals, their greatest fear was that somehow, by the normal working of the parliamentary system, they might contrive to defeat the Government and bring on an election—which would, they knew, be disastrous.

As things turned out, it was this very fear that ruined them.

For the first two months of the parliamentary session the Liberals appeared to be in a state of shock. Louis St. Laurent, who quite obviously had never really imagined himself in Opposition, sat on Mr. Speaker's left—with unfailing dignity but with no heart for combat. Pearson, Pickersgill, and Paul Martin, the strongest surviving figures from the Liberal Cabinet, tried in vain to make the new ministers look foolish in the daily question period; aided by the same civil servants who had previously made the Liberals look good, the Conservatives managed to look good too.

The feeling of impotence in Parliament was aggravated by a realization, all the more painful for being so belated, of their unpopularity outside.

"Nobody seems to be sorry that we were beaten," said one of the delegates to the Liberal leadership convention in January. "I can remember grown men crying in the streets when Laurier was defeated. Nothing like that now. People seem to think it was good riddance."

That was certainly the consensus, at the party convention that chose Lester B. Pearson (on the first ballot over Paul Martin) to succeed Louis S. St. Laurent, retired. One after another they warned the new Leader of the Opposition not to move votes of no confidence, not to give Diefenbaker a pretext for the early election that he obviously wanted and would certainly win. (It didn't seem to occur to them that he didn't need a pretext, that his minority position was reason enough.)

It was this kind of advice that prompted Pearson, on his first day in the House as Opposition Leader, to make the worst tactical error of his entire parliamentary career. The order of the day was a motion to go into supply, traditionally the occasion for Opposition parties to air grievances and voice their want of confidence in the government. Pearson had to make some kind of motion, and he was unanimously advised against the conventional motion of non-confidence (on the ground that he might inadvertently win). Against his better judgment he adopted a device contrived by Jack Pickersgill—a motion that "in view of the fact that unemployment has risen drastically, and . . . in view of the desirability at this time of having a government pledged to implement Liberal policies, His Excellency's advisers should, in the opinion of this House, submit their resignations forthwith," i.e., without dissolving Parliament and without another election, but simply handing over to a Liberal Government.

Diefenbaker tore him to shreds. It was the greatest debating performance of his life, perhaps the greatest Canada's Parliament had ever seen, certainly the greatest since the confrontations of Mackenzie King, J. L. Ralston, C. G. Power, and the rest in the conscription debates of 1944. He began with a scorn that was almost lighthearted: "Don't have an election, but give us back our jobs." Then, as he warmed to his theme, he grew stern. So unemployment had drastically increased, had it? And this was said to be the new Government's fault? (One of the Liberal ex-ministers had told the party convention: "They didn't inherit unemployment from us, they invented it.")

From the desk in front of him Diefenbaker picked up a white mimeographed booklet. This was the famous "Hidden Report," the prediction by Mitchell Sharp's economists that unemployment and not inflation was the real threat in 1957, and in the context of that debate it was utterly damning. Pearson slumped lower and lower in his seat as Diefenbaker read out the terrible quotations:

Increases in unemployment had been "clearly greater than seasonal" in the autumn of 1956; "no renewed strengths in corporate profits are expected. . . . The possibility of a more pronounced decline cannot be ruled out. . . . The lower level of exports is likely to result in a decline of cash income on the prairies again. . . . A higher average level of unemployment seems likely in 1957 than in 1956. . . ."

It was devastating. Conservative MPs were in ecstasies of triumph and applause. Liberals were crushed. When, a fortnight later, Diefenbaker without ever having been defeated or even challenged in the House asked the Governor-General for a dissolution anyway, and a new election, he strode forth to a victory as certain as tomorrow's sunrise, and much of his campaign consisted of minor variations on the great speech of January 20. From that day until March 31, election day, was unquestionably the zenith of Diefenbaker's long political career, just as it was Pearson's nadir. The Government came back with 208 seats out of 265, the largest majority in history.

Yet even the moment of triumph contained one seed of disenchantment. The alienation of the federal civil service, which was to become one of the Diefenbaker Government's gravest weaknesses, began with the speech of January 20 and the production of the "Hidden Report."

Mitchell Sharp was horrified when he learned from his new minister, Gordon Churchill, that the Government was considering use of this report as a political weapon. It did not really deserve to be called a "hidden" report at all, since he himself had given it to Churchill in the previous September, but it was a confidential communication from civil servants to the Cabinet and never intended for publication.

Sharp remonstrated with his minister as vigorously as he knew how. The report was, he pointed out, a polemic rather than a balanced document, deliberately prepared to counter the differing views of the Finance Department. It contained many statements and predictions the authors would not have made in public. Finally and above all, it was part of the vast, essential fabric of trust between the government service and the Government itself, and to publish it would unravel this fabric more seriously than the new Cabinet seemed to realize.

Churchill was not convinced. After all, he said, this document related to the past. Its predictions had been put to the test of events, and had proved to be correct in the main. Why should anyone be embarrassed to be shown as an accurate prophet?

"Do you intend to publish the same report for next year?" Sharp inquired.

Churchill wasn't sure about that; it would depend on circumstances.

"If you do intend to publish it," Sharp went on, "I'd be grateful to know as soon as possible just when you propose to do so. And we shall need your advice on what we should say.

"Actually we have already prepared for the present Government several reports of this nature," he added, "which I don't think you would wish to have published."

"Such as what?" Churchill asked.

"For example, an analysis of what would be involved in a fifteen per cent shift of imports from American to British products."

Churchill was sufficiently impressed with this point that Sharp believed, perhaps rightly, he had won the argument with his own minister. It wasn't until the morning of January 20 he learned that, if he had won that argument in the minister's office, he had won it in vain. The Prime Minister had decided otherwise.

Meanwhile Robert Bryce, then clerk of the Privy Council and one of the few civil servants who never lost the confidence of either the Liberal or the Conservative Government, had learned of the plan to use the "Hidden Report." He went to the Prime Minister himself to beg him not to do it. Diefenbaker was unmoved.

In the gallery that afternoon, Sharp noticed with grim amuse-

ment one small detail. He had delivered all available copies of the
report to the Government intact, with a blue cover bearing the
word "SECRET" in capital letters. The flyleaf inside, he remembered, carried the lower classification "CONFIDENTIAL." As
produced in the House of Commons, the report had no blue
cover, just the bare flyleaf. (He learned later that the covers had
been torn off by a team of stenographers in the East Block, whose
lunch hour had been canceled for the purpose.)

Stanley Knowles, the sharp-eyed CCF Whip, noticed a wisp of
blue cardboard under the staple of the copy tabled in the House,
and asked if the report had been tampered with in any way. "We
should be told," he said, "whether the covers were torn off."

"Mr. Speaker, there was no deletion whatever," the Prime
Minister replied. "The document I tabled was the one which
came into my possession in its entirety."

Alienation of the civil service was continued, and aggravated,
by other incidents. There was the Newfoundland loggers' strike
in the winter of 1958–59, when Prime Minister Diefenbaker
vetoed Justice Minister Davie Fulton's decision to send reinforcements to the RCMP in Newfoundland as requested, and as
stipulated by the contract under which the RCMP worked there;
RCMP Commissioner Leonard Nicholson resigned, at substantial personal loss, rather than countenance what he believed to be
a serious breach of faith. There was the dismissal of James Coyne,
governor of the Bank of Canada, in 1961—civil servants were
outraged, not because Coyne was dismissed (though that seemed
a bit superfluous since his seven-year term was about to expire
anyway) but because of the manner in which it was done, the
attempt first to intimidate him into resigning by threatening to
smear him personally, and then the unsuccessful attempt to carry
out the threat when Coyne stood his ground and fought. There
was also the general and growing habit of indecision, the interminable discussions in Cabinet arriving at no conclusion.

Alienation of the business and financial community, which also
began to develop quite early in the Diefenbaker years, had different origins. Ironically, the Government lost a lot of ground

with business by *not* dismissing James Coyne, or at least over-ruling him, long before they did. Coyne was preaching somewhat the same brand of economic nationalism for Canada as later was adopted by Walter Gordon, Pearson's first Minister of Finance, and its reception in the business community was much the same. Also, Coyne persisted in following a tight-money policy at the Bank of Canada at the same time Donald Fleming's Finance Department was piling up huge budgetary deficits in the attempt to stimulate the economy, so that the two policies tended to cancel each other out. Business disliked both of them—the tight money and the budgetary deficits alike. Moreover business, too, felt its confidence shaken by the amount of time and effort required to get any decision, however trivial, out of the new Government.

Peter Newman, in *Renegade in Power,* offers the following observation on the reasons underlying Diefenbaker's reluctance to come to a decision: "Each unresolved national problem represented an addition to his power, since it left the advocates of alternative solutions at his mercy. A decision once taken, on the other hand, represented a dilution of that power, since it lined up the dissatisfied factions against him. . . . He came to regard commitments on important issues, or appointments, as highly dangerous intrusions into his state of self-imposed siege."

Alienation of French-speaking Quebec, perhaps the most important single element in the erosion of Diefenbaker's power, came about more gradually. It was not entirely the Government's fault, either.

Quebec in 1957 had voted one last time for a Liberal Party still led by St. Laurent. As a French-Canadian MP explained at the time: "We French Canadians have never got over feeling guilty for having deserted Laurier in 1911, and we weren't going to desert another one of our own." But when St. Laurent retired and Pearson took over, Quebec's inhibitions were relieved. French Canadians felt as free as everyone else to express their long-pent exasperation with the Liberals. Also, it was obvious the Conservatives were going to win and, like every minority, French

Canadians prefer to have their representatives on the winning side. Fifty of Quebec's seventy-five seats went Conservative.

The quantity was there, the quality was not. For too long, a Quebec Conservative had been almost a contradiction in terms. Members of Conservative families were active in the Union Nationale party of Maurice Duplessis, but not in federal politics. The platoon of MPs that Quebec sent to the Conservative benches in 1958 was, broadly speaking, a seedy lot.

Moreover they were generally assumed, and some of them assumed themselves, to be followers of Duplessis rather than of Diefenbaker. In the spring of 1958, shortly before the new Cabinet appointments were announced, the Montreal *Gazette* carried a story by its Quebec correspondent, Wilbur Arkison, saying which Quebec MPs were to have what Cabinet posts in Ottawa. Noel Dorion, who had been chief Crown Prosecutor for Duplessis and was now MP for the rural county of Bellechasse, was to be leader of the Quebec group and Minister of Justice. Arkison's pipeline to Duplessis' office was very reliable, and nobody mistook this report for idle speculation—it was evidently *le chef's* decision on who should get what.

Naturally, every single one of Arkison's selections turned out to be wrong. Noel Dorion not only did not become Minister of Justice, he did not become a minister at all until three years later. The new men from Quebec were Raymond O'Hurley, an inoffensive timber cruiser from Lotbinière, and Henri Courtemanche of Labelle, a man who'd been an MP before and whom Diefenbaker at least knew, even though he didn't like him much.

None of these had the makings of a Quebec leader, but the new Government did not despair. Surely, among fifty Quebec MPs, somebody of stature would emerge. One man that caught several eyes was a big, handsome, fluently bilingual, wounded war veteran named Pierre Sevigny. Some shrewd observers, including the Prime Minister's chief political counselor, Allister Grosart, thought Sevigny might develop into "a Conservative Ernest Lapointe." They were delighted when, in August 1959, Diefenbaker chose him as Associate Minister of Defense.

Hindsight makes it clear enough what Diefenbaker should have done. He should have gone outside the parliamentary group, found some French Canadian of established eminence—as Mackenzie King had found Louis St. Laurent in 1942—and opened a seat for him. The fact seems to be that Diefenbaker didn't know any French Canadians, eminent or otherwise. Even in his own parliamentary group two of the best of them, Paul Martineau and Martial Asselin, didn't become ministers until the Government they joined was in its expiring stage.

Alienation of the groups above mentioned does not mean that Diefenbaker alienated all Canadians. Far from it. Among certain groups of voters, and in certain regions of Canada, he became if anything stronger than ever. His own Saskatchewan had given him only two seats besides his own in 1957, but in 1958 he carried all but one and in three elections thereafter he won every seat. Alberta was almost equally loyal. The maritimes and rural Ontario, though not as solid as the prairies, were nevertheless reliable Diefenbaker territory in five consecutive elections.

What kept these areas loyal was partly Diefenbaker's own personality, partly his Government's record of consistent generosity to western farmers and to the poverty-stricken maritimes, partly the fact that in Alvin Hamilton he had the best Minister of Agriculture since Jimmy Gardiner's best days, which were a long time before his eventual defeat in 1958. Hamilton had (and has) the ability to convince the farmers that he really has their interests at heart. He shares their suspicion and resentment of eastern city slickers, to whom he talks back with the salty and earthy candor that farmers applaud. Some of Hamilton's ideas sound very farfetched, especially to the orthodox and the conventional, but even they agree that Hamilton *has* ideas, which is more than can be said for many more conventional politicians.

One exploit in particular for which Hamilton gets great credit is the sale of Canadian wheat to China, probably the largest single commercial transaction ever consummated anywhere. As Conservative Minister of Agriculture at the time, Hamilton deserves a lot of credit, but in fact the whole Diefenbaker Government—and especially its first Trade Minister, Gordon Churchill—is entitled to at least an equal share.

Maxwell Forsyth-Smith, then Canadian trade commissioner in Hong Kong, had been trying for years to persuade his minister, C. D. Howe, to let him go to mainland China on a trade-seeking mission. Howe refused. He had been persuaded to consent, reluctantly, to a trade agreement with Soviet Russia, but the Communist Chinese in his view were too far beyond the pale. When Gordon Churchill took over from Howe in June 1957 Forsyth-Smith renewed his request, and this time the answer was "Go ahead."

At that time, of course, neither he nor anyone else thought of China as a big market for Canadian wheat. China was supposed to be self-sufficient in grains. Nevertheless that first trade mission, and the personal contacts it established, made it easy for the Chinese to turn to Canada when, in 1960, they found themselves in urgent need of food.

The first three-year contract, signed in 1960, was for a maximum of 200 million bushels, for which the Chinese paid nearly $400 million. Alvin Hamilton flew to Hong Kong to sign the contract, and was the target of Opposition jibes because in fact it was signed (by representatives of the Canadian Wheat Board) two days before he arrived. The ridicule didn't hurt Hamilton a bit—in fact, it boomeranged to some extent. The western farmers knew whom to thank for this bonanza, and still do. Since that first contract the Liberals have sold 187 million bushels more, and contracted for a third three-year period a maximum of 280 million bushels. But the Chinese wheat sale is still counted a Conservative feat.

To the astonishment of most Americans, and the unconcealed horror of many, this trade with Communist China has never been a political issue in Canada. (Neither has trade with Castro's Cuba, with which the Conservatives established and the Liberals have maintained relatively normal relations.) Nominally Canada does not recognize the Communist regime in Peking, nominally it does recognize that of Chiang Kai-shek in Formosa (though no

Canadian representative has ever been posted there). But little attempt is made to disguise the fact that these nominal postures are struck solely to avoid offending Washington, and that if Canada followed her own bent there would have been a Canadian ambassador in Peking at least ten years ago. Conclusion of a massive trading contract with an "unrecognized" government did not raise even a whisper of protest in Canada; if anything it helped to unify rather than divide the country, since everyone is in favor of selling wheat.

Some of the other achievements of the Diefenbaker Government did not have this unifying effect. The strengthening of its hold on the rural and small-town voter, and on the provinces of west and east, was accompanied by an alienation of the metropolitan areas of central Canada. Its massive aid to western farmers and to the Atlantic Provinces prompted frequent references, in the more right-wing papers of the central cities, to the "Robin Hood Government" that was robbing the rich to reward the poor. And the writers seldom failed to point out that by this reckoning a millionaire wheat farmer in Saskatchewan was counted as "poor" while a newly arrived Italian construction worker in Toronto was one of the "rich." To this extent even the accomplishments of the Diefenbaker Cabinet tended to aggravate rather than correct the growing disunity of the country. The seeming unanimity of 1958, with its three-to-one majority in Parliament, concealed a fragmentation which, between 1958 and 1962, became embittered by disenchantment.

Abroad, disenchantment became even more pronounced.

The British were willing to overlook, but not entirely to forget, the unfortunate episode of September 1957—the free trade offer that got no response from Ottawa. If the incident did nothing else, though, it confirmed the Macmillan Government's belief that the only way Britain could expand her export market adequately was to join the European Common Market.

By mid-1960 this British decision, not yet public, had nevertheless created an almost open dispute between Whitehall and Ottawa. When the British Parliament in July 1961 voted formally in favor of seeking Common Market membership, the break with Canada was no longer concealed.

At a Commonwealth meeting in Accra, Ghana, in September 1961, Canadian Finance Minister Donald Fleming and Trade Minister George Hees were the most vehement of all in denouncing the British intention. New Zealand and Australia, who would have suffered far more had the British plan been carried out, were relatively mild in their language.

Hees's executive assistant, Mel Jack, handed out copies of the Hees speech to Canadian reporters in Accra. Fleming's speech, though not published verbatim, was paraphrased at length at the same press briefing. Both were printed at considerable length in both Canadian and British papers. This leakage from a nominally closed meeting caused a storm of indignation.

"We didn't mind what they said at the conference table," a British civil servant said in London months later. "That's what these conferences are for, to let people speak frankly. Publishing these frank words is a different matter. Not that there's any real breach of secrecy (delegates are quite free to publish their own views if they like) but the public isn't used to hearing this sort of talk. Civil servants and politicians don't mind it, but the British voters were furious."

Meanwhile Diefenbaker himself had tried British patience on a different issue, one which did him more credit and on which he spoke for a much higher fraction of Canada's people and Parliament, but which probably did him as much harm in the eyes of British officials and ministers. This was the status of South Africa in the Commonwealth.

When the Commonwealth Prime Ministers met in London in 1961, South Africa's policy of _apartheid_ was almost as explosive a question as Rhodesia's unilateral declaration of independence was in 1966. Britain, however, hoped other members would refrain from rocking the boat, and leave it to Whitehall to pour the customary oil on the troubled waters. Had Canada listened to this advice, the result probably would have been—as at the time of Suez—a breach in the Commonwealth along the color line. Instead, Diefenbaker spoke out vigorously against *apartheid* and took a leading part in drafting the statement of principle to which, in the end, the South Africans decided they could not subscribe. It might therefore be said that Canada took the lead in shutting South Africa out of the Commonwealth.

Back home, Diefenbaker was applauded by other political parties for the stand he had taken—it was one of the rare moments of near unanimity in the Canadian Parliaments of recent years. But in Britain and in South Africa it is still Diefenbaker in particular rather than Canada in general that they blame for the ouster of South Africa.

These various resentments came to a head at the Commonwealth Prime Ministers' Conference in London in September 1962. The election of the previous June had already reduced the Diefenbaker Cabinet to a minority position in Parliament, which may have led the British to think it even less representative of Canadian opinion than in fact it was. Diefenbaker, for his part, continued to speak and act as if he were speaking for all Canadians. The result was a considerable collision.

Diefenbaker at the conference table adopted the role for which he is ideally suited by temperament and experience, that of Leader of the Opposition. In the Common Market debate, he attacked the British proposal as the British had never been attacked before in these rather polite sessions at Marlborough House. This can be said with assurance, even though the meetings were closed, because Diefenbaker himself briefed Canadian reporters with lengthy excerpts from his own speech (as he had a perfect right to do under the normal conference rules) while the British Commonwealth Secretary, Duncan Sandys, was equally forthright and considerably less accurate in briefing British reporters. According to Sandys, Diefenbaker had succeeded in "isolating" Canada at the conference. The truth was exactly the opposite. He had succeeded in isolating Britain. In the whole Commonwealth only Trinidad-Tobago took the British side.

References to Diefenbaker in the British press were so virulent that, when relayed back to Canada, they roused indignation and sympathy for him even among political foes. The reaction was: "They can't talk that way about our Prime Minister." But although in this sense he may be said to have won the engagement, it was a pyrrhic victory for one who had come into office only five years before with the declared intention of "restoring" Canada's good relations with the Commonwealth in general and Britain in particular.

With her other great ally and relative, the United States, Canada's relations deteriorated even more calamitously. But since this became in the end the principal cause of the Diefenbaker Government's downfall, the story deserves a chapter to itself.

XIX

Nuclear Weapons: The Five-year Time Bomb

THE ROOTS OF the nuclear weapons issue go back to 1957, in the Diefenbaker Government's earliest months in office.

In midsummer came the question of setting up NORAD—the North American Air Defense command. In practice it was already operational. The physical means of instant communication between RCAF stations at St. Hubert, Quebec, or North Bay, Ontario, had been installed several years before. All arrangements had been made whereby, in an emergency, Canadian and American defense forces would work as one.

All that remained, and it was a gap that the military men in both countries wanted to close, was the formal integration of command—an American general as commander, a Canadian air marshal as his second in command, and a neatly coordinated chain running down from these two men and their headquarters in Colorado Springs, Colorado.

When General George Pearkes took over as Canadian Minister of Defense, his military advisers told him the previous Government had already decided to take this final step and had merely put off the signing of it until after the election. This was not quite accurate. It was true that the previous Defense Minister, Ralph Campney, had been persuaded of the wisdom of this move. It was true he had written a letter to someone in the Pentagon, saying "formal approval" would have to wait until after the election, lest it become "a political issue"; (Prime Minister Diefenbaker gleefully paraphrased this Campney letter in a speech to the House of Commons later, when the Liberals had challenged his decision to go ahead with the NORAD agreement). But the fact is that Campney had not sold the idea to his colleagues, that some of them (notably L. B. Pearson) would have opposed it vigorously, and that the signing of the agreement by a Liberal Government had been very far from a foregone conclusion. The probability is that it would have been refused.

The reason for the reluctance became clear to the Conservatives in the course of time. Without the formal agreement, adequate arrangements had been made for joint action in an emergency. But the key decision as to what *is* an emergency was left open. Real emergencies like invasion would, of course, have been unmistakable. Artificial emergencies, the results or even the incidental tactical moves of American foreign policy, would not be automatically treated as if they were equally serious. Without the agreement, consultation was compulsory. With it, as Diefenbaker learned to his great resentment in the Cuba crisis of 1962, consultation became more or less optional.

Next step in setting up the origins of the nuclear issue came in December 1957, at the annual meeting of NATO ministers in Paris. This was the meeting at which the crucial decision was taken to stockpile American nuclear weapons for the use of NATO troops in Europe. It was a decision to increase firepower instead of manpower, to give up the attempt (already proven futile) to match the Soviet Union's deployment of ground troops, and instead to multiply the striking power of NATO's few divisions by arming them with nuclear tactical weapons.

Canada accepted this decision. Later it became apparent that, in doing so, the new Canadian ministers had not quite realized all the implications of this step. From then on, the Canadian brigade and the Canadian air division in Europe would have either nuclear weapons or none. The RCAF's aircraft, the CF-104, was so designed that it could not carry conventional weapons at all. For the ground forces the principal offensive armament was the Honest John, a short-range ground-to-ground rocket for which no conventional warheads were available. Of course these changes did not take place instantly. It was several years before the new nuclear weapons were ready. But when the old conventional ones were phased out toward the end of the 1950s, there were no new conventional weapons to replace them.

Another step in Canada's nuclear commitment came in 1958 when the Diefenbaker Government decided to abandon the RCAF's most ambitious project, the supersonic fighter that would have been called the Avro Arrow. The A. V. Roe Company at Malton, near Toronto, had been at work on development of this aircraft since 1953. It was to have taken the place of the highly successful CF-100, then in process of being phased out, and the unit cost was to be two million dollars a copy—costly, but not exorbitant for a highly sophisticated weapons system.

But this unit price was based upon the assumption that other air forces, notably the American and the British, would also buy the Arrow and make possible a production run of at least five hundred aircraft. The RCAF had made inquiries in both London and Washington, and brought back encouraging reports. Later, critics were to say the RCAF exaggerated these, and interpreted merely polite congratulations as acceptance of the Arrow. However that may be, the acceptance did not in fact come through in the end. The United States decided (reversing a previous decision) to make an interceptor of its own that would fill the gap for which the Arrow was intended, and would of course be vastly cheaper because of its great production run. This competition, plus the fact that the Arrow development program had consistently fallen behind schedule and gone over its budget, made the Arrow's unit cost fantastic—almost eight million a copy, according to the estimate Prime Minister Diefenbaker eventually gave the House of Commons.

He decided the price would be prohibitive, and in retrospect few would quarrel with his decision. In September 1958 he announced that the Arrow contract would be "reviewed" in six months, but the announcement was widely interpreted as warning that the program would be scrapped and, the six month delay as an adjustment period for Avro and its fourteen thousand employees.

To replace the Arrow the Diefenbaker Government bought, not another manned fighter, but an air-breathing missile called the Bomarc B, designed to knock out air-breathing bombers by means of a nuclear warhead. Its predecessor, the Bomarc A, had included the option of a conventional warhead, but no conventional warhead was ever designed for the Bomarc B. This point was not made very clear in public statements at the time the Bomarc B arrangement was concluded—an arrangement whereby the United States would pay for the fifty-six Bomarcs to be deployed on Canadian soil, and Canada would pay only the local labor costs of building the sites.

The combat value of the Bomarc was always somewhat dubious. At one point during the interval between Canada's decision to take the weapons and their actual delivery, the United States decided to scrap the Bomarc altogether. This would have left Canada in the same position as the U.S. abandonment of Skybolt left Britain in late 1962—dependent on a weapon that was never to be produced. Urgent representations from Ottawa led Washington to change its mind, and the Bomarc program continued.

But when the time came to provide the nuclear warheads, without which the Bomarc was nothing but an expensive blank cartridge, misgivings developed. Howard Green, who had become Minister of External Affairs after Sidney Smith died in 1959, was passionately devoted to the cause of disarmament, and he believed Canada's influence in this field would be impaired if not destroyed by acquisition of nuclear weapons. Other ministers realized, apparently for the first time, that American nuclear warheads on Canadian soil would require American soldiers on Canadian soil to guard them, since U.S. law forbade their being released from American custody. The result was a protracted deadlock in Cabinet which amounted, in effect, to a refusal to accept the nuclear warheads for which approximately $700 million worth of carriers—Bomarcs, CF-104s and Honest Johns—had already been bought.

The crisis of indecision lasted one full year, from the completion of the Bomarc base at North Bay, Ontario, in February 1962, to the overthrow of a much-diminished Diefenbaker Government by vote of non-confidence in the House of Commons on February 5, 1963. The interval was marked by a weird variety of complications.

One was the near collapse of the Government itself in the general election of June 18, 1962. The Prime Minister requested dissolution on April 19 of a Parliament in which he still commanded two hundred and three seats against the Liberals' fifty. He came back with only a hundred and fifteen followers to face a Liberal Opposition that had doubled its strength, plus two resuscitated splinter parties for a combined Opposition that outnumbered the Conservatives by thirty-three. The causes of his decline were mainly domestic, but they had international overtones. For example, the depletion of Canada's gold and U.S. dollar reserves compelled a sudden, drastic devaluation of the Canadian dollar just as the election campaign began. Scornful Liberals and vengeful Conservatives were equally ready to see this monetary crisis as an effect of the rapidly worsening relations between Prime Minister Diefenbaker and President John Kennedy.

The two men were not personally congenial. There was a brief interval of enthusiasm when Diefenbaker visited the White House, on Kennedy's invitation, shortly after the inauguration in 1961, but it ended within days—Kennedy made a sardonic remark in private which was soon relayed to Ottawa, and which reached Diefenbaker's ears at once. When Kennedy visited Ottawa in May of the same year, the breach was further widened. The President made a speech to both Houses of Parliament in which, among other things, he suggested Canada ought to join the Organization of American States. Before making this statement he consulted Arnold Heeney, Canadian ambassador to Washington, and asked whether Canadians might resent it. Heeney said no, he was sure they would not. For most Canadians his advice may well have been correct, but for two important exceptions it was not. Prime Minister Diefenbaker and his Minister of External Affairs, Howard Green, were both indignant at this "interference." This was also the trip during which President Kennedy mislaid the memorandum with the allegedly scurrilous remark about his host allegedly scribbled in the margin in the President's handwriting. Altogether the visit was less than a success.

So far, though, differences were merely personal and social. The major collision came during the Cuban missile crisis of October 1962, when Washington asked Canada to put the Canadian share of North American Air Defense on alert status. When the Diefenbaker Government stalled for forty-two hours before complying, it did major and permanent damage to that Government's relationship with the United States.

Diefenbaker's Minister of National Defense, Douglas Harkness, endured this period with increasing frustration and decreasing confidence. A man of great integrity and courage, he took it for granted that Canada had accepted a binding commitment when, in 1957 and 1958, it acquiesced in the nuclear weapons policy of the Western Alliance and in the nuclear defense system of the North American continent. His inability to persuade his Cabinet colleagues to translate this commitment into action depressed him but did not discourage him utterly. He kept hoping, until January 1963, that eventually he would carry his point and that Canada thereby would keep her word.

On January 3, 1963, General Lauris Norstad came to Ottawa for his farewell visit before retiring as supreme commander of NATO forces in Europe. At a press conference he was asked whether Canada had, in fact, committed itself to equip the CF-104 aircraft with nuclear weapons. Norstad answered, "Yes." Whether or not he realized how short a fuse he was lighting with that answer, only General Norstad knows. At any rate, the fuse burned smokily for three weeks, until Parliament reconvened on January 21.

Meanwhile a dramatic change had taken place in the Liberal Opposition's policy on nuclear weapons. Up to the end of 1962 the Liberals, or most of them including Pearson, had inclined against the acquisition—in other words, they had supported the Howard Green faction against the Douglas Harkness faction in the Conservative Party. But by December 1962 those Liberals who disagreed with this stance, notably Paul Hellyer and Mitchell

Sharp, had persuaded Pearson that it was more important to honor Canada's international commitments than to maintain a nuclear virginity that did not really exist. He announced this change of mind in a speech to a Liberal audience in Scarborough, a suburb of Toronto, early in January 1963. For the first time defense policy emerged as a clear-cut issue between the major parties.

Diefenbaker's defense of his policy, as delivered to Parliament January 25, included a vague reference to the recent conference between President Kennedy and British Prime Minister Harold Macmillan, to the closing stages of which Diefenbaker had invited himself. He said the nuclear strike role of Canada's CF-104 Starfighters in Europe had been "placed in doubt by the recent Nassau declaration concerning nuclear arms."

This was more than the U. S. State Department could tolerate. To the other NATO allies, especially West Germany, it sounded like a hint that the nuclear policy of 1957 had been scrapped by a bilateral deal between the U.S. and Britain, which of course was quite untrue. So the State Department's press spokesman, Lincoln White, issued a press release January 30 flatly denying several of the key statements in the Diefenbaker speech of January 25.

Whether this did Diefenbaker more harm or more good politically, with the Canadian voter, is still a matter for argument. In any case it brought Doug Harkness' dwindling patience to the breaking point. He sent the Prime Minister a letter of resignation which, though it was said to be much milder than Harkness' first draft, was nevertheless stinging enough.

Harkness' resignation was submitted on Sunday, February 3, and published in the morning papers of the following day. That afternoon the Government introduced a supply motion—traditionally the Opposition's chance to air grievances and move nonconfidence. Lester Pearson moved an amendment: "That this Government, because of lack of leadership, the breakdown of unity in the Cabinet, and confusion and indecision in dealing with national and international problems, does not have the confidence of the Canadian people." After two days of furious debate the amendment was carried by a vote of 142 to 111. For the first time in thirty-six years, and only the second time since Confederation, a Canadian Government had been overthrown by defeat in the House of Commons.

To all outward appearances the Government's position was hopeless, as it prepared to face the electors for the second time in ten months. George Hees resigned as Minister of Trade and Commerce, Pierre Sevigny as Associate Minister of Defense, a few days after Parliament was dissolved—their letters of resignation, though too late to earn them the same honorable status as Doug Harkness', were equally devastating in their reflections upon the Diefenbaker Government and its policies. Hees announced he would not be a candidate at the forthcoming election. Donald Fleming and Davie Fulton, by that time Ministers of Justice and Public Works respectively, had also withdrawn for reasons that were different but not wholly dissimilar. His Cabinet no more than a rump of its former self, his policies repudiated by five of his ex-ministers, even his veracity impugned by a formal statement from the U. S. Administration, Diefenbaker appeared to be doomed not merely to defeat but to political extinction.

This judgment, commonplace at the time, turned out to be fantastically premature. Almost singlehanded—though with the useful help of a few loyal stalwarts like Alvin Hamilton—the Prime Minister conducted a political rear-guard action that has no compare in history or legend since Horatius held the bridge.

He had some assistance from circumstances. The Liberal campaign was unbelievably inept. The allegedly bright young men who had contracted or volunteered to relacquer the image of Lester Pearson and his Liberal Party came up with a series of maneuvers that were cheap, derivative, and absurd—weak imitations of devices that had been effective in the Kennedy presidential campaign of 1960, but in the Canadian context were merely preposterous. Pearson himself was subjected to a campaign schedule that did nothing to enhance his dignity. Toward the end of it he said to a visitor from Britain: "This campaign has been the most degrading experience of my life."

Also, Diefenbaker got some unexpected help from Robert Mc-

Namara, U. S. Secretary of Defense. A week before the election, the U. S. House of Representatives released the edited transcript of a secret committee hearing held a month before. McNamara testified, among other things, that one purpose of the Bomarc bases in Canada was to attract the fire of Soviet missiles that might otherwise have been aimed at American targets. Diefenbaker made great hay with this, in the few days that remained to him—"the Liberal policy is to make Canada a decoy for intercontinental missiles."

But in the main his appeal was personal. He campaigned in his favorite role—the persecuted, traduced, victimized representative of the Common Man, slandered by the servile press of the rich central provinces and the rich big cities, sneered at by the egghead intellectuals, undermined by the highly paid agents of Bay Street and St. James Street, but still bravely speaking up for the Little Man of, for instance, Prince Albert. He came out of the campaign defeated, true, but far from demolished. He still had ninety-five seats to the Liberals' hundred and twenty-nine (four short of a clear majority) but he had better than that—still a solid hold on the prairies, where the Liberals got only three seats to the Conservatives' forty-one, and a fair grip on the maritimes, where he held the Liberals to a thirteen–thirteen tie. Rural Ontario was still Diefenbaker territory in the main. And Quebec, where the once formidable Conservative platoon was reduced to a mere ten seats, at least did not go Liberal.

Coming back to oppose a minority Government instead of leading one, Diefenbaker seemed in many ways stronger than before.

XX

The Quiet Revolution: New Brooms in Quebec

IT WAS THE DEFECTION of Quebec that deprived the Liberals of the victory they expected in 1962. It also deprived them of an over-all majority in 1963 and 1965, but by then the blow was expected. The 1962 result was the traumatic shock.

Until about a fortnight before election day, Liberals viewed Quebec with a revival of their old complacency. They observed, correctly, that Quebec voters were disillusioned and alienated by the Diefenbaker Government, which had never understood French Canada and in its later years seemed to stop trying. Liberals therefore inferred, incorrectly, that Quebec would have no alternative but to swing back to them as it had always done in the past. They were disdainful of the strident noises made by Quebec's peculiar version of the Social Credit movement, a party that had operated in Quebec for about twenty years without ever electing a candidate (except once, by accident, in a north-country by-election).

This complacency was somewhat eroded as the campaign wore on and both old parties began to realize the depth of Quebec's disaffection. They also began to realize the reasons for it. Ten days before the election I was talking to the wife of a Liberal candidate, a man who became a minister when the Pearson team took over the following year.

"We've been canvassing in Lower Town," she said, "and frankly I was horrified. Neither of the old parties has done anything for those poor people. Nobody pays any attention to them, nobody ever calls on them—not even the priest. We found one old lady of seventy-two, illiterate, living in complete destitution on the charity of neighbors—why? Because she didn't know about the old-age pension! Nobody had ever told her she could get fifty-five dollars a month from the Government, so how was she to know?"

That conversation took place on a Saturday evening. The following Monday, a week before election day, the Liberals got the bad news. A costly public opinion survey, which they had commissioned, reported a dramatic upsurge in the strength of Social Credit, and predicted that the Créditistes would win nineteen seats. They won twenty-six.

The Créditistes had not yet separated formally from the national Social Credit Party, based in Alberta and British Columbia and led by a bland, voluble, ex-chiropractor named Robert Thompson. Nevertheless, the Créditistes were as different from the Social Crediters as caviar is from porridge. They were led by a fiery, eloquent used-car dealer from the northern mining town of Rouyn, Réal Caouette, whose campaign slogan was a telling one:

"What have you got to lose?"

What, indeed? In the neglected back concessions of rural Quebec, in the equally neglected slum ridings of the smaller industrial towns, French-Canadian voters by the thousand came to the conclusion that both old parties had been neglecting them long enough. Réal Caouette came to Ottawa at the head of a group of twenty-six militant, violently discontented French-Canadian nationalists. His "leader," Robert Thompson, headed a group of four, two from Alberta and two from B.C. Effectively from the start, and formally after the 1963 election, the two wholly disparate groups became two parties; the handful of French-Canadian MPs who stayed with Robert Thompson were all wiped out in the 1965 election.

This revolt of Quebec against the major national parties was all the more startling to the Liberals because two years before, in the provincial election of 1960, a Liberal Government had come to power in Quebec City under Jean Lesage, formerly a junior minister in the St. Laurent Government. It looked as if a new era of Liberal power had dawned in both fields.

Maurice Duplessis, the despotic old Union Nationale chieftain who had ruled Quebec with a rod of iron since 1944, had died suddenly in September 1959—suddenly but not altogether unexpectedly, for although he remained in harness until the lethal stroke that felled him during a tour of the iron mines of Ungava, his colleagues had been aware for some time of his failing health. They were ready with plans for an orderly succession. Paul Sauvé, Minister of Youth and himself still youthful-looking at fifty-two, had long been known as the Union Nationale's crown prince and heir apparent, and he had no rivals who dared to make themselves visible. When *le chef* died the take-over was smooth and uneventful. It was taken for granted that 1960 would be an election year, since the last provincial election had been in 1956, but it was also taken for granted by friend and foe that the Union Nationale under its popular new leader would win as usual.

The event for which nobody was prepared was the death of Paul Sauvé, on the night of New Year's Day 1960. The disarray of the Union Nationale was complete. Finally the Minister of Labor, Antonio Barrette, a harmless soul of sixty who'd been in the Quebec legislature since 1936 and in the Duplessis Cabinet since 1944, was chosen as the new Premier. Jean Lesage and his Liberals, whose hopes of beating Duplessis had been nil and of beating Paul Sauvé only slender, beat Antonio Barrette by the adequate margin of fourteen seats—fifty-four Liberals to forty Union Nationale, with one independent.

But as the Lesage Government began to develop its policies, it became obvious that these Quebeckers were not "Liberals like the others." René Lévesque, Lesage's Minister of Resources, was and is a Liberal in name only. A fierce Quebec nationalist whose attitude toward any Ottawa government is one of suspicion and hostility, Lévesque gave the federal Liberals as much trouble as Duplessis used to do at federal-provincial meetings. This confrontation did not become fully apparent, of course, until 1963 when the Liberals took power in Ottawa, but there were signs of it as early as the spring of 1962. Jean Lesage did not appear on a single platform with his old friend and colleague L. B. Pearson. He explained rather lamely that it would have done neither of them any good for him to be linked too openly with any Ottawa party. To other observers it seemed obvious that it would have done Pearson a great deal of good, but would not, in Lesage's opinion, have helped Lesage. And this opinion itself, right or wrong, was significant of the change of weather in Quebec.

Separatism, for the first time, became an openly proclaimed cause in the early 1960s. A now forgotten federal civil servant named Marcel Chaput, a physicist employed by the National Research Council, defied his employers by taking unauthorized leave of absence to attend a meeting of the separatist group he was in process of organizing. Subsequently dismissed for this insubordination, he made a brief parade of martyrdom but quite obviously had decided anyway to make a full-time job of his advocacy of Quebec separatism. Chaput has since been left by the wayside, in the course of the numerous fissions through which Quebec separatist parties have gone, but the sentiment was and is more powerful than any of its organizations. To some extent, separatism now permeates all political parties in Quebec —even those who denounce it most vigorously.

For brief periods in 1962 and 1963, the separatist movement took an exceedingly ugly turn. Terrorism, Algerian style, was attempted in various ways. Plastic bombs left in mailboxes killed one man and maimed another. Banks were robbed by young "patriots" of good family, to raise funds for the cause. Militia armories were raided and robbed of various types of small arms, most of which were mere dummies for parade-ground use but some of which were lethal weapons. One gang murdered a Montreal gunshop owner during a futile attempt to steal arms and ammunition; several accused are awaiting trial for capital murder as these lines are written.

Quebec Provincial Police, attempting to penetrate the presumed organizations behind these atrocities, found themselves baffled. They could not find any evidence that such organizations existed. Eventually they came to the conclusion, which seems to have been borne out by events, that in fact no organizations did exist—that the atrocities were carried out by a handful of young men representing nobody, and when (as happened in due course) the police arrested the individuals responsible for the crimes, they wiped out the "organizations" *in toto* at the same time.

But it would have been a great mistake to infer that therefore the separatist movement had no importance. Even the above-ground organizations, campaigning quite legally to elect candidates to Quebec City and failing to elect a single one, were a misleading measure of the strength of separatism. The true measure was not the vote polled by far-out parties demanding "independence now," but the extent to which orthodox political parties in Quebec based their appeal on separatist policies and tendencies.

Daniel Johnson, leader of the Union Nationale who in 1966 defeated Jean Lesage and became Premier of Quebec, wrote a book called *Equality or Independence,* a book that stops well short of issuing any ultimatums to English Canada but that certainly contemplates an independent Quebec as the alternative to a satisfactory revision of the British North America Act. Jean Lesage himself remained vehemently anti-separatist in all his public utterances, and gave no reason to doubt the sincerity of his disagreement with those who wanted to lead Quebec out of Confederation, but he also made it amply clear that his concept of a true Confederation called for much more autonomy for the provinces, or at any rate for Quebec (which was not, he insisted, "a province like the others," but the homeland and stronghold of French Canada). As for René Lévesque, by the time he got through enumerating the fields of authority that should be turned over to the provinces (or at any rate to Quebec) he had left as little for Ottawa to do as for a late Holy Roman Emperor, and considerably less than the central jurisdiction of the Austro-Hungarian Empire.

It was an entirely new mood, a mood of self-assertion. In the past French-Canadian nationalism had been primarily defensive, a vigilant protection of rights won in the Quebec Act of 1774, and in subsequent constitutional documents down to the British North America Act of 1867 and all its later amendments. Now it was ceasing to be merely protective and becoming aggressive, demanding not only the old rights but new ones as well.

Daniel Johnson, in a conversation in the summer of 1966, put it in terms that his political rival Jean Lesage would certainly have accepted: "We have not closed any of the avenues to Confederation except two. One is the *status quo*, which nobody wants any more. The other is assimilation [of French Canada by the English-speaking majority]. Any other alternatives, we are prepared to consider and discuss."

But all this concerns the relationship between Quebec and the rest of Canada, on which the great majority of French Canadians seem to be agreed at least in principle. More important, and productive of much less unanimity, was the impact of the so-called Quiet Revolution on the traditional society of French Canada itself. As the election of 1966 made clear, the Lesage Government grossly underestimated this impact, and the resentment it aroused in a society that still cherished its traditions.

An achievement of which the Lesage Government was justly proud was the elimination, or at any rate the dramatic reduction, of political patronage, bribery, and corruption in the Quebec Government service. Shortly after it took office the Cabinet set up a Royal Commission of inquiry under Mr. Justice Elie Salvas of the Superior Court of Quebec, to look into the Duplessis machine's methods of purchasing, issuing contracts, and the like. Mr. Justice Salvas reported on June 27, 1963, as noisome a system of kickbacks, under-the-counter deals, general and systematic looting of the treasury for private profit and political advantage, as ever has been exposed anywhere in Canada at any time. Two Duplessis ministers, a powerful Union Nationale official, and several civil servants of high rank were successfully prosecuted for fraud (though most of the convictions are in appeal at the time of writing and one has been reversed). It might be supposed that the traditional system of logrolling, back-scratching, and paying unearned "commissions" on provincial contracts and purchases would have been stamped out forever.

It was stamped out for a while. The Lesage Government hired Jean Fournier, a foreign service officer in the federal Department of External Affairs who had attained the verge of ambassadorial rank, to set up a provincial civil service and a system of merit competition for official posts. For the more routine jobs, such as highway labor, union organization was permitted and even encouraged, partly with the idea that in future the unions would be able to prevent the spoils system from going back into operation.

The new purity had some unforeseen side effects. When all contracts were let by tender, all of them went to the big city contractors who had the machinery and the skilled men to do a job cheaply. The small local contractor, who used to get "his share," got nothing. Neither were there any jobs for the local farmer-laborers, who didn't know how to operate a sophisticated machine but who had always been accustomed to supplement their meager cash incomes with "road work."

As one small-town contractor rather pathetically said to a reporter from the Montreal *Gazette* in 1966: "Those big companies should not be allowed to bid in wholesale prices. We can't compete with that. They ought to quote retail prices, as we do."

Another confrontation in which the Liberals' assumption of victory was somewhat premature was that with the Roman Catholic Church over control of education. Ever since the days of New France, Quebec schools had been run by the Church. (The Protestant schools were, and are, solely for the English-speaking minority, which is allowed to do as it likes with its own children. There are no public schools for French-speaking Protestants or French-speaking Jews, who must attend Catholic schools or pay for private ones.)

Lesage's young Minister of Education, a former Rhodes Scholar named Paul Gérin-Lajoie, set out to bring the schools under

secular authority. His first task was to create a department and
a title for himself—Quebec had never had a Minister of Education, but only a Council of Public Instruction composed mainly
of, and dominated wholly by, the Roman Catholic bishops. Gérin-
Lajoie set up an Education Department to which the council of
bishops became merely advisory. He also addressed himself to
modernizing the classical curriculum which, in the secondary
schools and colleges, had changed little since it was laid down by
the great Bishop Laval in 1663.

The effect of these changes among the young intellectuals of
French Canada was exhilarating. Stifled as they had been during the long dark night of the Duplessis era, they burst forth with
a renaissance of every kind of cultural activity—new books, new
plays, new films, new broadcasting programs, and a mushroom
crop of new places of entertainment in Montreal and Quebec.

The dominant quality of these young people was their pride,
a wholesome pride. They felt they could do anything. They
thought—and many English Canadians agreed—that they were
the cultural leaders of Canada, that Quebec was the one place in
Canada where exciting things were happening and progress could
be seen with the naked eye.

It was easy, in those days of high endeavor, to overlook the fact
that not all of Quebec acquiesced in this headlong rush forward.
The parish priests, temporarily by-passed but by no means shorn
of their old authority, saw the changes with very understandable
resentment. Mothers, especially in the rural areas, were roused to
alarm by charges that the schools were to be "de-Christianized."
The young agnostics of Montreal and Quebec City were neither
so loved nor so trusted as they thought they were.

But probably the biggest handicap to the Liberal regime was
the simplest—money.

Quebec in 1959 had expenditures of $533 million, and a rev-
enue of $556 million—the kind of tidy surplus that Maurice
Duplessis, who had old-fashioned ideas of finance, liked to see.
The provincial debt was $469 million.

By 1966 provincial revenues were well over a billion and a

half, and expenditures had crossed the two billion mark. The debt by 1965 was $1,088,469,933, and the province was running out of the credit that had been so readily available in 1960. New schools, new roads, new projects of every kind were matters of pride, but few were actually completed and fewer still had been paid for. The Quiet Revolution was proving inordinately expensive in a province which, though always short of modern government services, had also been unaccustomed to paying taxes. Many a farmer and rural tradesman found his tax bill tripled over what it used to be in the bad old days of Duplessis. And the promise of better education for his still numerous children, to the Liberals' dismay, left him unmoved.

The fatal error of the Lesage Government was to pay too little attention to this rural discontent, while at the same time neglecting to carry through a real redistribution of seats in the province to diminish, if not entirely eliminate, the heavy advantage of the farm voter over the city man. The Liberal bill to redistribute ended as a compromise, an addition of urban seats that left the basic structure undisturbed.

Thus in the election of June 5, 1966, it was possible for the Union Nationale to gain a decisive majority of seats with only forty per cent of the popular vote, while the Liberals were defeated with forty-seven per cent.

However, the anomaly was not as great as it appeared to be. For one thing, there was truth in the words indiscreetly spoken on the French-language television network by Daniel Johnson on election night: "Take away the Montreal English vote, and the Montreal Jewish vote, and the Montreal immigrant vote, and you'll find we have a good majority of French Canadians." One Montreal riding with a substantial Jewish and English population, Mount Royal, voted ninety per cent Liberal.

The other mitigating factor in the Union Nationale's minority victory was the fact that two splinter parties, both separatist, probably took more votes away from the Union Nationale than from the Liberals. Between them they polled approximately thirteen per cent of the total vote. It is a fair inference that if a run-off election had been held to establish an over-all popular majority, the Union Nationale might well have got a majority of all Quebec voters, and would almost certainly have got a majority of all French Canadians.

How much of the ambitious Liberal program the Union Nationale will complete had not become clear as Centennial Year opened. The most spectacular of Liberal plans, the quarter-billion-dollar steel complex called SIDBEC that was to have been built at Betancourt, was dropped in August 1966, apparently from despair of raising enough capital. Whether the Liberals would also have dropped it, there is no way of knowing for sure. A perceptible slowing down occurred in other fields of activity, but no dramatic changes of direction. Union Nationale ministers went to Ottawa to the autumn federal-provincial conference accompanied by the same officials, and prepared to make the same case for a greater share of tax resources, that the Liberals would have had.

From the general standpoint of national unity, it was not yet clear as 1967 began whether Quebec's relations with the rest of Canada had changed substantially—and if so, whether it was for better or worse. In opposition, Daniel Johnson had sounded rather more like a separatist than Jean Lesage ever did, but in office he began at once to sound much more cautious. Lesage, for his part, resisted the temptation to enter a contest of extreme nationalism, and continued to speak as a Canadian first and a Quebecker second.

Perhaps more seriously in question, for the first time since World War II and perhaps even since World War I, was the attitude of English Canada toward Quebec. Evidence had been growing for several years that the considerable pool of good will for French Canada, which had built up during the St. Laurent regime, was being sadly depleted.

One incident in particular, in the autumn of 1964, left a very bad taste in the mouths of English Canada. This was the visit of Queen Elizabeth II to Canada to help celebrate the centenary of the Confederation conferences, which opened in Charlottetown and continued in Quebec City in 1864. Separatists chose to make a major issue of the royal visit, calling it a provocation to Quebec's national feelings, and although elaborate (and rather humiliating) precautions by the RCMP prevented any harm or even serious embarrassment to Her Majesty, she was greeted in Quebec City by crowds of booing separatists, mostly students, and some mild disorder in the streets.

This would have been hard enough at best for English Canada to bear, for English Canadians are almost as sentimental as the English themselves about the royal family. What made it still worse was the fact that it was the Lesage Government of Quebec, not the Pearson Government in Ottawa, that invited Her Majesty in the first place. She was originally asked by Premier Walter Shaw of Prince Edward Island to come to his capital, Charlottetown. Jean Lesage personally, at tea at Buckingham Palace in 1963, added a pressing invitation to come also to Quebec City, where the Charlottetown conferences a century ago were carried to a successful conclusion. Lesage could have done himself, at least, a great deal of good had he gone on television before the royal visit to explain this to the people, and tell them it was he and no one else who was her host.

He did not do this. Instead he allowed one of his ministers, René Lévesque, to absent himself without rebuke from the state dinner given by the Government of Quebec to the Queen. Students from Laval University were first allowed to conduct a number of rowdy demonstrations, some in university buildings, and were then dispersed by Quebec municipal police with an ugly, unnecessary violence that made the day of the royal visit, October 10, a day of bitter memory all over Canada.

The whole episode was dismal in the extreme. Unfortunately it continues to stand, three years later, as a kind of dreary symbol of mutual feelings beteen the two major ethnic groups. Only pessimists believe the unity of Canada has been destroyed, but even optimists admit it was rather sadly impaired in the first half of the 1960 decade.

XXI

Days of Decision: The Renewal of Disenchantment

OF ALL THE CAMPAIGN DEVICES that the Liberal tacticians employed in 1963, the one they most bitterly regretted in the end was the slogan "Sixty Days of Decision." More than the homing pigeons that never reached home (they were supposed to fly into a Pearson rally at London, Ontario, but where they did go nobody knows to this day), more than the silly and vulgar coloring books, more than the "Truth Squad" that was to correct Conservative lies, and that Diefenbaker mocked out of existence in a matter of days, Liberals had reason to wish they had never stolen the "Days of Decision" from their campaign Bible, Theodore White's book *The Making of a President 1960.*

No sooner was the Pearson Government sworn in on April 22, 1963, than the press began counting off the days. It was already Day Twenty-two when the new Parliament met for the first time, and the minority Government started the run toward its first major hurdle—the vote of confidence that follows the Address in Reply to the Speech from the Throne.

On Day Twenty-seven, May 18, the new Minister of Finance, Walter Gordon, held the first meeting of senior officials to plan the new Government's first Budget. No Budget at all had been adopted by Parliament in 1962, nor had any departmental estimates been voted; the urgency to get a public statement of the nation's finances was genuine enough. But the preparation of a national Budget begins in late autumn and goes on until early spring, and even the special urgencies of 1963 did not oblige Gordon to produce a Budget in fewer weeks than the usual allotment of months. Only the "Days of Decision" slogan required the fatal haste.

Day Fifty-three, June 13, was the almost incredible deadline that the new minister actually met. On Day Sixty, by an ironic coincidence, he offered his resignation to a confused and dismayed Prime Minister. Sixty days had been enough to shatter the myth of Liberal supercompetence, and to convert the Walter Gordon image from that of an infallible economic wizard to that of a myopic dunce.

By profession Walter Gordon is a chartered accountant and management consultant, a partner until he joined the Government in two of the most respected companies in Canada. He is a former governor of the University of Toronto, former chairman of several important Royal Commissions, chairman most notably of the Royal Commission on Canada's Economic Prospects which, after some three years of study, produced the most thorough appraisal of the economy present and future that had ever been attempted. Reluctantly but energetically he had flung himself into politics to help and advise his old, close friend Lester Pearson, for whom he became chief fund raiser, election campaign planner and, above all, economic counsel. Within the Liberal Party his opinions on all matters economic had almost the authority of Scripture.

For years, and especially since his study of Canada's economic prospects, Gordon had been concerned about the maintenance of Canadian identity on a continent increasingly American. He became convinced that, if existing trends were allowed to continue, Canada would be totally absorbed before long into a continental economy in which everything would be owned, controlled, or directed from the United States, and the façade of political independence (if it continued to exist at all) would become more and more unreal. It was his firm resolution, and a major reason for going into politics, to do what he could to reverse these trends, and he had very definite ideas how to set about it.

Even before the Liberal accession to power, some of his old friends in the business community were suspicious of these no-tions. On the day the Diefenbaker Government fell and the Liberal victory seemed more assured than in fact it turned out to be, one company president remarked: "I'm worried about having Walter in Finance. He's the sort of fellow who will try something to see if it works." Prophetic words.

What he tried in that first Budget was the use of frankly discriminatory taxation in order to discourage further take-overs of Canadian companies by American buyers, and to encourage Canadians to buy back those enterprises already under American control. He put a tax of thirty per cent, a forbidding penalty, on the sale of shares in Canadian companies to foreigners or to foreign-owned companies. He also put a discriminatory penalty on wholly owned subsidiaries of foreign corporations. Companies with less than twenty-five per cent Canadian ownership were to pay twice as high a withholding tax as companies that did have Canadian ownership of twenty-five per cent or more.

These measures (as well as an attempt to extend the eleven per cent sales tax to industries previously exempt, especially the construction industry) set off an explosion of furious protest. Eric Kierans, who three months later became a minister in the Lesage Cabinet in Quebec but who was then president of the Montreal Stock Exchange, fired off an open letter to Gordon that began: "The financial capitals of the world have just about had enough from Canada," and went on to describe Gordon's views on foreign take-overs as "complete and utter nonsense."

Gordon had, of course, expected strong opposition, though he may have been taken aback to find *how* strong. Certainly his colleagues were. And even Gordon was disconcerted to be told, and indeed to be shown, that the take-over tax as drafted was simply not administrable. It could not be made to work.

Civil servants had warned him of this, though apparently the warnings were not strenuous enough. Some ministers, including Prime Minister Pearson himself, believed the failure to dissuade Gordon from the course he chose, and to convince him that the administrative difficulties were insurmountable, was deliberate on the civil servants' part—a kind of passive sabotage. This charge is furiously denied by the suspected officials, and there is no evidence that it had any basis in fact, but in 1963 at least it was believed. The reason for the suspicion was a fact that nobody denied—the fact that senior officials in the Finance Department were resentful of the way their new minister was treating them.

Gordon had decided, as he started his helter-skelter attack on the Budget problem, to bring in three advisers from the business community in Toronto—D. C. Stanley of the investment firm of Wood Gundy, M. P. O'Connell of Harris & Partners Limited, and a young tax specialist who was then taking a doctorate in economics at Harvard, G. R. Conway. None had any experience in the civil service, but all were familiar with Gordon's economic views—they had worked with him on the economic planks of the Liberal campaign platform, which he now intended to translate into law.

Gordon probably knew, since he knew them all well, that the permanent officials in the Finance Department and the Bank of Canada would disagree with him. He certainly knew there would be little time for the protracted discussion and the working out of detail that would normally have preceded a Budget. What he evidently did not know was how strange this unprecedented intrusion of outsiders into Budget preparation would look to the officials, to Parliament, and to the general public.

The Budget debate had barely started when Douglas Fisher, then New Democratic MP for Port Arthur, happened to see one of the three "advisers" in the House of Commons cafeteria, a man he had known at university. Fisher asked casually what his old acquaintance was doing in Ottawa, and was startled by the answer he got. In the House that afternoon he rose to ask whether the Minister of Finance could assure honorable members that "he and his Government officials alone prepared the Budget without the assistance of outside consultants or ghost writers from Toronto." Gordon, apparently acting on the whispered advice of his seat mate Jack Pickersgill, gave a rather evasive answer, which he soon had cause to regret.

Later the same day he interrupted debate to make a supposedly "clarifying" statement, which sounded to many like an admission that his previous reply had been incorrect. He explained that the three outsiders had taken the oath of secrecy and thereby acquired the technical status of Government officials. Thus, in the strictly literal meaning of the words, "Government officials alone" had helped him with the Budget. But Gordon also revealed that two of the three outside "officials" had remained on their own companies' payrolls while doing their volunteer stint for Gordon. To say the whole thing sounded rather odd was an understatement—the more so because of Gordon's less than frank answer to Doug Fisher's original question.

The oddity was accentuated the following day. Convinced at last that his take-over tax could not be administered in its then existing form, Gordon announced its withdrawal. The announcement was made, by oversight, some twenty minutes before the Montreal and Toronto stock markets closed and therefore, of course, when the Vancouver exchange had more than three hours of trading left in its day. Share prices rocketed, a windfall for the alert or the merely lucky.

Nothing like this had ever happened before. True, there was a precedent for "voluntary" amendment of his Budget by the Minister of Finance—J. L. Ilsley withdrew a proposed tariff increase on steel pipe in 1946, after a rebel band of Prairie Liberals threatened to vote against the Budget and defeat the Mackenzie King Government if he didn't. But the steel pipe tariff was a minor and relatively trivial item, which the minister hadn't even bothered to mention in his Budget speech. Gordon's take-over tax was part of the very core of his Budget and his policy. Its removal almost amounted to a defeat to the Budget—which, if it had happened formally as the result of a vote in the Commons, would have meant defeat of the Government and a third general election within a year. (This prospect, horrifying to politicians and voters alike, may have been a major reason why the Government was not formally defeated.)

In any case it was certainly a defeat for Gordon, and he took **it** as such. The next morning—Day Sixty—he called on the Prime Minister and offered his resignation.

Pearson was upset like every other minister, but he didn't want to let Gordon go—suggested instead that perhaps his old friend would be happier with a different portfolio. This Gordon declined. He would cheerfully resign and disappear from public life entirely, he said, but if he stayed it would be in the department he had already.

After some thought, Pearson decided not to accept the resignation. No Government can ever afford to let any group, and perhaps especially the financial community, believe it can decide the fate of ministers—and by this time every voice of Canadian business and most of the Canadian press were clamoring for Gordon's head on a charger. Morever Gordon still had the loyal devotion of many Liberal MPs who would have been sadly disconcerted and disillusioned if he had been thrown to the wolves then howling at his heels.

Nevertheless, the decision was costly in both the short and the long run.

The immediate effect was a Budget debate more grueling, probably, than any Canadian Minister of Finance had ever faced. Day after day from all three Opposition parties came a steady barrage of derision. Naturally it was the bruised Conservatives, whose own competence in financial affairs had been so contemptuously impugned by Liberal speakers during the campaign, who sprang most joyously to the attack upon Gordon the ex-wizard. Conservative financial critic George Nowlan was, and remained, a personal friend of Walter Gordon, but this did not deter him from arraigning the Gordon Budget as a masterpiece of ineptitude, unsound in concept and preposterous in execution.

Other Conservative speakers, including Opposition Leader Diefenbaker, went further. At least by innuendo if not quite explicitly, they questioned the integrity of a minister responsible for such Budget leaks.

Until then Gordon had got little support from his own party. Only one minister, his close friend and policy ally, Maurice Lamontagne, had spoken in his defense. Normally, of course, this was only to be expected. The Minister of Finance does not need any help from colleagues in an ordinary Budget debate. But when a minister is getting the kind of personal fire that Gordan suffered that week, it is usual for other members of the Government (all equally responsible, constitutionally, for the policies under attack) to join the battle. This time it was widely rumored, and is still recalled with bitterness by Gordon's more devoted friends, that some of Gordon's colleagues disagreed with his Budget and did not mind hearing him roasted for it.

Hearing his character impugned was another matter. The Government decided someone other than Gordon should deal with this, and the choice fell on Mitchell Sharp. It was a somewhat ironic choice, for nobody in the Cabinet disliked the Gordon Budget more than Sharp did, but in this debate he was Gordon's ablest defender.

Sharp found it helpful, though, that he did not have to deal with Budget policy, only with the question of integrity. Probably other Liberals, and certainly some members of the minor Opposition parties, felt equally relieved to have some pretext for not voting against this ill-starred Budget and thus defeating the minority Government. On the formal vote of confidence, Gordon and the Government survived—but in truth confidence in the Pearson Cabinet and especially in its Minister of Finance had been sadly impaired, not only in Opposition parties but also in the not too secret hearts of many Liberals. Things were never quite the same again. The epithet "accident-prone," which before long was to become a cliché, first cropped up in the gossip over the Gordon Budget.

So much for the short-run effects of Gordon Budget number one (his second and third, in 1964 and 1965, were so quietly orthodox they have been completely forgotton). Long-term effects were even more serious for the Pearson Government.

On July 18, 1963, even before that first Budget debate had got to its sticky end, Canadians went through a dramatic demonstration of how heavily their economy depended on the cooperation and good will of the United States. That was the day President Kennedy announced his Administration's intention of putting a fifteen per cent tax on the export of American capital, as an emergency measure to stop the drain on the United States' balance of payments.

Instant panic swept Canadian stock exchanges. In the wave of selling on the Toronto market the index of Canadian industrial securities dropped fifteen points in the first hours of trading, a faster plunge than the exchange had ever registered before, even in the crash of 1929. Canadian affiliates of American corporations started moving their case reserves home to the United States, fearing (and therefore contributing to the danger of) devaluation of the Canadian dollar. Between noon on Thursday, July 18, and the closing of the banks Friday afternoon, Canadian foreign exchange reserves dropped by $110 million, a greater reduction than had taken place in any two-day period during the foreign exchange crisis of 1962.

Emergency consultations ensued, first in Ottawa and then in Washington. Louis Rasminsky, governor of the Bank of Canada (a Government-owned central bank), flew to Washington with two senior Government officials to meet Douglas Dillon, then Secretary of the United States Treasury, and Under Secretary of State George Ball. The Canadians were able to convince their American friends that to include Canadian investments in the U.S. capital export tax would actually harm rather than help Washington's own foreign exchange problem, because Canada ran a huge annual deficit in its trade with the United States made up, in large part, by its surplus in trading with the rest of the world.

Rasminsky's point was that if the proposed fifteen per cent tax were levied on American investments in Canada, it would not only ruin the Canadian economy but actually *reduce* rather than augment American reserves of gold or foreign exchange. The first thing Canada has to do, in any serious exchange crisis, is to impose stringent controls or outright prohibitions on imports from the United States, of which Canada is the world's biggest foreign buyer. Dillon and Ball saw the point, and even had the grace to be a bit sheepish about not having seen it for themselves in the first place. It was duly announced from Washington that Canada would be exempted from the fifteen per cent levy, when or if Congress should accede to the President's request to pass the legislation. Gordon and R. B. Bryce, who was soon to become Gordon's deputy minister, made sure this American decision was well publicized in Canada before the stock markets opened on the Monday morning.

That was the end of the great panic, or near panic, of July 1963. Its tangible effects were slight—stock prices recovered quickly, Canadian foreign exchange reserves more slowly but still fast enough, and Canada's economic equilibrium was not seriously upset. Intangible effects were more lasting. As a proof of how vulnerable Canada is to American interventions, even inadvertent ones, it has not been forgotten and isn't likely to be.

To Canadians who agree with Walter Gordon it is an argument for immediate action, drastic if necessary, to reduce Canada's dependence on American capital. To those who disagree with Gordon—and they include the whole of the Canadian financial community, the midwestern prairies, and a British Columbia booming on foreign investments—it is an argument for an exactly opposite policy, and even greater solicitude for the sensitivities of American investors.

But this alone would not account for the opposition, often rising to a hysteria of hatred, that Canadian businessmen developed toward Walter Gordon from that time on. It was rooted in a very personal emotion.

Many of the leading figures in Canadian business were themselves directing American-owned corporations. All automobile companies, most oil and gas companies, many mining and manufacturing companies, and some important lending institutions are wholly owned or majority-controlled by American parents. The Canadian executives in charge of these firms felt that Walter Gordon was somehow impugning their patriotism by attacking or even doubting the values of foreign ownership. So their reaction to his proposals, then and since, went far beyond mere disagreement. The result was a permanent impairment, and in many cases total destruction, of businessmen's confidence in the Pearson regime.

Inside the Cabinet and the Liberal caucus, the wounds of June and July healed slowly but they did heal, superficially at least. Gordon recovered his status as the Prime Minister's closest adviser, not only on fiscal but also on political matters. It was he more than anyone else who, two years later, persuaded Pearson to ask for dissolution of a Parliament less than two and a half years old, and bring on a needless general election for no other purpose than to achieve the parliamentary majority he had missed by four seats in 1963. Gordon had public opinion polls to show that the Pearson Government would get its long-desired majority in November 1965. He was wrong, as things turned out—the Liberals came back after an exhausting campaign with only two more seats than they'd had before, and Gordon resigned from the Cabinet on the ground that he had given the Prime Minster bad advice.

Even this was by no means the end, either of the Gordon story or of the issue of American control over the Canadian economy. But meanwhile other issues, some of them even more sensational if not more important, had moved into the center of Canada's political stage.

XXII

Armed Forces: The Fight over Unification

NO CAUSE FOR ALARM was apparent to the senior officers of Canada's armed forces when Paul Theodore Hellyer, the young MP for Toronto-Trinity, was named Minister of National Defense in the Pearson Cabinet on April 22, 1963.

True, it was an unorthodox appointment. Not since before World War I had the defense portfolio been given to a man who himself had never heard a shot fired in anger. During and after World War II the office had been held by two ex-generals (one of them a winner of the Victoria Cross, the highest military decoration in the Commonwealth), three ex-colonels, three ex-subalterns, and an ex-sergeant major, Brooke Claxton, who had given up a captain's commission in order to go overseas and had there won the Distinguished Conduct Medal in the field.

Hellyer was an ex-lance corporal. In his two years of undistinguished military service he did not manage to get overseas. When finally discharged, a year after VE-Day, he was still in Petawawa, Ontario, learning to be a gunner. He had been made Associate Minister of National Defense in the St. Laurent Government for two short months in 1957, but not until the Twenty-second Parliament had already been dissolved. The popular belief at the time was that Hellyer got the job in order to reduce the average age of the rather elderly St. Laurent Cabinet (58.5). Hellyer was only thirty-three, the youngest member of the last House of Commons.

It may have seemed rather a comedown for the services to have such a military apprentice for their minister, but it had also a major consolation—or so they thought. An ex-private who had never seen action was surely unlikely to argue with generals, admirals and air marshals about defense policy. Except in the special case of conscription (and even then, in the end) the chiefs of staff had never had too much trouble in persuading the minister to their point of view, however distinguished his own military record may have been. "Military mastery of ministers" was an established art among Canadian service chiefs.

Nobody then seemed to remember that the higher a minister's former rank the easier it was to persuade him. Nor, apparently, did any senior officer recall that the average private's opinion of the average general is not necessarily reverential. But even if they had remembered these things, they would still have been unprepared for the horrendous shocks of the Hellyer regime at National Defense. Tho most important part of the new minister's military experience, in shaping the views he was about to put into effect, was something they did not know about.

Hellyer originally enlisted in March 1944, not in the artillery but in the Royal Canadian Air Force. He went through the basic training that was essentially the same for all three services, then wrote and passed the examination to start learning to be a pilot.

By that time, though Aircraftman Hellyer had no way of knowing it, the RCAF had more men and especially more pilots than, quite literally, it knew what to do with. There were not enough aircraft in the whole Commonwealth for the stream of young airmen pouring out, at last, from the British Commonwealth Air Training Plan in Canada.

Meanwhile, the Canadian army, after more than a year of action in Italy and now heavy fighting in France, was running desperately short of reinforcements. Casualties were higher than estimates had predicted. It was the first sign of the crisis that led some five months later to the resignations of J. L. Ralston and C. G. Power from Defense and Air Ministries respectively, and to the near downfall of the Mackenzie King Government.

But in the summer of 1944 Ralston and Power were conferring, with a slowly rising sense of urgency, on the problem of tranferring from the RCAF to the army some 4500 young men whom the

RCAF did not need and the army did. It turned out to be impossible. The only way to make a soldier out of an airman, they found, was to give the airman a discharge and let him re-enlist, as a civilian, in the army.

Hellyer was one of the 4500 who did this. It was explained to the young would-be pilots how urgently they were needed in the infantry, how imperative the duty to take off their air force blue and put on a foot soldier's khaki. But these patriotic appeals were not borne out by what happened next.

First, the young army recruits were put through basic training— the same basic training they had just completed in the RCAF, but that made no difference. The book said basic training comes first, so basic training came first. RCAF training didn't count.

Then, young Hellyer's academic record showed he was above average in mathematics. The book said that recruits with above-average mathematics should go to the artillery. In 1944 the artillery did not need men, at least not acutely, and the infantry's need was desperate, but that made no difference. Hellyer was sent to the artillery.

Thus it was that, when Lance-Bombardier Paul Hellyer finally emerged from the armed services in April 1946, he took away a vivid impression of military organization and military thinking. According to his personal experience, it was not merely stupid, it was imbecile. Seventeen years later when he was sworn as Minister of National Defense, this impression had not entirely disappeared.

Nothing happened in the first few weeks to warn senior officers that their new minister's views might be unorthodox. On the day he took office he did what the services had been hoping for, and announced that Canada would immediately acquire nuclear warheads for the weapon carriers already in place. ("Immediately" turned out to be a slight overstatement, but deliveries did begin before the end of 1963. The first Bomarc warhead arrived on December 31.)

Hellyer then went overseas, as George Pearkes had done six years before, to see the Canadian deployment in SHAPE and get the top-secret briefing on NATO strategy. The professionals were impressed by his anxiety to learn and his ability to absorb large masses of unfamiliar facts. Spirits rose in all three services.

Not until late August or early September did signs begin to emerge of the storm that lay ahead. Each of the three services needed, and requested, a lot of expensive new equipment. The navy wanted a fleet of frigates which, according to the navy's own estimates, would cost $450 million for eight ships. (Other estimates put the final cost nearer $600 million, or about $75 million per ship.) The RCAF wanted a follow-on order of its fighter-bomber, the CF-104, or preferably a more advanced aircraft with which it could continue in its nuclear-strike role in Europe. The army wanted more money to complete development of its armored personnel carrier, the Bobcat, on which millions had been spent over ten years without bringing the program to the production stage.

All three requests were turned down. Cancellation of the navy's frigate program was formally announced on October 24, though the navy had got the bad news privately more than a month before. On November 5, Hellyer told the defense committee of the House of Commons that the army would buy the American personnel carrier M-113 and scrap the Bobcat program altogether. RCAF hopes for another fighter-bomber dwindled sharply when the minister decided to discontinue even the replacements for the existing CF-104s. Canada's future role in the air defense of Europe remained, for the time being, undefined, but it became increasingly obvious that, whatever the role might be, it would not require another manned bomber.

The main reason given for these decisions was the "cost-effectiveness ratio"—bluntly, the equipment that the services had requested would cost far more than it was worth. The M-113 would be vastly cheaper than the Bobcat (exact cost of which could never be determined) and just as good. Cheaper ships could be bought to do all the things the navy had proposed to do with its eight "all-purpose" frigates. As for the fighter-bomber that would succeed the CF-104, it would not only be fantastically expensive but it might also prove quite useless, because airstrips are so vulnerable to an enemy "first strike." Missiles would be better as well as cheaper.

Along with these common-sense points went another, similar but not identical—the wasteful inefficiency of a triplicated defense force.

For example, one of the declared purposes of the navy's multi-purpose frigate was troop transport. The new frigate was designed to carry up to two hundred soldiers, but the navy did not consult the army on whether this little ship would ever be used for this purpose. When the minister did ask the army, the answer was "Good heavens, no." Frigates had room for only the lightest equipment, the soldiers pointed out, and they would also be forbiddingly uncomfortable, especially for seasick-prone landlubbers. Moreover, it was hard to conceive any operation that would require infantry in units of only two hundred, and without heavy gear. Yet, when the navy's frigate problem was discussed and approved by the chiefs of staff committee, the army had made no comment. Apparently it was not considered good form for one service to comment unfavorably on the plans or proposals of another.

Hints began to leak out of National Defense Headquarters that a complete reorganization of the armed services was under study. There would be a single commander-in-chief for all three forces. There would be an end to such obvious anomalies as three separate paymaster corps (and three scales of pay), three procurement services (with three sets of specifications), three information and public relations services with a grand total of 152 all ranks, plus 37 civilians, and a budget of $1.6 million a year.

Plans to correct these redundancies were not new, of course. Sixteen years before, when Brooke Claxton took over National Defense in the last Mackenzie King Cabinet, he too had tried to integrate certain common services like, for example, the chaplain service. Each of the three forces had a chaplain-general with a rank equivalent to full colonel. After "integration," a top chaplain-general was appointed for all forces with rank equivalent to brigadier. Under him the three chaplain services continued intact, each headed by its colonel-or-equivalent.

Early attempts to integrate medical services had results not quite
so ludicrous—military hospitals, for instance, were opened to all
armed forces—but in all other respects separation remained complete. The highest military authority was something called the
chiefs of staff committee. It comprised the heads of army, navy,
and air force, the chairman of the Defense Research Board, the
deputy minister who looked after civilian administration in the
department, and a senior officer as chairman. For many years
the chairman was General Charles Foulkes, a former chief of
the general staff (army). His successor (and, as it turned out, the
last to hold the post) was Air Chief Marshal Frank Miller, former
deputy minister and, before that, chief of the air staff.

The chairman of the chiefs of staff was the minister's senior
military adviser, but he had no personal authority over any chief
of staff. He could not settle interservice arguments, he could only
report to the minister that the chiefs had failed to agree. In theory
the minister could settle them, but in practice it was difficult because no common chain of command existed. Tri-service matters
were handled by tri-service committees, in which few tri-service
disputes were ever resolved. The serious ones, as a rule, were not
even brought up.

This was the *status quo* that senior officers had contrived to
defend, or at least maintain, since World War II. Hellyer's plan
to dismantle it was cautious. There were adroit leaks to the press,
which blossomed forth with stories of the new defense program
that were substantially correct, but committed the minister to
nothing. Public reaction, though apathetic, seemed favorable. A
special defense committee of the House of Commons, which had
been at work since June, toured Canadian defense establishments
at home and in Europe, interviewed NATO strategists as well as
Canadian commanders, and thus provided an all-party core of
well-informed MPs for the defense debates that were to follow.
The committee report had little actual effect on the new defense
policy, since both documents were written about the same time,
but they proved to be not dissimilar.

Finally, in March 1964, the new policy was officially unveiled with the tabling in the House of Commons of a White Paper on Defense. It announced "integration of the armed forces of Canada under a single Chief of Defense Staff and a single Defense Staff," this to be "the first step toward a single unified defense force for Canada." Legislation creating the integrated command structure was passed on July 16, and on August 1 Air Chief Marshal Frank Miller, until then chairman of the chiefs of staff committee, became the first chief of the Canadian Defense Staff. This meant, as the minister explained later, that "the three services were no longer independent entities for the purpose of control and administration."

So far, no strong opposition to the new system had made itself heard. Nobody in or out of uniform seriously tried to defend the more preposterous of the triplications that were being removed. There was a natural concern for the personal welfare of men who had spent the best years of their lives in the armed forces and whose jobs were now about to be abolished, but this problem was met by a range of lump-sum retirement bonuses which, if not fully adequate in all cases, were not ungenerous. Broadly, the first year of integration was as smooth as could reasonably have been expected.

The atmosphere began to change in June 1965, when the new integrated command structure was announced. Canadian forces in Europe were not affected, but at home the changes were drastic. Eleven military commands were reduced to six—a training command for all recruits, a materiel command for all supply (or logistics), a maritime command over all forces on both coasts, an air transport and an air defense command, and something new called mobile command, primarily army but including all necessary services, which looked like the egg from which the Canadian armed force of the future might eventually hatch.

Mobile command was established in 1965, at St. Hubert, Quebec, a former RCAF station on the outskirts of Montreal. Its mission, as officially defined later, was "to maintain combat-ready land and tactical air forces, capable of rapid deployment in circumstances ranging from service in the European theatre to UN or

other peacekeeping operations." It was to be responsible for providing a "rotational brigade" for NATO's land forces in Europe,
plus two additional air-portable brigades (still to be trained) that
would be "designed for rapid deployment." Its air component
would include something the Canadian armed services had entirely lacked in the past, "four squadrons of tactical ground support
aircraft" equipped with the RCAF's new CF-5, a supersonic
fighter designed for close support of ground forces and particularly suitable for so-called "brush-fire wars." It would also be
equipped with a new Canadian transport aircraft, the Buffalo,
and with light and heavy helicopters for maximum mobility in
any zone of combat. To move the heavy gear such a force would
require, the navy would be assigning more men and money to
supply ships like the present HMCS *Provider*.

Obviously the navy and air force were being nudged further and
further toward the role they had always tried to avoid—that of
sea-borne and air-borne army service corps. But that was only one
reason for the growth of misgiving as "integration" of the forces
went into effect and "unification" became nearer and more clearly
visible as the ultimate objective.

As army, navy, and air force personnel were put to working more
closely together, curious anomalies among the different forces became apparent. This wasn't exactly new (away back in World
War II some people had wondered aloud why non-commissioned
airmen slept between sheets, while non-commissioned soldiers
slept between blankets) but the new intimacy made the contrasts
more noticeable. Why, for instance, should each service have its
own set of stipulations for men to be considered for promotion to
commissioned rank? As Hellyer told Parliament later:

"These differences could well result in the least qualified of three
persons, in the three services, being commissioned in a particular
trade common to all services."

To remove or diminish this danger, a common personnel structure was worked out. Among the three services there had been
more than three hundred occupational classifications; these were
cut to about a hundred. Titles for various ranks were continued for

the time being—a group captain remained a group captain, not a colonel—but rates of pay, stipulations and qualifications for promotion, and similar rules became standard for all members of the Canadian armed forces.

What had formerly been remote and hypothetical became suddenly obvious and imminent: Canada was about to have, in Hellyer's words to Parliament, "one force with one common name, a common uniform, and common rank designations."

This was further than many senior officers and ex-officers, in all three services but especially in the navy, had ever intended to go. The dissidents included many who had not opposed, and in some cases had even applauded, the initial step of "integration at the top." They'd had no objection to a single commander-in-chief and a single defense staff, or to the removal of such absurdities as three separate pay corps and postal services.

But elimination of their service itself, as a separate entity, was something else again. This ran counter to all the traditions in which professional servicemen had been bred. Admiral William Landymore, then senior officer commanding maritime command in Halifax, Nova Scotia, summed up the arguments against it in an article in *Maclean's Magazine* in September 1966:

"Within the services the threat of this single force is devastating. It strikes at the heart of all existing military organizations. It means abolishing proven military institutions and adopting a scheme improvised in Ottawa and as yet untried anywhere in the world.

"By destroying the institutional structure of the armed services, the single force threatens the pyschological basis of military life. The confusion and insecurity already caused among career-conscious officers and men is the immediate reason why so many more are leaving the service and not being replaced by recruits. By definition, servicemen are not civilian workers, a little pay increase doesn't make everything all right. Hence, the manpower shortage. . . .

"The concept of the single force is based on a naïve and limited view of the armed services—not as forces to defend the nation in time of war, but primarily as a special peacetime force to undertake small police actions in foreign countries. Historically, police actions form an insignificant part of the life-and-death tasks of the armed services in protecting the nation. Yet Canada is being asked to dismiss her armed services as they are now, and form a new force to concentrate on police work.

"The frightening thing about this aspect of the single-force plan is that it assumes that present conditions among the nations of the world will remain basically as they are. But what happens when the *status quo* alters? And we can be sure that it will, for international conditions and military planning have changed several times since the end of World War II. Instead of the flexible military organization we have at present, are we to be left with no more than a contingent of unemployed constables, in green suits?

"The absurdity is that our armed services have shown their existing organizational framework is eminently competent in fighting police actions. The new force does not derive from military necessity, but from political expedience. . . . We know from experience that our armed services work well in all phases of military operations, but we really don't know whether the new force will work at all."

Admiral Landymore added a Parthian shot: "Senior officers who have tried to inform the Defense Minister of dangers in the program, and in the haste with which it is being carried out, have, like myself, been retired. It has boastfully been said that other nations are watching closely Canada's progress in unification. This is true—but they are watching in horrified fascination."

In the autumn of 1965 Admiral Landymore and the other senior officers of whom he spoke had not yet retired, or been retired. They were still in uniform, therefore still publicly silent, but presumably more and more vocal in the privacy of their own messes and in the secret councils of National Defense Headquarters. Landymore himself wrote a long memorandum in February 1966 which was published after his retirement (or dismissal) in July but which when written was a secret document, setting forth his arguments against unification at much greater length and in detail. No doubt other officers in other services, especially the RCAF, did the same. (The army, numerically the largest service and the one most likely to dominate a unified force, has always been more receptive to unification than the others.)

But the Canadian public heard nothing of this argument. The Commons committee on defense, chaired by a retired naval captain, held sixteen meetings between March 1 and June 29 without ever discussing unification. Hellyer did mention it, in his testimony before the committee on May 12: "We have now reached the stage for final steps toward a single unified force, as forecast in the White Paper [1964]." Nobody commented on this reference. Later General Frank Fleury, comptroller-general, outlined the extent to which integration had been "achieved" in the Canadian armed forces, reporting that Canada had gone "further and faster than any other country" toward "the final goal of unification." Nobody challenged General Fleury's statements, or his choice of language. The only questions from Opposition members, relating to unification, were rather vague queries about morale in the armed services.

On June 23, Landymore himself was a witness before the Commons committee. The session was *in camera* at Landymore's request (he wanted to present highly classified material) but according to MPs who were there, and to an edited version of his testimony published later, he did not then make a direct criticism of the unification program—except to say, in answer to a question, that he did not agree with it.

This point became, within a few weeks, a matter of violent controversy. Landymore said the statement he intended to make was "censored" by Hellyer and his personal staff. Hellyer said there was no censoring. He didn't really care what Landymore might say, he explained later, because he had already decided to dismiss him, believing his failure to implement the program amounted to insubordination. ("Consistent disloyalty," Hellyer imprudently called it at another hearing seven months later— a phrase which he retracted with apologies.) However, Hellyer did point out that Landymore's statement contained figures different from those provided by the headquarters staff. Landymore's figures showed such a falling off in enlistment and re-enlistment as to jeopardize Canada's naval commitment to NATO. Headquarters' statistical picture was much less glum. Both were derived from the same facts; the difference was one of interpretation.

In any event, censored or not, Landymore did make a statement different from the one he originally drafted. Shortly afterward, his patience ran out. On the day Parliament rose for the summer, he gave an interview to the Canadian Press blasting the unification program—even though he was still in uniform and still, at least nominally, head of maritime command. Thereupon Hellyer did what he had intended to do anyway and dismissed Landymore from the service, though without penalty and without loss of pension rights.

With that the whole dispute, which had been smoldering for a year or more, burst into the open. Landymore's example prompted others to follow. The naval officer commanding on the west coast, Rear Admiral Michael Stirling, announced his own premature retirement for reasons similar to Landymore's. In Halifax the entire naval establishment paraded to honor Landymore's departure from the service, all ships flying signal flags that said, "Well done, Landymore." Several senior officers of the RCAF, who had retired within the previous year without giving any reason, now proclaimed their disagreement with the unification policy. In Toronto an organization of ex-officers, some ex-professionals and some veterans of World War II, was formed for the preservation of the three services' "identity." It was called TRIO (Tri-Service Identity Organization).

In addition, some other admirals and a couple of generals retired prematurely, but without any public statement of their reasons for so doing. Spokesmen for TRIO said, or assumed, that these too were disgusted or defeated opponents of unification. Spokesmen for Hellyer said this was not true—each of the men had his own personal reasons for wishing to leave the service (e.g., in one case, his wife's health) which had nothing to do with the unification controversy.

In Parliament the Conservative Opposition, and especially certain individual MPs like the member for Halifax, Michael Forrestal, took up the battle on the ex-officers' side. The debate developed into a personal attack on Hellyer himself and on the "arrogance" with which he was pushing unification through. But colleagues including Prime Minister Pearson made it clear that unification was not just a Hellyer policy, but one on which the whole Government was willing to stand or fall. Since the minor parties were willing to back the Government on the issue there was no serious doubt that the unification bill would become law, with no more than minor modifications.

Whether it will work, as a military policy, is a different question that only time and events can answer. But what did become clear during the long debate, in and out of Parliament, was that the two sides were arguing from different premises, and that there were at least two fundamental contradictions between them.

One concerned the nature and purpose of the Canadian armed forces. Opponents of unification argued, like Admiral Landymore, that the very concept of a unified force was naïve—suited only to a peacetime, peace-keeping force that would be useless in a major war. Advocates retorted that it was the opponents who were naïve. They were assuming that a "major war" would be similar to World War II, in nature if not in scale. They talked of the need for mobilization, for patrolling coastal waters, for dispatching troops overseas. To the advocates of unification, this was the traditional military vice of preparing to fight the last war instead of the next one. If all-out World War III ever does break out, they argue, no home-based Canadian troops will ever get into action. World War III will be an exchange of nuclear weapons delivered essentially by intercontinental missiles, and possessed by great powers alone. Canada will have no consequential role to play. The only useful function of a Canadian armed force will be in conflicts which may be serious and may be bloody, but which will not reach the scale of major thermonuclear war.

The other fundamental difference turns upon the word "identity."

Traditional servicemen have demanded preservation of the identity of the three services with which their emotions and loyalties are engaged. But each of these services becomes, in war, a part of another service in another country. Canada's army, navy, and air force have worn the uniforms respectively of the land, sea, and air forces of Great Britain. Only shoulder flashes, illegible from distances of more than a few feet, distinguished the Canadian serviceman from the British.

More was involved here than a matter of national pride or vanity. Senator C. G. Power, Canada's wartime Minister for Air, has recounted in his memoirs (*A Party Politician,* 1966) some of the complications that arose when Canadian pilots and other air crew were posted to service in the Royal Air Force. The Royal *Canadian* Air Force had different scales of pay. Even more important, it had different standards and procedures of promotion—Britain still had an "officer class" from which most commissioned ranks were drawn as a matter of course, even though humbler "sergeant pilots" might have more important jobs, whereas in the RCAF the general principle was that men doing the same duty, and having the same seniority, should bear the same rank. Perhaps most important of all, Canadian parents and wives looked to the Canadian Government for word, and immediate word, of where and how a wounded son or husband might be, and it often proved difficult to get this information from the Royal Air Force.

Experience in two world wars had convinced a great many Canadian citizens, and two generations of Canadian politicians, that no Canadian *individuals* should ever again be placed under the direct command of another country, however friendly or closely related. It is of course taken for granted that a Canadian force would usually, if not invariably, form part of some larger force, and to this there is no objection. But it has also been taken for granted, increasingly since the intergovernmental arguments of World War II, that Canadian troops would be under Canadian command up to a fairly senior rank—senior enough to make its own views unmistakably clear, and if necessary to refer a disagreement to its own Government.

Above and beyond these specific and practical matters, there is the question of "identity" in the broader sense. Some Canadian servicemen, in wartime at least, did not like being mistaken for men of another country. They would have preferred to wear a recognizably Canadian uniform, to fly a distinctive Canadian flag, to be instantly identifiable as Canadians. This sentiment lay at the root of another bitter controversy in 1964.

XXIII

The Great Flag Debate: Maple Leaf Rampant

THE LONG BATTLE over the Canadian flag, which paralyzed Parliament and Government for six months of 1964, loosed a torrent of invective as harsh as that of the pipeline debate eight years before. For a while it seemed to many people as if it would have the same effect on the new Liberal Government as the pipeline had had upon the old. And in that protracted exchange of harsh words, the commonest charge against the Pearson Government's flag project was that it repudiated Canada's history and destroyed symbols of Canadian nationhood as old as the nation itself.

In one sense the charge was true. The Canadian Red Ensign, the flag of the British merchant marine with the Canadian coat of arms in the fly, had been commonly accepted as a Canadian flag since a year or two after Confederation. Two generations of Canadian soldiers, in two world wars, had regarded it as their battle standard. After VJ-Day it was proclaimed, in the typically tortuous language of a Mackenzie King Order in Council, as the banner to be flown "wherever place or occasion may make it desirable to fly a distinctive Canadian flag." This was to prevail "until such time as action is taken by Parliament for the formal adoption of a national flag." And it was the Red Ensign, thus sanctified by time and circumstance, that the Pearson Government intended to set aside and replace by a banner with its own strange device.

In another sense, though, the new flag project was in line with a national tradition which also was as old as the nation itself. The first Canadian Prime Minister to fight for a distinctive Canadian flag was the first Prime Minister of all, Sir John A. Macdonald. True, the particular flag for which he fought was the Canadian Red Ensign, but the principle was the same. The issue lay between those who wanted Canada's symbols to be British and those who wanted them to be Canadian.

What brought it up was an action of Canadian shipowners. On land it is anyone's right to fly any flag he pleases—it may be improper but it is not illegal—and the new Canadian Government soon began to fly the Canadian Ensign over its Parliament Buildings. At sea it was a different matter. Laws do apply to the flying of flags at sea; a British ship, not a naval vessel, flying the White Ensign of the Royal Navy is liable to be boarded by an Admiralty officer and even to be fined up to £500 sterling. So when Canadian ships began flying the Canadian Ensign, the Admiralty took indignant notice.

Any "defacement" of the ordinary Red Ensign, the flag of the British Merchant Marine, was most improper, it told the Colonial Secretary in a stiff note. "The Ensign without any badge" was the only proper flag for a "colonial" ship. This message was conveyed in due course to the Government of Canada, which paid no attention.

The Admiralty refused to let the matter drop. After several such protests over a period of years, the First Lord of the Admiralty introduced an imperial statute at Westminster in 1889. It formally declared the Red Ensign "without any defacement or modification of any kind" to be the proper colors for "all ships and boats belonging to any subject of Her Majesty" Queen Victoria.

John A. Macdonald's Government reacted instantly, applying for an Admiralty warrant to legalize the Canadian Red Ensign, and meanwhile passing its own Order in Council authorizing Canadian ships to fly the Canadian Ensign as before. The battle went on for three years. Finally in 1892, a year after Sir John A.'s death, the Admiralty gave in. A warrant authorized the Canadian Ensign for ships of Canadian registry. This made it Canada's national flag to all intents and purposes, since it had already been flown on land for more than twenty years without attracting comment either at home or abroad.

Perhaps it would never have become a topic of dispute within Canada, but for a curious incident in 1902. Sir Joseph Pope, the former private secretary and first biographer of Sir John A. Macdonald, by then was Under Secretary of State and responsible for ceremonial. He wrote to the Deputy Minister of Public Works, whose duty it was to buy the flags for Parliament's tower (they wear out about every three months), to tell him that the Union Jack and not the Canadian Ensign was the proper flag to fly over the Parliament of Canada. (To prove it, he cited an editorial in *The Times* of London.) The deputy minister did not argue, he merely bought a Union Jack.

Nobody noticed it, apparently, for two years. Then in 1904 Henri Bourassa, the fiery French-Canadian nationalist, asked in the House of Commons why the Canadian Ensign had been replaced. Sir Wilfrid Laurier, the Prime Minister, said he did not know. But the Minister of Public Works, James Sutherland, intervened to explain that the Red Ensign was "a merchant marine flag, not the national flag of any nation." This seemed to have satisfied Bourassa. Nothing more was heard about the flag, officially, for seven years.

Then in 1911 one John Stedman, a schoolteacher in Saskatchewan, wrote to the Secretary of State for official guidance. What flag should he fly in his school yard as the flag of Canada? This time the question went all the way to Westminster, and a clear answer came back. The Colonial Secretary in Britain "directed" the Governor-General of Canada to state that "the Union Jack is the national flag of Canada as of all other parts of His Majesty's Dominions."

That until VJ-Day in 1945, remained the final word on the national flag *within* Canada. Abroad, the situation was more troublesome. How could anything Canadian be identified, in any other country but especially in Britain, if the only banner it could display must be the flag of Great Britain? In 1924 the first Mackenzie King Government quietly authorized the display of the Canadian Ensign on all Canadian government buildings abroad.

This roused no protest, since the common sense behind it was obvious to all. At home it was a different matter. There the imperial loyalists, as always more royalist than the King, cried, "Hands off the Union Jack!" whenever any attempt was made to give Canada's own flag an official status on its own soil. During the twenties and thirties no fewer than six full-dress debates were held on resolutions for a national flag (usually sponsored by French-Canadian nationalists) which were all either dropped or defeated.

In those days, oddly enough, nobody objected to inclusion of the Union Jack as *part* of a Canadian flag. Even the fiercely nationalist Armand Lavergne, a firebrand of his day, protested in one debate that he would not wish to exclude the British symbol from its place in Canada's ensign. The Orange Loyalists never believed this, and perhaps they were right, for by the time English Canadians were ready to accept the Red Ensign almost unanimously, French Canadians had moved on to a firm stand against "foreign symbols" of any kind.

It was always assumed, in the days before World War II, that this was primarily an argument between the English and the French. Therefore it was a threat to Canadian unity. Therefore, in Mackenzie King's book, it should be touched only rarely and with the greatest care.

In the spring of 1944 *Maclean's Magazine* submitted policy questionnaires to all party leaders, in anticipation of the election that was expected that year (though it didn't come until 1954). One of the questions for Prime Minister King was:

"Should Canada have its own flag and national anthem?"

Brooke Claxton and Jack Pickersgill, then King's parliamentary secretary and executive assistant respectively, drafted the Prime Minister's answers to all the questions, and for that one they needed only one word:

"Yes."

But when King saw the draft, he inked a comma after the

word and scribbled a brief addition. As published, the amended answer read: "Yes, at an appropriate time."

Even Mackenzie King thought the "appropriate time" had come when World War II ended. He passed the Order in Council authorizing use of the Red Ensign "until such time as action is taken by Parliament," and two months later he set such action in motion. A parliamentary committee was set up to choose the design for a Canadian national flag.

To the motion creating the committee, the Conservative Opposition moved an amendment: Let the Canadian Red Ensign be adopted straight away, without further inquiry or fuss. At that stage such a motion would probably have passed the House of Commons unanimously. But the Speaker of the Commons, Dr. Gaspard Fauteux (known to the Press Gallery as Dr. Ghastly Faux-pas) ruled the Conservative amendment out of order and thus destroyed the last chance for amicable agreement.

The committee began its work early in 1946. It received 2695 suggested designs from the general public—1600 had a maple leaf motif, 116 had beavers, 231 stars, 49 crowns, and 22 crosses. One memorable design consisted of a mother beaver and seven little ones, following nose to tail like a family of skunks; the sender appended a note to say the little beavers "represented the seven [sic] provinces." The Union Jack figured in 383 designs, the French fleur-de-lis in 184.

The committee made a solemn mummery of studying all the 2695 suggestions, which were put on public exhibition for several weeks. In private, however, the Commons chairman Walter Harris (later Minister of Finance) had got the word from Mackenzie King. The Prime Minister wanted a Canadian Red Ensign with a large gold maple leaf, instead of the Canadian coat of arms, in the fly. That was what the Liberal majority was instructed to support, and that is what the committee recommended.

But meanwhile, opposition had been stirring. In the Quebec legislature, the Duplessis Government introduced a resolution demanding that "all foreign symbols" be excluded from any Canadian flag. It passed unanimously, the Liberal Opposition not daring, or perhaps not wishing, to vote against it. In the federal Parliament not only Conservatives but Ontario, maritime, and western Liberals as well were letting it be known that, no matter what design was finally adopted, it *must* include the Union Jack in the same place of honor, the upper left-hand corner, that it held in the Red Ensign.

Confronted with this impasse, the Government did nothing. The committee report was tabled, and that was all. Twice during the 1946 session, questions were asked as to when the report would be debated. The answers were evasive. In the next and subsequent sessions of the Twentieth Parliament the subject was not mentioned at all.

It was not forgotten, though. French Canadians were not the only ones who wanted a distinctive Canadian flag. By this time, indeed, they were no longer even the greatest enthusiasts, for Quebec had rather lost interest in the subject. The dedicated flag men were English-speaking war veterans, and one of them was L. B. Pearson. So the Liberal Party platform adopted in 1961 included a clause:

"A Liberal Government will establish a distinctive Canadian flag within two years of taking office."

It was the kind of blunt, firm, imprudent promise that Mackenzie King had always tried to avoid. Once the Liberals took office on April 22, 1963, their 730 days began ticking away like the "Sixty Days of Decision," and the Conservatives licked their chops and bided their time. They expected, and freely predicted, that the Liberals would ignore the flag commitment when the deadline came, but Her Majesty's Loyal Opposition was not about to let them do it quietly.

The cynical prophets were wrong. Pearson had never had any intention of forgetting or ignoring his pledge about the flag. On the contrary, he decided to take action well before the two-year deadline to make sure it would be completed, not merely commenced, by the due date in April 1965. Early in the spring of 1964 he set heraldry experts working on suitable designs. The one he himself liked best was a banner with three red maple leaves conjoined on a single stem, on a white field with wavy lines of blue at top and bottom.

There was good historical and heraldic precedent for this. The cluster of three red maple leaves had appeared in the coats of arms granted by Queen Victoria to Quebec and Ontario in 1868. They also appeared in the Great Seal of Canada, and in the Canadian coat of arms proclaimed as Canada's national symbol by George V in 1921. More recently, the same cluster had appeared on the personal banner for Canada of Queen Elizabeth II, designed in 1962. (The purists of heraldry were less enthusiastic about the wavy lines of blue, but these were accepted as symbolizing the sea-to-sea motif.)

Having decided which flag he preferred, Pearson took a series of carefully planned steps to introduce it to the public. He accepted an invitation to speak to the annual meeting of the Canadian Legion, the principal association of Canadian veterans of both wars, in Winnipeg on May 17. A few days before this event he invited a small group of parliamentary correspondents for a drink at his official residence, 24 Sussex Drive, and showed them a number of designs, indicating his own preference. Press and radio blossomed with reports from "an authoritative source" that this was the design the Government intended to introduce.

On Sunday, May 17, the Prime Minister made it official. This was the subject of his address to the Canadian Legion—an address that turned out to be quite an extraordinary affair.

Membership in the Legion is open to all war veterans, but the majority and the dominant group are those of World War I. Their loyalty to the Canadian Red Ensign was as fierce as that of any Canadian. Forewarned of the Prime Minister's intentions by the news stories of a few days before, they were ready to let him know in no uncertain terms what they thought of his flag proposal.

The speech was broadcast live, and also recorded for rebroadcast later. Thus for two or three days the radio and television audiences of Canada were able to see and hear their Prime Minister being hooted, jeered, and howled down by an angry mob of

Legionnaires, not all of whom appeared to be quite sober. It was an unedifying spectacle.

Pearson took it with composure. He had expected trouble, and he was ready for it. At press conferences after the Legion meeting he showed western reporters the same flag designs that he had already displayed in Ottawa. Partly because of the boomerang effect of the Legionnaires' rowdyism, he got at the outset a fairly good press.

Before long, however, the battle lines were drawn. Except for their small group of French-Canadian MPs, the Progressive Conservatives were solidly for the Red Ensign and against any tampering with it. Liberals were equally solid (with one maverick exception) for the new flag. The NDP suggested a different design, but most of its members favored some kind of a distinctive Canadian flag. So did the Créditistes, the Quebec wing of Social Credit. Thus the Liberals were assured of a parliamentary majority if the question could be brought to a vote, but the Opposition was strong and self-confident enough to delay that moment indefinitely.

Also, the Government's attitude was rather ambiguous. Pearson had said it would be a "free vote"—one in which members would not be required to vote under party discipline—but he also said the Government would "stand or fall" by the decision, which seemed to mean the flag resolution was an issue of confidence and therefore not, in the usual sense, a free vote at all. (Any vote is "free" if the Government's own members don't care whether or not they defeat their own leaders and bring on an election in which they're likely to be defeated themselves.)

Then there was the matter of the design. Pearson had said it was for Parliament to decide, yet the resolution under debate described the proposed design quite precisely—it was the three-maple-leaf flag, which the Opposition derisively called "the Pearson Pennant."

But these were details for parliamentarians and pedants. The general public and the press hardly noticed them. There, the discussion was all upon the main point: "New flag (any new flag) or Red Ensign?"

Strangely, although the Liberal Party's intention had been well known and frequently remarked upon for three years, many papers and people deplored the "suddenness" of the Government's action. The Edmonton *Journal* wondered dolefully "why Mr. Pearson has so suddenly and so persistently taken up the flag issue." Nevertheless, the *Journal* went on, "with infinite sadness we have come to the conclusion that if a new flag is needed to save the country, then a new flag we must have."

It was this very point that alarmed some of the editors in central Canada, and especially in Quebec. The Montreal *Gazette* said: "The danger in the flag issue is that it may make serious emotional demands upon many Canadians to accept the solution offered. And having made what they feel is a 'massive concession' they may feel less disposed than ever to make any more, for a long time. In this way the country's resources of good will may be lowered, just when they ought to have been carefully guarded."

The Winnipeg *Free Press* struck a note of alarm that had wide echoes in the west:

"The arguments Mr. Pearson has advanced for getting rid of the Red Ensign could be applied with equal force to getting rid of the monarchy. Is this the ultimate goal of the policy and program initiated by Mackenzie King and carried on by his successors? Is the Liberal Party dedicated to turning this country into a republic?"

But if some editorial writers were a bit hysterical, they were all cool and calm compared to the people who wrote them letters for publication. One wrote from Ottawa:

"The Karl Marx plan for world conquest decreed that national corruption and spiritual decay must be the first fruits of ultimate victory. . . . We now understand the Liberal Party's desire to strike the Canadian Red Ensign."

From Toronto, another called the suggested new flag "a rag of appeasement, thrust upon us by a dictator who has split the country."

Not all citizens had entirely lost their sense of humor, though. A reader in Oakville, Ontario, wrote to the Toronto *Star:* "If all Canadians will fight as vigorously *under* the new flag as they have *over* it, there is still hope for us as a great nation." And William Arthur Deacon, the retired literary critic of the Toronto *Globe and Mail*, offered a philosophical reflection upon protests that the maple leaf grows in only one quarter of Canada's land surface, and therefore isn't truly representative as a national symbol:

"Industrious and ubiquitous, the beaver alone represents us all. The visual objection to this overgrown rat is that its shape is ugly. The bull moose, weighing up to 1800 pounds, is also ugly but is a creature that inhabits all regions except the civilized south. As farms and towns move north there will be fewer moose, but choosing this beast now would postpone the flag controversy for a century, and I am all for us getting back to our regular jobs."

Others were beginning to feel the same, especially around Parliament Hill where the flag debate had settled down into a steady, repetitive drone. Charles Lynch, the political columnist for the six Southam newspapers across Canada, remarked as early as June 17, only two days after the debate began:

"The flag debate may be the stuff of which history is made, but if it is the historians are going to be bored stiff."

For a while the Government seemed to count this universal boredom as an ally, and to think the Opposition would give up through sheer weariness. It was wrong. Even though the Government threatened to, and did, keep Parliament in session all summer without the usual break that tired spirits and testy tempers sorely need, the Opposition kept pegging away at the same few points—keep the Red Ensign, or anyway put the question to a plebiscite and let the people decide.

Finally it was the Government that gave way. Instead of forcing the debate through to a finish on the resolution then before the House, it turned the whole question over to a select committee of seven Liberals, five Progressive Conservatives, and one each from the three minor parties. Of the five Conservatives, one was a French Canadian.

The committee was to review the whole question of flag design and come back with a recommendation. Both the Red Ensign and the "Pearson Pennant" would be considered, but the committee was also free to recommend any other design that it might choose.

After weeks of study, and testimony from a battery of heraldic experts, the committee got down to the task of voting. The Red Ensign was soon disposed of—defeated by a vote of ten to four, with the French-Canadian Conservative voting with the majority. This left the "Pearson Pennant" and a new design, a single red maple leaf on a white ground with bands of red on either side. The decisive vote was the one taken between these two, and it presented the Conservatives with a problem in gamesmanship.

They assumed that the Liberals would still feel themselves committed to the "Pearson Pennant" with its three maple leaves. They assumed that the NDP and perhaps the two Social Credit MPs would prefer the new, one-leaf design, and they knew their own French-Canadian member would vote for it. There was a chance, therefore, that an Opposition majority might deal a nominal defeat to the Liberals by rejecting the "Pearson Pennant" by a vote of eight to six. (The chairman, a Liberal, could vote only in the event of a tie.)

What the Conservatives did not know was that the Liberals had changed their minds. Convinced at last that the "Pearson Pennant" had too much political flavor to become an acceptable flag for all Canadians, they too decided to vote for the new, single-leaf design.

The result, to the Conservatives' horror, was a unanimous vote of fourteen to zero.

"They were aghast, they were horrified," Liberal MPs chortled later, as the details of what had happened at the closed meeting began to leak out. The reasons for their horror were plain enough. The Opposition had no intention of letting the new design, or any design, go through Parliament without a filibuster. The fact that they had actually voted with the Liberals and the minor parties for the new design was bound to be embarrassing to them. They did what they could by putting a new motion, and voting that this new design should *not* become the national flag of Canada, but their faces remained red for some time.

Not that it made much difference. As before, the public was not interested in details. The pro-Ensign voter, minority though he seemed to be, still relied on the Conservatives to block the Liberals' dark designs upon Canada's traditional symbols. As autumn advanced into winter the renewed flag debate dragged on, and the Conservatives introduced a new amendment whenever an old one was voted down, a process that could go on forever.

More and more frequently, in the corridors and cafeterias of Parliament, the word "closure" was heard—uttered by Liberals in dread, by Conservatives in glee. Since the pipeline debate in 1956 an almost superstitious horror had grown up against using the ultimate weapon of closure to choke off debate. Both major parties, or large sections of them, really believed the Liberals had been turned out of office in punishment for using this sinful device, and to use it in so emotional an issue as the flag seemed to be, was considered doubly dangerous.

So as day followed day and week followed week, the Government put off the horrid decision. Gradually it was the Conservatives who became apprehensive, resentful. They were being blamed, they discovered, for "holding Parliament to ransom," in the Montreal *Star*'s phrase. Yet they did not dare simply cave in, for fear of the vengeful wrath of their Ensign-loving voters.

"The Liberals have got to use closure, to get us off the hook," George Nowlan said one day, in perfectly genuine indignation. "We can't just quit, our people would never forgive us for it. They've got to take the responsibility of forcing us."

Finally on Monday, December 14, the long-dreaded moment came and the closure motion was put. The debate ground on to its appointed end, 1 A.M. the following day, and the flag then passed the Commons with nobody but the Conservatives voting against it. In the Senate the debate was brief. The resolution having passed both Houses, no legislation was necessary; the red maple leaf on its red and white banner became officially the flag of Canada on February 15, 1965.

The event was celebrated in various ways around the world. In Ottawa a large crowd gathered on Parliament Hill to see the new flag hoisted for the first time. A Conservative secretary was detected in the act of applauding; she was threatened with dismissal for this act of disloyalty, but saved her job by the counterthreat of making public the reasons why she was being fired. In London a handful of Canadians gathered on the sidewalk beside Trafalgar Square while Lionel Chevrier, the High Commissioner, made a brief speech into a microphone, which was audible to the radio audience if any, but not to those standing five feet away. To a NATO base in Germany the Canadian ambassador to the North Atlantic Council came all the way from Paris for a flag-raising ceremony, which was marred when someone let go the halyard so that the flag couldn't be raised until a corporal had shinnied up the flagpole to recover its loose end. In Jamaica, High Commissioner Graham McInnes introduced a little originality and style. Instead of holding the ceremony in the blazing heat of high noon he called it for 5 P.M., not too early for cocktails; the whole Canadian colony was invited, and sang "Auld Lang Syne" as the Red Ensign was struck for the last time and then "O Canada" while the new flag went up. There was not a dry eye on the lawn, they say.

In Ontario, Conservative Premier John Robarts quietly made the best of both worlds. He said or did nothing against Canada's new flag, but he adopted the Red Ensign with a provincial instead of the all-Canadian coat of arms to be the flag of Ontario, where it therefore continues to fly as of old, side by side with the new maple leaf. In Newfoundland, Liberal Premier Joey Smallwood harrumphed that, no matter what the rest of the country did, his province would always fly the Union Jack. Some Canadian Legion posts vowed never to disfigure their flagpoles with anything but the old Red Ensign.

But soon these attitudes softened. Within a year an Ontario judge, Mr. Justice W. S. Lane, refused to hold court in the Prince

Edward County Council building in Picton, Ontario, because only the Ontario flag was flying above it and he presided, the judge said, over a Canadian court. But he was mollified to learn that the Picton County Council had already ordered a new Canadian flag and erected a flagpole to fly it on. The Canadian Legion's national executive recognized the new flag and enjoined all its posts to do likewise.

As for Premier Smallwood, he still flies the Union Jack on his lawn, but he also flies the maple leaf beside it. The Jack is now not only the flag of Britain and the Empire, but also the official flag of Newfoundland.

Voters didn't forget the flag controversy entirely. John Matheson, MP for Leeds, a badly wounded war veteran who was one of the leaders in the fight for the new flag, had his majority cut from 2214 in 1963 to only 229 in 1965, by the fiercely loyalist voters of his riding.

In general, though, the whole fuss seemed to be forgotten within weeks. An issue which had terrified Canadian governments for forty years, and been a burr under Canada's saddle blanket for a century, had at last been disposed of forever.

XXIV

The Tangles of a Ten-horse Team

TENSIONS IN Canada are never merely two-way. Nothing so simple as north against south, English against Irish, French against German. In Canada the patterns of hostility are a kaleidoscope of regional and religious, personal and political, social and economic, cultural and linguistic prejudice in which no combination is reliably predictable. It is partly a cause, partly an effect of this condition that sovereignty itself is divided between two levels of authority, each supreme in its own sphere. Ten provincial governments, each a working model of Her Majesty's Government in Westminster, are wholly independent of each other and partly independent of the central government in Ottawa that exercises its own kind of authority in all provinces.

In this situation it is hardly surprising that tension is chronic and crisis frequent. Canadians are used to it—so used to it that they may not even notice when the nation's normal malaise becomes suddenly acute. Such a moment of high fever came in the spring of 1964.

It was the eve of All Fools' Day, a coincidence that seemed more appropriate in retrospect than it did at the time, when Prime Minister Pearson and four of his colleagues met the ten provincial premiers in Quebec City. The atmosphere was cordial enough, at least at the outset. Even though they represented four political parties, the men around the table were old acquaintances, and most of them were friends. Their host, Jean Lesage of Quebec, was the most aggressive of spokesmen for provincial rights, but he had also sat in a federal Cabinet beside

Pearson for four years, and had been his parliamentary assistant
for two years before that. Some of the federal ministers were
newcomers, but none was a stranger, and all fifteen were masters
of the same craft, politics. Altogether, a congenial group.

On the first evening Lesage had them all to dinner—ministers
only, no civil servants. Already the opening statements had shown
considerable differences among them, but these were not allowed
to mar the mood of good-fellowship. As the party broke up
Lesage said to a friend: "You know, an evening like this does
more good than all our formal sessions put together."

Pearson was more clearsighted. Talking to the same friend
about the same occasion, he said: "These dinners are a little
misleading. Jean Lesage is such a good host, the atmosphere is so
pleasant and congenial, and he himself says all the right things
about being a Canadian first and not just a Quebecker—it's easy to
let yourself think we really have no serious problems, none that
can't be dissolved in a bath of good will. We have to remind
ourselves that none of us came here as an individual. Lesage has
all kinds of pressures working on him, and so have we all, and
the differences among us are very real."

Some of the pressures were dramatically visible. About two
thousand students of Laval University marched on the Quebec
legislature building with placards that said "Lesage, the Queen's
Jester," and "John, Judas of Quebec," as well as the more ordinary
"Pearson Go Home." (Six months later the same boys were out
booing Queen Elizabeth II, and having their heads broken by
Quebec City police for doing so.) Provincial spokesmen let it
be known that the anti-Lesage and anti-Pearson placards had
been censored by university authorities, and only the milder ones
permitted. The outright separatist slogans, of which there had
been several, were suppressed.

But if Lesage looked like "Ottawa's Valet" to the students at
Laval, he certainly did not to the Ottawa delegation, or even to his
fellow provincials. The demands he laid before the conference
next day were peremptory and extreme. One correspondent,
Charles Lynch of the Southam newspapers, was moved to a wry

simile: if Quebec and Ottawa had fought a war and Quebec had won, he said, the peace terms might be very like Lesage's new proposals.

Ottawa ignored them. When he delivered the final communiqué to the press, and answered questions about it, Pearson had John Robarts of Ontario sitting beside him but not Jean Lesage, the equally senior premier from Quebec. Lesage was holding his own press and television conference, and issuing his own communiqué. Its tenor was one of controlled rage:

"One thing must be understood: We want our rights under the Constitution! We want justice!"

To the reporters who were taking it all down with their notebooks and tape recorders, it sounded like one of Lesage's routine TV tantrums, by that time a fixture of every federal-provincial conference. We knew before we came to Quebec City that Lesage needed a lot more money to finance his grandiose Quiet Revolution. We knew that Walter Gordon, the federal Minister of Finance, was determined not to give him any. Therefore Lesage would have to impose massive new taxation on his own people. Naturally, he would try to blame it on Ottawa.

But at least three men in the federal delegation thought that the trouble was more serious, and that Confederation itself was in graver danger than it had ever been. Two were bureaucrats— Gordon Robertson, whose title was Clerk of the Privy Council and whose function was to be the Government's chief adviser, and Tom Kent, special assistant and economic counselor to the Prime Minister. The third man who felt concern was Pearson himself.

They realized, as no outsider then did, how deep were the roots of this controversy, how long it had been developing, and how complex were its origins and effects. It was much more than a routine dispute between Ottawa and Quebec, or between the English and the French.

One aspect of it was as old as Confederation itself, for it began with the British North America Act. In 1867 the Fathers gave to provincial Governments "direct taxation within the province," which in those days meant property taxes, as their only source of revenue. They allowed the central Government "the raising of money by any mode or system of taxation," but in nineteenth-century practice this was mainly customs and excise, and so it remained for half a century.

When, in 1917, Sir Thomas White introduced his Income War Tax Act as a "temporary" emergency measure, the provinces were hardly in a position to complain. It was the darkest period of World War I, and opponents of the war effort were saving their fire for the imminent threat of conscription. Besides, the very idea of income tax seemed an outrage that could be tolerated only in time of war, and would of course be withdrawn in peacetime. Several years went by before the objections became coherent, and provincial premiers began to complain that the "direct" federal income tax was a clear invasion of provincial rights and violated the spirit of the Constitution. Some of them are continuing to say it to this day—and not only in Quebec.

But Ottawa had no intention of giving up this rich tax field. Not only did it bring in about half of all federal revenues (and more than this in emergency periods of high taxation) but it also gave the central Government an instrument of control over the national economy, alternately a stimulus and a brake. As the economic theories of Lord Keynes became accepted during and after World War II, this second advantage became the more important of the two.

Instead of giving back to the provinces this most lucrative of all "direct" taxes, Ottawa began a series of tax-sharing devices— equalization formulae, they were called. The theory was that certain rich provinces, notably Ontario and Quebec where most corporations have their head offices, were really catch basins for wealth that was earned all over Canada, and that the taxes on this wealth should be pumped back to the hinterland whence it had come. Also (a supplemental theory that developed later, along with the concepts of the welfare state) all Canadian citizens should enjoy reasonably similar standards of public service, regardless of where they lived.

This sounds fairer on paper than it turned out to be in practice. Quebec has the rich metropolis of Montreal, home of many corporate headquarters, but it also had some of the worst pockets of poverty in all Canada, and its non-tax revenues (mining royalties and the like) are relatively small. Oil-rich Alberta, at the other extreme, has been able for twenty years to maintain a high level of provincial services and also to pay off the entire provincial debt with what it gets from the oil industry—yet until 1961, Alberta was listed among the "have-not" provinces getting "equalization payments" from the federal treasury. No proper definition or standard of fiscal capacity had been worked out; hence the anomalies.

But in the late 1950s and throughout the 1960s even the rich provinces have been increasingly desperate for money. The same British North America Act that limited their tax revenues to "direct taxation within the province" also gave them a range of responsibilities—education, local works such as highways, municipal institutions, and a ragbag item that in 1867 did not amount to much: "Hospitals, asylums, charities and eleemosynary institutions." A century of court rulings had determined that "charities and eleemosynary institutions" included most if not all social welfare legislation.

These were all rapidly expanding fields. School costs, university costs, highway construction costs, welfare costs were all being multiplied by fantastic factors while provincial revenues were not being multiplied nearly so fast. And provincial embarrassment was aggravated rather than relieved by a device that was growing very popular with federal Governments, the "shared-cost program." This was an offer by Ottawa to pay a share, usually fifty per cent but sometimes as high as ninety per cent, of some new and costly project in the provincial field.

Quebec was the most outspokenly indignant, but all provinces disliked these programs, or Ottawa's way of handling them. As a former provincial civil servant once explained it:

"If you're a provincial treasurer and you've got your budget all worked out, and then suddenly, without consulting you, Ottawa announces a shared-cost program that will add $10 million to your expenses—I tell you, you don't have to be French Canadian to be mad."

That is how it looked to the provinces. From Ottawa the view was quite different. The provincial fields had become not only the most expensive but also the most attractive—it was by promising more money for schools, universities, hospitals, medicare, and welfare programs in general that politicians could win friends and influence people. Ottawa suspected the provincial Governments (all but three of which were then non-Liberal, and one of the nominal Liberals was the refractory Jean Lesage) of wanting to make themselves popular by spending money that Ottawa made itself unpopular by collecting. There was some truth in this. Every provincial premier came annually to Ottawa, demanding more money from the central treasury to avoid having to raise his own taxes and risk thereby his own political neck.

Walter Gordon and his colleagues decided this had gone on long enough. At their first dominion-provincial conference in November 1963 they were resistant to provincial demands—Lesage, for example, came stipulating that he must have $150 million more, and all he got was $43 million. Other provinces were similarly served, and all were surly about it.

Behind this quarrel another one smoldered, over something called the Canada Pension Plan.

Canada had had a government pension system since 1927, but in its first twenty-six years it was distinguished chiefly by stinginess and hardness of heart. A maximum of twenty dollars a month, at the outset, was paid to elderly folk who could prove themselves utterly destitute and without near relatives able to support them. In 1953 this Bumble-worthy scheme was replaced by a universal old-age pension with no means test, paid to every citizen of either sex, rich or poor, who reached the age of seventy. The auction process of four general elections had raised this dole from forty to seventy-five dollars a month by 1963—which meant, for many an elderly couple in the poorer regions like Newfoundland, a higher cash income in retirement than they had ever earned in their working lives.

In the election campaign of 1963 the Liberals promised to supplement this universal, flat-rate payment with a graduated, contributory pension scheme in which the rate, both of benefits and of contributions, would depend on the earner's income before retirement. No sooner was the election over and the Liberal Government in office than work began on the details of the Canada Pension Plan.

Obviously it depended on cooperation from the provinces. The constitutional amendment of 1953, which had made the existing pension scheme possible as a federal activity, defined pensions as a joint field—no federal plan should be allowed to interfere with a provincial one, if any. Therefore any province that was big and rich enough could block Ottawa's plans for a national scheme by introducing one of its own.

There was some fear that John Robarts in rich Ontario might do just that, since he did bring in a new law to make private pensions "portable" within Ontario, from one employer to another. Also, Robarts called a provincial election for September 1963. The federal Minister of Health, Judy LaMarsh, saw fit to intervene at the side of John Wintermeyer, Ontario Liberal leader, and attack Robarts as the enemy of the Canada Pension Plan.

Robarts was furious. Federal ministers do not normally take any part in provincial elections, for one thing—they have to work with whatever Government is elected, no matter what its party, so they remain relatively neutral. Moreover, it was not true that Robarts was then blocking, or sabotaging, the Canada Pension Plan. He had not yet made up his mind what to do about it, and didn't intend to until he had seen its details. When in the September election Robarts was returned with an increased majority, the Ontario Liberals slaughtered and John Wintermeyer defeated in his own constituency, the outlook for collaboration between Ontario and Ottawa did not improve.

But what really infuriated Robarts was Ottawa's reaction when Jean Lesage, out of a blue sky, suddenly announced that he wanted no part of the federal pension plan; Quebec would have one of its own. After a few initial gulps, the federal Liberals smiled bravely and said the Premier of Quebec was merely exercising his constitutional right. The Premier of Ontario took this badly.

In public statements he was formal and cool: "To us," he said in his opening speech at Quebec City, "cooperative federalism cannot mean a system under which some provinces can stay out of programs, with federal approval, while against others that also elect to stay out is levelled the accusation that they are breaking up Confederation."

Privately he put the same thought in blunter language: "I'm mad as hell at being made the fall guy, after Quebec had opted out altogether!"

He still didn't say whether he would or would not join the federal scheme, but he certainly made the doubts a lot livelier. Meanwhile, Lesage played another card, which turned out to be a trump.

Details of the Quebec plan had not then been published, but it was known that the big difference between it and the federal scheme was the size of the reserve fund—Quebec's would be bigger. At the conference on April Fools' Day, Lesage explained to his dazzled fellow premiers just *how much* bigger. Ottawa's plan would have raised about $2½ billion in ten years, of which, rather grudgingly, Ottawa had offered to make half available for provincial borrowings. Quebec's plan would raise about the same amount in the same time for Quebec alone. On an all-Canada scale it would amount to between $8 and $10 billion, of which Ontario could count on about $3 billion.

Prospective pensioners, had they too been studying the details, might not have been so pleased with the Quebec plan—they'd be paying about twice as much in contributions for the same rates of benefit. But to nine provincial premiers hungry for capital and yearning to be free of the tyrannies of the money market, it looked like a godsend. Joey Smallwood of Newfoundland expressed the thoughts of all:

"How can we get in on it too?"

Robarts made no public announcement during the Quebec City conference, but a few days later he let it be known that Ontario would be opting out of the federal scheme just like Quebec. "Were we to join the federal plan," he told the Toronto Canadian Club blandly, "we would be surrendering our constitutional rights as a province." Jean Lesage couldn't have put it better.

But at Quebec, Lesage was also asking for things no other province requested, among them, Ottawa's complete withdrawal from a long list of "shared-cost" programs, and he wanted to have the money instead, a total of about $212 million a year. In addition he wanted $150 million as compensation for Quebec's refusal, in Duplessis' time, to have anything to do with shared-cost programs. (It was this demand that prompted Charles Lynch's remark about "peace terms.")

For all these requests he got precisely nothing. The nearest approach to a "concession" was the appointment of a thirteen-man committee to examine tax structures and make a new definition of the provinces' fiscal capacity. When this committee made its report two and a half years later, Quebec was the major gainer by the new standards it set, but this was cold comfort for Jean Lesage in 1964.

Cold was what it was meant to be. Walter Gordon's decision to "hold the line" had not wavered. He had served public notice of it by making his own Budget speech unusually early, two weeks before the Quebec conference opened. Judy LaMarsh had done the same, introducing her Canada Pension Plan bill the following day, March 17.

To all outward seeming, therefore, none of the rigid positions had given an inch when the Quebec conference broke up in open bitterness and anger. Beneath the surface, though, a change was already well advanced.

Four men were working on it over the weekend, unbeknownst to each other. Tom Kent and Gordon Robertson each prepared, independently, a memorandum for the Prime Minister suggesting negotiations on the pension plan be reopened with Quebec.

Maurice Sauvé, the young Minister of Forestry who had been in the Cabinet only two months, had not gone down to the Quebec conference (he was detained in Ottawa by an NDP filibuster that prevented the Easter recess) but he was in closer touch with the Lesage Government and its officials than any other federal minister. He gathered information about what had gone on in Quebec, and planned to reopen the whole subject in Cabinet. Meanwhile Pearson was doing his own brooding at 24 Sussex Drive, and coming to similar conclusions unassisted.

By Tuesday evening of the following week the Cabinet had been persuaded, and Kent and Sauvé took off for Quebec City. After a hard day's work with Claude Morin, Lesage's Deputy Minister for Dominion-Provincial Affairs, they went in to see Lesage himself. He was non-committal, but agreed to postpone his own Budget speech in which he intended to blast Ottawa's intransigence. Kent and Sauvé went back to Ottawa with the compromise to which he had more or less agreed—a national and a Quebec pension plan, still separate but now identical and interchangeable, and resembling the original Quebec much more than the original Ottawa project.

But in return for the concessions he did make, Lesage got massive payments from Ottawa on the tax-sharing side. About $60 million were to be added to the $87 million worth of tax rebates given to the provinces in November, and Quebec would get $17.5 million of the new money. More important, the rate of increase in payments to the provinces would be accelerated, so that by the time existing tax agreements expired the provinces would be getting about $200 million more than they had received in the past. None of this counted whatever money might be turned over, in lieu of "shared-cost" programs, to any province that exercised its privilege of "opting out."

Pearson announced the new deal in the House of Commons on April 20. Diefenbaker and his Conservative followers were predictably scornful, but there was never any questions that Parliament would approve. Tommy Douglas, the NDP leader who used to be Premier of Saskatchewan, called it "a real victory for national unity and common sense." W. A. C. Bennett, the Social Credit Premier of British Columbia, publicly pronounced it "an enlightened approach," which was enough to ensure the backing of Robert Thompson and his federal Social Crediters. The minority Pearson Government had no cause to worry about getting majority support.

Whether the support was deserved is still an open question.

To Conservative critics the whole idea of provinces "opting out" of national welfare schemes was part of the "Balkanization of Canada," which they saw as the inevitable end of Liberal policy. Many a Liberal in his secret heart agreed with them. It could hardly be denied that the looser its reins and its traces, the harder the ten-horse team would be to drive.

But Pearson had no doubts, then or later. He was convinced that, if matters had been left where they were when the Quebec conference ended, Confederation would either have broken up or become meaningless. The Quebec pension plan, and the one that Ontario would certainly have modeled upon it, would have divided the central provinces from the rest of Canada to a lethal degree, and made it prohibitive for men to move from one part of Canada to another. The welfare programs from which any province already had the right to withdraw would have lost any semblance of similarity, and turned Canada into a crazy quilt in which nobody would know for sure what his rights were in any part of the country.

If he'd been asked then what was the most important achievement of his Government after a year in office, Pearson would have said, "Breaking the deadlock at Quebec." Three years later, as his own political career was nearing its close with many more spectacular events behind him, he would almost certainly have said the same thing.

The year 1964 saw the end of another deadlock of many years' standing—a feat that was somewhat obscured at the time by the excitements of the flag debate and the fact that there was no stubborn or strident opposition, but one that changed the political face of Canada perhaps more than any other. This was the new electoral redistribution act, which took the allocation of constituency boundaries out of partisan and regional politics.

Redistribution had been a headache ever since Confederation. The British North America Act provided a formula for the allotment of parliamentary seats to each province, on a basis of population, but nothing regulated the distribution of seats *within* the province. The grosser forms of gerrymander had been abandoned, since the days when Sir John A. Macdonald could boast cheerfully of "hiving the Grits," but if the impact of party politics had diminished, the resistant power of sheer inertia had correspondingly increased.

The result, by 1964, was an assortment of rotten boroughs almost as fantastic as those before the British Reform Bill of 1832. Bruce County, Ontario, had 17,075 electors in 1965 who returned one Member of Parliament, Conservative Whip Eric Winkler. York-Scarborough, the suburban riding on the eastern edge of Toronto, had 190,698 electors who returned one Member of Parliament, Liberal Robert Stanbury. NDP Candidate Edward Phillips, who ran third in York-Scarborough, got 33,815 votes —or almost one hundred per cent more than the entire electorate of Bruce County.

Examples such as this could be found in every province, varying only in degree. Canada in 1900 was about two thirds rural, but by 1961 it was nearly three quarters urban. Parliament did not begin to reflect this change. It was more like half rural, half urban by even the broadest sense of the word "urban." Country and small-town members combined were an overwhelming majority, for the bigger the city, the more it was underrepresented.

What perpetuated this absurdity was the fact that each redistribution was carried out by the Members of Parliament themselves, the men directly affected. Naturally they did not readily redistribute themselves out of existence. Even political enemies could band together for self-preservation. Except when the shrinking population of a province made reductions in the number of its seats unavoidable (and even for that there were various constitutional brakes) few ridings, however tiny, were ever actually abolished.

The 1961 census showed these anomalies had reached such a pitch that everyone agreed something had to be done. The solution, reached after protracted but not too acrimonious debate, was to set up ten electoral commissions, one for each province and each headed by a judge. The chief electoral officer, Nelson Castonguay, as the only technically qualified expert on the subject, would be a member and adviser of all ten. They would draft new electoral boundaries on a basis of equal population, with an agreed tolerance up or down for thickly and sparsely settled areas. Their draft would be returned to the House of Commons for comment and advice, but the commissions could take the advice or leave it as they saw fit. After a certain time the new boundaries would go into effect automatically.

The waiting time was considerable. The general election of November 1965 had to be held on the old basis, though almost a year had gone by since the act received royal assent. But after the next general election and forever thereafter, the Parliament of Canada will represent a Canada that actually exists.

Passage of the redistribution bill gave the accident-prone Pearson Government a new sense of confidence. The flag debate had not yet been completed, but closure had already been decided upon so the result was a foregone conclusion. What with the flag question settled, the perennial dispute between Ottawa and the provinces settled for the time being, a fair batch of housekeeping legislation disposed of, and now redistribution, the Liberals had some reason to hope their luck had turned.

This euphoria lasted seven days. The redistribution bill passed the Commons November 16, 1964. One week later, on November 23, the roof fell in on the Pearson Government with the loudest crash in recent parliamentary history.

XXV

Shady Trails of Scandal

TO MOST OF the 265 Members of Parliament, and to all but a handful of the spectators in the galleries, the opening of the afternoon sitting of the Commons on November 23, 1964, was an occasion of unclouded cheer.

First item of business was the introduction of a new member. It is customary that party hostilities are put aside for this ceremony, and the House revealed as the exclusive, congenial club that it really is, but on this day there were more than the normal reasons for a show of good-fellowship. The new member was Margaret Rideout, the attractive blonde widow of a popular backbencher who had died suddenly a few months before. She had won the by-election for the seat his death made vacant, and the House outdid itself to bid her welcome as she walked down the center aisle, the Prime Minister at her right hand and the New Brunswick Cabinet minister, Hedard Robichaud, at her left, to be presented to Mr. Speaker and then shown to her seat.

Next came the daily question period, and now a hint of mystery did arise. Tommy Douglas, leader of the NDP, put a question to the Minister of Justice, Guy Favreau: Had he received any complaints that "persons in high places" had been trying to exert improper pressure, to get bail for two men held in Montreal's Bordeaux Jail? But Favreau was obviously ready for this question. He would be making a statement on this matter later in the day, he said, and Douglas did not press the question further. The estimates of Favreau's Department of Justice were that day's order of business.

When they were called, at the end of the question period, Favreau launched upon an hour-long speech about his plans for penitentiary reform, a worthy but dreary performance that sent most MPs and reporters to the fifth-floor cafeteria for their usual afternoon coffee. They were back in their seats by 4:30 P.M. for word had filtered around, from the few who had known it for several days, that fireworks would begin as soon as Favreau sat down.

Tommy Douglas rose again as the minister finished, seeking an answer to his previous question: Had there been charges of political pressure in a criminal case? Yes, Favreau said without embarrassment, there had been certain charges to that effect. He had ordered an inquiry, which had indicated no evidence on which to base a prosecution. He was sure the honorable member would not wish to damage individuals by linking their names with unsupported accusations.

It was evident that Favreau thought his answer sufficient. Douglas politely disagreed. Would the minister not order a fresh, independent inquiry, preferably by a judge, and thus dispel any possible suspicion? Favreau had no objection, provided the inquiry was conducted *in camera* to protect innocent men from public obloquy.

This appeared to satisfy Tommy Douglas, who subsided. But the ordeal of Guy Favreau had not even begun. The next man on his feet was Erik Nielsen, Conservative MP for the Yukon.

Nielsen is a lawyer, the son of a Danish immigrant who was a sergeant in the Royal Canadian Mounted Police. He was first elected to Parliament in 1957, but as a Government backbencher he attracted little notice. Not until the Conservatives went into opposition did Nielsen's special talents get full play, but by mid-1964 he had already earned some reputation as a scandal-hunter and scourge of wrongdoers. Twice he had been able to charge, and then triumphantly prove in the face of official denials, that certain Liberal ministers had been indulging in petty political patronage.

There was nothing petty about the charges he had to make now. They were harsh and specific:

A notorious gangster named Lucien Rivard, charged with smuggling narcotics into the United States, was being held for extradition in Bordeaux Jail. The Canadian lawyer representing the U. S. Department of Justice in the extradition proceedings, a young Montrealer named Pierre Lamontagne, had been offered a bribe of twenty thousand dollars if he would refrain from opposing Rivard's application for release on bail. The man who offered the bribe, said Nielsen, was one Raymond Denis, executive assistant to the Minister of Immigration and formerly assistant to Favreau himself. Additional persuasion had been attempted by a member of Favreau's present staff, Guy Lord.

At Nielsen's first mention that a man "in the minister's office" was involved, Favreau was stung to a rejoinder he later regretted: "That is an absolute lie. No one involved in this case, implicated as an offender by the honorable member, is a member of my department or ever has been a member of my department."

It was true no member of the Justice Department had been implicated "as an offender," since no charges had been laid against anyone. But of the men "involved," one was still on Favreau's staff and another was a man Favreau had brought to Ottawa when he joined the Cabinet. Favreau was convinced that Guy Lord's involvement was innocent and trivial, and this opinion was confirmed by subsequent inquiry (Lord was "an innocent dupe," according to the report of a Royal Commission seven months later). Raymond Denis, though eventually charged, was never convicted—the case ended in a mistrial, and no further steps have yet been taken against him. But to call Nielsen's overstatement "an absolute lie" was itself an overstatement, and did Favreau's cause more harm than he seemed to realize.

Indeed, the whole affair was graver for himself and for the Government than Favreau seemed to realize. His behavior from beginning to end was lamentable proof that an honest man's consciousness of his own rectitude can be a dangerous thing.

He had known about the bribe allegation since mid-August,

when Pierre Lamontagne first told his story to the Royal Canadian Mounted Police. RCMP Commissioner George McClellan reported it immediately to his Cabinet superior, the Minister of Justice. Favreau ordered an immediate investigation, and specifically that Lord, Denis, and Favreau's own executive assistant, André Letendre, should be "questioned immediately and simultaneously." But he was visibly upset that such charges should be laid against men he knew well, and had himself brought into Government employment. When all three men denied any wrongdoing, Favreau believed them. His chief preoccupation seemed to be that they should not be "smeared" with unsupported accusations, and he did not even tell his colleague René Tremblay, the Minister of Immigration, of the charge against Tremblay's assistant, Raymond Denis. (Tremblay first heard of it from Denis himself, two weeks later.)

More important, Favreau said nothing to the Prime Minister about the affair. For all of the second half of August it was a secret known only to the accused and their accuser, to the RCMP, to Favreau himself, and to a few senior officials. To repeated suggestions that he should, indeed must, tell the Prime Minister what was afoot, Favreau remained curiously reluctant.

Finally, though, he agreed. There was to be a meeting with provincial premiers in Charlottetown, Prince Edward Island, over the Labor Day weekend; he would find an opportunity there to tell Pearson about the bribery charge. When he came back he took a weight off the officials' minds by assuring them that he had in fact done so.

It turned out to be a slight exaggeration. Pearson was sitting with another Cabinet member, Senator John Connolly, and both their wives on the plane coming back from Charlottetown. When Mrs. Pearson left her seat for a few minutes, Favreau sat down in her place. There was something he'd been meaning to tell the P.M., he said—someone had made a charge of bribery against a former assistant of his, but the man denied it, and the RCMP were investigating. Pearson thanked him, asked for a further report when the RCMP inquiry was completed, and then forgot the brief conversation.

Nothing happened to remind him of it until the day before the story broke in the House of Commons. For a full week the facts had been leaking out bit by bit. Fear of libel actions prevented any actual publication, but at least two newspapers had the story already in type, and at least two radio stations were ready with taped reports, for the moment when a mention in Parliament might put the whole affair under the libelproof shield of parliamentary privilege. Worried friends kept phoning Favreau to warn him that a scandal of major proportions was about to break.

Favreau remained unconcerned. He was deeply preoccupied with his departmental estimates, the first he had ever presented as Minister of Justice, and the annual occasion for cross-examination of the minister in Parliament on the affairs of his department. Favreau held long conferences with his officials to acquaint himself with every detail of his new responsibilities, which (as a former assistant deputy minister in the same department) he took very seriously indeed.

The so-called scandal did not appear to him as important. He knew that he himself had done nothing wrong, he was confident his officials were equally innocent, and he seemed to recoil from even discussing the distasteful subject.

It was not until the Saturday evening he was persuaded to warn the Prime Minister of what might happen on Monday, and to request an interview for the purpose on the Sunday afternoon at the Prime Minister's residence. Even then his briefing was strangely cursory, offhand, and incomplete. He did not remind the Prime Minister of their casual talk on the plane three months before. He did not say, perhaps did not even know, that Erik Nielsen was in full possession of the most damaging facts. Worst of all, he failed to mention what to Pearson was the most vital point—that one of the men involved, who also had tried to get bail for Lucien Rivard, was Pearson's own parliamentary secretary, a Montreal MP named Guy Rouleau.

So the parliamentary week that began November 23 was, for
Pearson, one devastating shock after another. Until he heard Erik
Nielsen put the "case for the prosecution" he had had no idea
of the gravity of the affair. Favreau was asked whether, before
deciding not to prosecute, he had sought advice from the Law
Officers of the Crown. No, he had not. He was asked whether the
case involved "anyone else higher up in the Government." Unaccountably, Favreau said he was not sure. He still did not tell
Pearson that the "person higher up" was Guy Rouleau—who was
not, strictly speaking, "in" the Government but was obviously a
close associate.

Pearson did not hear about Rouleau until the following morning. Once informed, he called Rouleau to his office, extracted
from him the admission that he had intervened in Lucien Rivard's
favor, and fired him on the spot. Rouleau was permitted only the
grace of announcing his own resignation as the House met Tuesday afternoon, instead of having it announced from the Prime
Minister's office Tuesday morning.

No sooner had Rouleau finished his statement than Favreau
rose to make another one. A judicial inquiry would be held, he
said—an open inquiry, not *in camera*. Attempts during the question period to define the terms of reference drew no more than a
general statement from Pearson: "The terms of reference will
permit the widest possible inquiry." But toward the end of the
question period, a more precise query was put to the Prime
Minister by the Conservative ex-minister Douglas Harkness:

When had the Prime Minister first been informed about the
affair?

"Mr. Speaker," Pearson replied, "I think I was informed on
the day before the [Justice Department] estimates were brought
before the House."

Favreau listened to this in a stricken silence. He'd had no
idea that Pearson had forgotten their conversation on the flight
from Charlottetown in September. He could not believe that a
moment so painfully vivid in his own mind should have made no
impression at all upon Pearson's. But he said nothing at the time,

and had no opportunity later, for the moment the question period ended Pearson left the House of Commons for Uplands Airport. There the Government's new JetStar had been standing by since noon, waiting to fly him to Saskatoon for—of all things—a Liberal Party rally.

It was a political affair, but it was by no means trivial. Saskatchewan Liberals under the leadership of Ross Thatcher had unexpectedly won the provincial election in June, unseating the CCF (not changed to NDP in that ruggedly rural province) after twenty years. Thatcher had once been a CCF socialist himself. Now, with the zeal of a convert who also happened to be a millionaire hardware merchant, he headed a Government that was Liberal with a capital *L* only. On matters of policy it stood well to the right of the federal Conservatives, and even further to the right of its nominal allies in the Pearson regime. For this and other reasons the relations between Ottawa and Regina had not been warm. This Liberal dinner in Saskatoon was a long-planned exercise in mutual conciliation.

After the important engagement on the Tuesday, the Prime Minister was to spend two days making closer acquaintance with western farmers and then—another major event—address a fund-raising dinner in Winnipeg for which $50-a-plate tickets had already been sold. Then he was to fly to Toronto and go through the annual ceremony of kicking off to start the Grey Cup game, Canada's professional football championship and one of the two biggest moments of the year in Canadian sport (the other being hockey's Stanley Cup final).

Item by item, the week's program was defensible enough. The political engagements were important not only for the party but also for the nation—this was Pearson's first attempt to sell his policy of "cooperative federalism" and of sympathetic help to a renascent Quebec, in the so far unsympathetic prairies. As for the Grey Cup game, it was an annual fixture at which his attendance had long been expected, and on Saturday Parliament was not sitting anyway.

Nevertheless the effect of the whole week was bad. To the

general public he presented an image of cynical frivolity, un-
matched since Nero's violin solo. To the reporters and politicians who were watching at closer range, the impression was
even worse—not frivolity but indecision, ineptitude, and a state
of fluster bordering on panic.

Things went badly at Ottawa during his absence. With Paul
Martin, the dean of the House of Commons and Minister of
External Affairs, filling in as Acting Prime Minister, the Government had been forced back step by step on the terms of reference it proposed for the judicial inquiry, broadening them from
the narrowly limited scope that Opposition critics had decried as
"a whitewash." Moreover Guy Favreau was coming under heavi-
est fire, in press and in Parliament, for his "failure" to tell the
Prime Minister about the Rivard affair. After enduring this for
two days in silence, he told the Cabinet about the conversation
on the plane—Pearson was asked by long-distance telephone from
Paul Martin to confirm this incident, and was thus reminded of
it for the first time. He did confirm it to his colleagues but, unaccountably, made no public statement, an omission he had cause
to regret.

His immediate problem, though, was whether to cancel the
rest of his political fence-mending tour and go back to Ottawa
to resume personal command. In midafternoon on the Thursday
he decided the answer was yes, and authorized an announcement
to that effect to the press cavalcade traveling with him. The
decision stood long enough to be broadcast on the CBC national news that evening. Half an hour later it was reversed.
Things looked better at Ottawa; the Prime Minister would complete his western schedule, and the fund-raising dinner at Winnipeg would have its principal speaker after all. As it turned out,
the speech was not a great success. The Prime Minister seemed,
as he read his prepared text, to be thinking of other things.

There ensued an interval of quiet. Parliament having turned
the Rivard case over to a judicial inquiry, on the broad terms
of reference that the Opposition had demanded and got, the

House returned to the last, anticlimactic fortnight of the flag debate. Pearson considered, but unaccountably postponed, making the personal statement that would have cleared up the misunderstanding about whether, and how, he had been told about the Rivard scandal in advance. Instead he composed a letter to all members of his Cabinet that soon became public, and was known as "Pearson's code of ethics." The key sentences:

"It is by no means sufficient for a person in the office of a minister—or any other position in the public service—to act within the law. . . . There is an obligation not simply to observe the law but to act in a manner so scrupulous that it will bear the closest public scrutiny. . . . In order that honesty and impartiality may be beyond doubt, members of ministers' staffs, equally with ministers themselves, must not place themselves in a position where they are under obligation to any person who might benefit from special consideration or favor on their part. . . ."

Before the week was out, those words came back to haunt him.

On the very day the Pearson letter went out, an enigmatic question appeared on the House of Commons Order Paper. Donald MacInnis, the onetime coal miner who was Conservative MP for Cape Breton South, asked: "Has the Government any information . . . that the bankruptcy proceedings by Max and Adolph Selfkind [in Montreal] disclose contributions for campaign purposes to any Cabinet ministers or other Members of Parliament?"

MacInnis was acting on fragmentary information, as the errors in his question revealed. The men involved were named Sefkind, not Selfkind, and their "contributions" had nothing to do with campaign funds. Erik Nielsen's acquaintance with the facts was more precise. He was able to assist two reporters, George Brimmell of Southam News Services and Paul Akehurst of radio station CHUM, in tracking down the real story: two Cabinet ministers had incurred substantial debts to a bankrupt company formerly owned by the Sefkind brothers, who themselves had fled the country. The Sefkind name had been cropping up in newspaper reports of the Quebec Government's inquiry into fraudulent bankruptcies in Montreal.

The two ministers were Maurice Lamontagne, Secretary of State, (no relation to Pierre) and René Tremblay, Minister of Immigration. First in statements to the two reporters, later to the House of Commons, they told what had happened.

Tremblay's story was short, simple, and innocent. Wishing to furnish the home he had acquired in Ottawa after becoming a Cabinet minister, he had ordered some furniture from the Sefkind brothers' Montreal shop, a fashionable emporium called Futurama. There was then nothing to indicate the Sefkinds were on the brink of bankruptcy. However, they did go bankrupt before delivery of Tremblay's furniture order was complete, so that the first and only bill he ever got came from the receiver in bankruptcy, the Bank of Montreal. He paid the full amount, some $3600, within a week of receiving the bill. That, so far as he was concerned, was the end of the story.

No such luck. Even though no one, then or later, could point to anything Tremblay had done wrong, he had eventually to resign from the Cabinet with his political career in ruins. He'd been an innocent bystander too often. In Quebec he had been a deputy minister in the department that lent $1.2 million to a company owned by the Sefkinds. In Ottawa his executive assistant (whom he had not hired, but inherited from his predecessor Guy Favreau) was the principal suspect in the Rivard bribery case. Now, for no reason within his control, he was associated with Maurice Lamontagne in what came to be called "the furniture scandal."

Lamontagne's story was more complex. He had known the Sefkind brothers for some years. They were German-Jewish refugees who had set up business and prospered in Montreal, with a predominantly French-speaking clientele, and who had cultivated such socially distinguished acquaintances as the former Laval University professor, later economic adviser to Prime Minister St. Laurent, still later economist on the personal staff of Opposition Leader L. B. Pearson, and now Secretary of State.

While the Liberals were in opposition, and he himself was working in Pearson's office at a modest salary, Lamontagne had suffered a personal calamity. A fire in his home destroyed his furniture. He then discovered that, because his insurance agent had recently dropped dead, his insurance policies had lapsed without his knowledge. In this emergency it seemed natural enough that his friends the Sefkinds, respectable and presumed to be rich merchants, should say, "Come and pick out what furniture you need, and don't worry about the cost—pay us when you can."

At this time Lamontagne had no power to do political favors for the Sefkinds or anyone else. Later, when he was a minister of the Crown, he did buy some more furniture on the same easy terms—"nothing down and nothing a month"—but there is no evidence that the Sefkinds ever asked or received any benefits in return. Lamontagne, too, received his first and only bill from the Bank of Montreal, after the Sefkind brothers had fled. He arranged to pay off the account, a total of about $6800, in installments of $200 a month.

Lamontagne had done nothing illegal. Still, his arrangements with the Sefkinds looked odd in the light of the Pearson "code of ethics": "an obligation not simply to observe the law but to act in a manner so scrupulous that it will bear the closest public scrutiny."

Meanwhile still another matter had cropped up, petty in itself but embarrassing in the circumstances, involving another minister.

In June 1960 an Italian named Onofrio Minaudo came to Canada, settled in Windsor, Ontario, went into business there as a baker, and applied for the status of landed immigrant. Investigation revealed that Minaudo had previously been deported from the United States, that he had been convicted and sentenced in Italy for crimes including armed robbery and murder, that he was believed to be a leading member of the Mafia, and that he had entered Canada illegally, not once but many times. These facts were not published at the time, but Minaudo's application for citizenship was refused. Instead, he was ordered deported on February 9, 1961.

For some reason the deportation order was not carried out until March 11, 1964. During that interval Minaudo, who in

Windsor had tried to present the image of a respectable businessman, retained the services of two lawyers who were also Members
of Parliament for the Windsor area. One was a Conservative,
Richard Thrasher, parliamentary secretary to the Minister of Labor until his defeat in 1962. The other was Paul Martin, dean
of the House of Commons, a private MP when he acted for
Minaudo but now Secretary of State for External Affairs and
Deputy Prime Minister. Trivial, perhaps, but embarrassing.

Much more embarrassing was the device Pearson adopted to
reveal his prior but forgotten awareness of the bribery charges.
Having let two weeks go by without rising in the House of
Commons to correct his inadvertent misstatement, he wrote a
letter instead to Mr. Justice Frederic Dorion, Chief Justice of
Quebec, at the opening of the judicial inquiry into the Rivard
affair. Dorion, who was sitting as a one-man Royal Commission,
had the letter read into the record of his inquiry on Wednesday,
December 16—two days before the House rose for its Christmas
recess and, by coincidence, the same day as written answers were
produced to the questions about Onofrio Minaudo.

Because the flag debate was still going on, the daily question
period had been eliminated for technical reasons of procedure.
This did not prevent Douglas Harkness from raising, as a matter
of personal privilege, the incorrect answer he had got from the
Prime Minister November 24. Pearson's further explanations were
lame. Harkness suggested, and Tommy Douglas formally moved,
that the whole matter be referred to the Committee on Privileges
and Elections, an unprecedented affront to the dignity of a
Prime Minister. Mr. Speaker ruled the motion out of order, but
Douglas appealed the ruling, and the vote on this nominally
procedural issue became in fact a vote of personal confidence
in Prime Minister Pearson. The Government won, but narrowly
—122 to 105. Social Credit members sided with the Liberals. The
other Opposition parties were solidly against.

That night the closure motion on the flag debate took effect,
so that next day, the last of the pre-Christmas session, the question period was restored for the first time since November 27—

a fact of which the Opposition took full advantage. This was also the day when Maurice Lamontagne and René Tremblay made their formal statements to the House on the furniture deal. When Parliament adjourned at 7 P.M. for a two-month recess, it seemed to be bringing to an end an exchange of personal insults and innuendo that had reduced political debate to a new low. But the Government knew, and several Opposition MPs had cause to suspect, that worse was still to come.

Ten days before, Premier Jean Lesage of Quebec had come to Ottawa on other business, but had taken the opportunity for a private chat with his former chief and old friend, Mike Pearson. Lesage brought a warning: serious allegations of bribery were being made against another of Pearson's ministers, Yvon Dupuis. The bribery charge concerned a provincial matter, a license for a racetrack in St. Jean, Quebec, for which Dupuis was the federal member.

Dupuis at thirty-eight was the youngest member of the Pearson Cabinet, but he was nonetheless the favorite son and standard-bearer of the old guard in Quebec politics. His appointment to the Cabinet had been part of a typical Pearson compromise. When old guardsmen Lionel Chevrier and Azellus Denis resigned from active politics in early 1964, a fierce dispute about who should succeed them had racked the Quebec caucus. The new guardsmen, few in numbers but strong in virtue and press support, wanted Maurice Sauvé and Jean-Luc Pepin promoted. Old guardsmen, who hated Sauvé and distrusted Pepin, demanded that favor should fall upon Yvon Dupuis and Guy Rouleau (who also was a young old guardsman). Pearson chose one of each, Sauvé and Dupuis, giving Sauvé the small Department of Forestry and Dupuis no department at all—he became Minister without Portfolio.

As an old-style, rough-and-tumble campaigner Dupuis had been a great help to the party in Quebec, or so his backers said. As a minister he was no asset. He had already embarrassed the Government by offering for sale, from his House of Commons office, bumper stickers picturing the new Canadian flag—which Parliament had not adopted.

The bribery charges were more than a mere embarrassment. In the circumstances of December 1964 they could become a lethal blow to the Government. A St. Jean chiropractor named Roch Deslaurier had complained, to the Quebec Government, that he had paid ten thousand dollars to Yvon Dupuis to get him a racetrack license. Eric Kierans, Quebec Minister of Revenue, said he had confronted Dupuis with this charge and had got from him a partial admission, that he had indeed received "a brown paper package containing money," which he in turn had given to a man whose name he didn't know, "a representative of the [Quebec] Department of Revenue." This was supposed to have taken place during the regime of Kierans' predecessor Paul Earl, who had died in 1963. (Kierans put this into a letter to Guy Favreau as Minister of Justice, which eventually was produced in the House.)

Told all this by Lesage, Pearson had an immediate showdown with Dupuis and gave him a brief interval in which to show cause why the RCMP should not make an investigation. Dupuis failed to do so. The RCMP inquiry was duly carried out. By early January, preliminary reports from the RCMP were unfavorable. Pearson summoned Dupuis and told him to resign.

Dupuis refused. For almost a week a state of curious deadlock ensued, with Dupuis adamant in refusing to resign and Pearson threatening to fire him if he did not—yet reluctant, on the eve of the Quebec legislature's opening January 21, to set off another resounding scandal.

The deadlock was finally broken on Friday, January 22. The Cabinet published an official announcement that "effective today, Mr. Dupuis is no longer a member of the Government." The public was allowed to infer that he had resigned. He had not—but before the day was out he was persuaded that his cause was hopeless and that he had no real alternative but to resign "for personal reasons." The resignation, and Pearson's curt acceptance, were released to the press that evening.

Dupuis was arraigned in March on charges of accepting ten thousand dollars "for illegal purposes." After a preliminary hearing that went on all spring, he was committed for trial in July. In the autumn he was found guilty. Dupuis at once declared his intention to appeal, but the result has not yet been announced.

Meanwhile, in Ottawa, public attention had shifted to another ring of this grisly circus, the shabby little hearing room of the Board of Transport Commissioners which Chief Justice Dorion had converted into something like a court of law. No charges were laid, but they might as well have been—men's reputations were at stake in this tribunal, and exposed to damage that no subsequent acquittals could repair.

First, young Pierre Lamontagne told his story, in detail and under oath: He had been appointed special counsel for the United States Justice Department (on the Canadian government's recommendation) for the prosecution of a drug-smuggling ring of which Lucien Rivard was the chief figure. Rivard and three others were arrested in Montreal in June, and lodged in Bordeaux Jail pending extradition to Laredo, Texas. Their lawyers applied for bail and were refused.

On July 14, Lamontagne said, he got a telephone call from a friend in Ottawa, Raymond Denis, who used to work with him in the same law office. At Denis' request he went to Ottawa for an "urgent" conference at which, he said, Denis offered him twenty thousand dollars not to oppose the next application for bail for Lucien Rivard.

Lamontagne said he refused the bribe but did not at that time report it. Later he got several other telephone calls—two from Rivard's lawyer, Raymond Daoust; one from Guy Rouleau, the Prime Minister's parliamentary secretary; one each from two members of Guy Favreau's staff, a junior assistant named Guy Lord and the senior executive assistant, André Letendre. Lamontagne regarded all these calls as part of the pressure on him to let Rivard's application for bail go unopposed.

276 Shady Trails of Scandal

Raymond Denis denied, under oath, that he had ever offered Lamontagne a bribe. Guy Lord, Guy Rouleau, and André Letendre all denied putting any pressure on him—their calls had been simply requests for information, they said, and in the case of Guy Lord, at least, Judge Dorion accepted the explanation. Guy Favreau himself was a witness, presenting his usual appearance of rumpled, ill-organized integrity.

There was also another group of witnesses of very different type—Lucien Rivard himself and his wife Marie, his and her friend Eddy Lechasseur, a man named Robert Gignac awaiting trial on a charge of murder, a self-described "Liberal organizer" named Guy Masson who was, or claimed to be, a friend of many in high places and in low. The stories they told, some of them bizarre, neither confirmed nor refuted Lamontagne's testimony, but they showed clearly enough that something very odd had been afoot in the Rivard case.

From the very beginning of the scandal on November 23, but more and more insistently as the inquiry proceeded, one ugly fact was hammered home each day: all the men involved in this case were French Canadians. Pierre Lamontagne with his ugly story, Guy Favreau with his naïve trust and his concern to protect other men's names, Raymond Denis with the call to Lamontagne that he admitted (even leaving out the bribe offer that he denied), all these men in positions of trust were Quebeckers. So were the seedy, shoddy underworld and half-world characters who had tried —with whatever hope of success—to escape the attentions of the law through political favor.

As the Dorion inquiry went on, however, this particular shoe began to raise blisters on the other foot. And the lamest victim of the transfer was that hitherto impeccable, world-renowned force, the Royal Canadian Mounted Police.

The RCMP was shown to be, even in Quebec, an almost wholly unilingual force. Although every person involved in the Rivard case was French-speaking, the officer put in charge of the RCMP investigation neither spoke nor understood French. Some French-speaking witnesses had been questioned by the RCMP in

English. Others, questioned in French, were asked to sign summaries of their statements in English, since the higher officers for whom the statements were prepared could not read French. As if to draw special attention to this defect in their capability, the Mounties had retained for the Dorion inquiry a Toronto lawyer, Norman Matthews, Q.C., who also spoke no French and could understand neither witnesses nor counsel until the translation (not always accurate) came through his electronic earphone.

This, however, was only part of the ineptitude the RCMP revealed in the Rivard case. In one important episode, Pierre Lamontagne had tried with RCMP assistance to trap Raymond Denis into a repetition, over the telephone, of the alleged twenty-thousand-dollar bribe offer. Denis did not oblige—but even if he had, there would have been no corroborative evidence. One of the two RCMP officers who listened in made some rough longhand notes on the back of an envelope, which he subsequently lost. The other made no notes at all—he was holding the receiver with one hand, he explained, while with the other he was covering the transmitter so that Denis would not hear his breathing. For this and many similar reasons, RCMP testimony at the Dorion hearing was almost entirely useless. But what finally reduced the whole affair to the level of farce was something that had nothing to do with the Mounties.

On March 2, the day he wound up his hearings in Ottawa, Chief Justice Dorion had a cocktail party for the reporters who had been covering the inquiry for the past two and a half months. Dorion is a jovial host. He'd been an MP himself twenty years before (Independent, but of Conservative origins) and he enjoys political gossip. His party in the Château Laurier hotel was a great success.

It was nearing its end when, unexpectedly, a telephone call came for David MacIntosh of the Canadian Press. MacIntosh listened for a few moments, uttering occasional grunts of incredulity. Then he hung up, and turned to break the news:

"Lucien Rivard has just escaped from Bordeaux Jail."

Every detail that came in later made the story even more preposterous. Rivard had escaped, along with a companion, by asking and getting permission to flood the prison rink—in spite of the fact that the temperature in Montreal that evening was 40° Fahrenheit. He had then thrown the hose over the jail wall, used it as a hook-and-rope to climb over, stopped a passing motorist to "borrow" his car (not forgetting to give him two dollars for taxi fare, and to return the car in good condition later).

The nation was convulsed. Rivard became a folk hero, a good-natured joke, like a mixture of Robin Hood, Long John Silver, and the Artful Dodger.

Jails are under provincial control—only penitentiaries, housing prisoners already sentenced to long terms, are federal. The guards by whose incompetence or connivance Rivard escaped were not only provincial employees, they were holdovers from the old Duplessis regime. Moreover, Rivard was recaptured in due course, extradited shortly thereafter, convicted in Laredo on the drug-smuggling charge, and sentenced to twenty years in prison. None of these facts saved Guy Favreau from being pilloried as the man who "let Rivard go."

But in the early weeks it seemed that the escape might be a kind of relief—comic relief, perhaps, but no less welcome. Even scornful laughter was better than the savage bitterness of December. As the spring wore on, and especially as Chief Justice Dorion finished his week of listening to lawyers argue, and settled down to the long quiet task of writing his report, Canada recovered its calm and the Pearson Government its confidence. There was a tendency to think the Winter Scandals had already been forgotten.

This notion was rudely dispelled by Chief Justice Dorion's report, handed to the Prime Minister June 28 and tabled in the House the following afternoon. It was unexpectedly harsh. Between the contradictory statements of Lamontagne and Denis, Dorion had no hesitation in choosing: "It is that of Mr. Lamontagne which must be believed, rather than that of Mr. Denis. . . . There cannot be any doubt that Lawyer Denis did offer Lawyer Lamontagne the sum of $20,000 to obstruct the course of justice."

Neither could there be any doubt that "Mrs. Rivard, Eddy Lechasseur, Robert Gignac and Guy Masson conspired to obstruct the course of justice. . . . I find no difficulty in reaching the conclusion that there certainly is *prima facie* evidence of an offense under the Criminal Code."

He was equally harsh in his appraisal of the RCMP. The force had been incompetent in its handling of the Rivard case, he found—slow and inept in questioning witnesses, dilatory in following up leads, premature in discontinuing its investigation, presumptuous and inaccurate in giving legal advice to the Minister of Justice. Dorion was also, as a French Canadian, biting in his remarks about the RCMP's deficiencies in French.

All these criticisms implied a rebuke to Justice Minister Favreau, but Dorion did not stop with the implicit. He was precise in deploring the judgment Favreau had shown: "The minister, before reaching a decision, should have submitted the case to the legal advisers within his department." This was the very point the Opposition had made against him in Parliament.

Favreau was appalled when he read the Dorion report. He at once offered his resignation to the Prime Minister, who refused to accept it. Yet to retain him as Minister of Justice, in the face of such an attack on his judgment in a legal matter, and by a judge of the Superior Court of his own province, seemed impossible too. The compromise that was contrived, and that Favreau with great difficulty was persuaded to accept, was that he should resign as Minister of Justice but remain in the Cabinet in the easier, almost nominal post of president of the Privy Council.

With that, the storm subsided, at least in Parliament. So quiet did the political weather become, and so promising the forecasts of Gallup Polls and other soundings of public opinion, that Pearson was persuaded against his own inclination and judgment to call another general election in the autumn of 1965. The Liberals then discovered that the Winter Scandals were not yet as dead as they had seemed.

XXVI

Lively Ghosts from a Dead Past: The Munsinger Affair

IT WOULD BE AN OVERSTATEMENT to say that scandals were the main issue in the general election of 1965. The main issue was the record of the Pearson Government—to its friends, an imposing list of accomplishments; to its enemies (and to many of the disenchanted who voted Liberal without enthusiasm), a sorry tale of stumbling, bumbling confusion. An important, related issue was the very fact that the election had been called. Why subject the voters to the inconvenience, and taxpayers and contributors to the expense, of a third trip to the polls in only three years? Why did an undefeated Government suddenly decide it could not go on without a majority in the House of Commons? The answers smacked at best of opportunism, at worst of some dark design against the popular will, which only a docile Liberal majority could support.

But alongside these questions, on which men could argue with no loss of mutual respect, an uglier note was sounded throughout the two-month campaign.

John Diefenbaker undertook to repeat his exploit of 1963, and turn the tide of political battle singlehanded. In the one-man show he took across the country, by far the most popular turn was his denunciation of "wrongdoing in high places." Sometimes he was solemn: "I may have been wrong, but I have never been *on the side* of wrong." Sometimes he was hilariously funny—his impersonation of Lucien Rivard setting off to flood the rink in Bordeaux Jail became famous, and if he omitted it from a campaign speech his audience would clamor for it as an encore. He even converted his preposterous French into an asset with English audiences, by deliberately mispronouncing the names of French-Canadian Liberals and French-Canadian criminals, adroitly linked together in a litany of innuendo.

But the political drama of 1965, both before and after election day, had another star who in 1963 had had no more than a walk-on part—Yukon Erik Nielsen. The accuser who had exposed the "wrongdoers" in the Rivard case now gave broad hints of his intention to unveil other sinister links between "high places" and low. In particular he talked about fraudulent bankruptcies, arraigned the Government for its failure to tighten up the Bankruptcy Act, linked the bankruptcy racket in the Montreal area with an alleged arson ring which in turn was linked with a series of grisly murders in various parts of the province of Quebec.

Liberal reaction to all this was one of sullen fury. The 1965 election had ended in another stalemate—almost as dire a shock as defeat would have been. The Government had made a net gain of only two seats, a tantalizing two short of over-all majority, and moreover had lost two of the three seats it had held in the prairie provinces. This alone would have shaken Liberal self-confidence badly enough. For honest men to be made to feel, in addition, that they were accused of consorting with criminals, licensing the underworld, conniving at fraud and even murder, evoked not only a resentful but a vengeful mood. The Parliament that met for the first time in January 1966 contained deeper reservoirs of ill will than any in Canada's ninety-nine years of existence.

Especially resentful, and especially wary, was the new Minister of Justice, Lucien Cardin, who had taken over when Guy Favreau resigned in June. A small, quiet, mild-mannered lawyer who had done an unobtrusively excellent job as Associate Minister of Defense, Cardin was capable of rare but formidable bursts of anger. Four years before, from his seat in Opposition, he had delivered a blistering attack on the then Prime Minister which Diefenbaker had neither forgotten nor forgiven. Cardin therefore felt himself to be a personal target in the Conservative campaign against "wrongdoing."

He had been particularly worried about Nielsen's questions on the bankruptcy racket, for a curious reason: Cardin, Minister of Justice, had no official information about it. Criminal law is a federal matter under the Canadian Constitution, but the *administration* of justice is provincial, and the inquiry into bankruptcy, arson, and murder was being carried out by the police of Montreal and Quebec, not the RCMP.

However, Cardin had been making his own inquiries, and by a lucky accident had discovered Nielsen's source of information. He was partly relieved, but still more enraged, to discover that Nielsen actually knew very little—and nothing that wasn't known to the police. His dark hints of horrid revelations, unlike his famous exposures in November 1964, this time were mostly bluff. Cardin, knowing this, was waiting for him with vengeful eagerness when the estimates of the Justice Department came before Parliament on February 23, 1966.

But meanwhile, the attention of press and politicians had been caught by an entirely different case, one which developed into the most bizarre episode that ever consumed the time of a legislative body. This was the case of a hitherto obscure postal clerk in Vancouver, British Columbia, named George Victor Spencer.

Ten months before, in May 1965, the Prime Minister had informed the House that two members of the Soviet Embassy staff had been expelled from Canada for attempting to buy information from two Canadian civil servants. One of the civil servants had merely pretended to comply, while cooperating with the RCMP in setting a trap for the Soviet agents. The other Canadian had instead yielded to the Soviet blandishments and sold information for "thousands of dollars." He had not been prosecuted, but he was on sick leave and "in fact gravely ill." Neither the innocent nor the guilty man was named in Pearson's statement.

But in November a reporter of the Vancouver *Province*, Tom Hazlitt, tracked down the mystery man who had taken the Soviet money, and Cardin later confirmed his identity in a television interview. In the same broadcast Cardin revealed that although George Victor Spencer had not been charged with any offense, much less convicted, he had been dismissed from his job and was now under "surveillance" by the RCMP.

For Opposition parties this provided an ideal whipsaw with which to torment the Government. On the one hand it was an outrage against civil liberty, a man convicted without trial, dismissed without proven cause, and now condemned to spend the rest of his life under the baleful eye of the police. On the other hand it was an indictment of Canadian security precautions; if this man was indeed "a self-confessed spy," why was he left at liberty? Why wasn't he tried, convicted, and jailed?

Cardin knew that this was all poppycock. He knew Spencer couldn't have been prosecuted for espionage, because the information he sold to the Russians was not secret. (One item they wanted, for instance, was any classified advertisement offering property for sale along the United States border!) But Spencer deserved to be removed from his job because his conduct had been, for a civil servant, grossly improper. Some of the material he sold, though not secret within the meaning of the Official Secrets Act, had come to him in his capacity as a post office employee. Spencer himself had not even protested against his dismissal. The only argument between him and his former employer, the Government, was whether his money in the pension fund should be paid him as a monthly allowance or a lump sum. As for the charge that Spencer's personal liberty had been abused or invaded, Cardin knew the very opposite was true. The RCMP had handled his case with such compassion that this lonely, miserable, mortally sick man had come to look upon the Mounties as the only friends he had.

All this was later established by a Royal Commission inquiry—another one! But when debate on his departmental estimates began February 23, after a month of insistent and insinuating questions about the Spencer affair, another inquiry was the one thing Cardin was determined not to allow. He knew neither he nor the RCMP had been at fault, and he was resolved to protect the bruised Mounties from the humiliation of another inquisition. He had discussed the whole question with his colleagues, including Pearson, and they were agreed: no amount of badgering by the Opposition would be allowed to shake their decision.

Opposition parties were equally determined not to let Cardin's estimates go through Parliament without extracting this concession from him. As day followed day of repetitive debate, tempers grew shorter. On the morning of Friday, March 4, the House was still on Item 1 of the Justice estimates.

Any minister's patience would have been tried, but Cardin had a special reason to resent Conservative sneers against the handling of a security case. At 12:45 P.M., in the course of a heated exchange with John Diefenbaker, he let it out:

"I can tell the right honorable gentleman that of all the members of the House of Commons, he—I repeat, he—is the very last person who can afford to give advice on the handling of security cases."

There was a thunderous burst of desk-pounding from the Liberal front bench, and Diefenbaker said: "Again applause from the Prime Minister. I want that on the record."

Cardin paused. "I understand the right honorable gentleman said he wants that on the record," he said. "Would he want me to go on and give more?"

Another pause, and shouts from the Liberals: "Go on, he wants it."

"Very well," Cardin said. "I want the right honorable gentleman to tell the House about his participation in the Monseignor case when he was Prime Minister of this country."

Diefenbaker, who seemed to know what Cardin was talking about, called back: "I'm not worried. Have your commission [on security methods] look into it. Put it on the agenda."

More pandemonium, and then Cardin said: "I have spoken, let the right honorable gentleman speak. I think I have said all I have to say about the Spencer case."

He went on to talk about bankruptcies, while reporters dashed out of the gallery asking each other "What, or who, was the Monseignor case?"

Rumor soon began supplying answers. The wildest of them (which very nearly got broadcast on one radio station) was that "Monsignor" was a Roman Catholic prelate mixed up in a drug-smuggling ring. The Prime Minister's office, horrified by these proliferating fantasies, authorized one of its men to issue an oral correction: "Monseignor" had been a mispronunciation on Cardin's part. He'd been referring to the case of a Mrs. Munsinger.

With that, some of the pieces in the jigsaw puzzle began to fit—not that the name Munsinger meant anything, but a security case involving some woman, yes. That was faintly familiar. Hints had been dropped by Conservatives three years before (no details, just hints) to explain why, when Douglas Harkness resigned as Defense Minister, Diefenbaker had chosen not to promote the associate minister, a middle-aged playboy named Pierre Sevigny.

Later, after Erik Nielsen's bombshell about the Rivard case, Liberals began to leak a few enigmatic stories which, for obvious reasons of libel, were not published at the time. It seemed they had asked the RCMP to check the files of the past ten years to make sure there were no other time bombs, like the Rivard affair, lying in wait for them. The Mounties were asked to make a report of any security case that involved, even indirectly, any Member of Parliament or civil servant.

They produced only one, a liaison between a Conservative minister and a woman they had known as a security risk. The minister was Pierre Sevigny. The woman's name was seldom mentioned at the time, but gossips would refer to her as "Olga, the Beautiful Spy." This is probably why the first stories from Ottawa, on that Friday afternoon and Saturday morning, talked about "Olga" Munsinger. None mentioned Sevigny, of course.

Meanwhile in the Commons chamber, all Friday afternoon, the debate on the Justice estimates ground on to its own quite different climax. Tempers remained short. At one point Cardin shouted at Diefenbaker: "Why don't you shut up?" But moments later he apologized for his rudeness:

"I sincerely apologize to the right honorable gentleman. I think he knows, as I know, that sometimes one gets provoked beyond a certain point."

Diefenbaker accepted it gracefully: "We all do that." The debate then proceeded with better manners on both sides.

For Cardin the deadly blow that afternoon came not from the Opposition but from his own revered leader Lester Pearson. The Prime Minister had agreed to a "firm" stand in the Spencer case, but he felt uneasy about it. The argument that convinced and silenced him was the assurance, from men who should know, that Spencer himself did not want an inquiry. So when David Lewis of the New Democrats rose at 2:20 P.M. to produce a telegram from Spencer's lawyer, which bore Spencer's name as well and which said he did indeed want an inquiry into his case, Pearson was as deeply shaken as any other member in the house.

He said nothing for the moment, though. Instead he allowed two other ministers, Jean Marchand of Immigration and Lawrence Pennell, Solicitor-General, to endorse Cardin's stand against any inquiry or appeal in the Spencer case.

Not until ten minutes to four, after three members of his Cabinet had committed themselves to what they thought was Government policy, did the Prime Minister get to his feet with a most extraordinary proposal:

"I think it is my duty, now, to telephone Mr. Spencer myself. If Mr. Spencer is to be given the benefit of an inquiry into the nature of his dismissal and his superannuation rights, I think we in the Government have the right to ask him whether he wants such an inquiry. He has not said so before. . . .

"If Mr. Spencer says yes . . . I do not see any reason why we should not grant him this request. I am quite prepared to do that if this telephone call confirms that he would like an inquiry." And Pearson invited David Lewis to listen in on the telephone conversation, "to make sure we do not have any kind of misunderstanding."

Cardin was stunned. Pearson had called him out of the chamber a few minutes before to tell him what was intended, and had got from him a disheartened acquiescence, but he could hardly believe his ears when the Prime Minister spoke. He left the House at five o'clock, took the afternoon train to Montreal, and spent a weekend with his family in Sorel, during which he resolved to hand in his resignation from the Pearson Cabinet.

It took his colleagues three days to dissuade him. Not that they didn't sympathize (Jean Marchand was particularly angry) but they told him his departure would doom the Government to early defeat and lethal disarray. It might lead to the triumph of the man Cardin regarded as Canada's evil genius, John Diefenbaker. After much painful soul searching Cardin decided to swallow his pride, withdraw his resignation, and carry on in loyal silence. But the strain of those days had been too great to make the silence complete—he had to talk to someone. He talked to a couple of reporters whom he knew and liked, and they wrote sympathetic stories that reopened the whole issue.

Cardin intended to leave next day on a sorely needed holiday— he was exhausted in mind, body, and spirit. But his public relations officer pointed out, sensibly enough, that other correspondents would be furious if he went off having talked to a favored two or three and said nothing to the rest. So Cardin wearily agreed to a general press conference for the next morning, Thursday, March 10.

Pearson heard of this engagement only minutes before it began. He phoned Cardin in some alarm: "For heaven's sake, Lucien, take care. Don't say any more than you've said already."

"Don't worry, Prime Minister," Cardin replied. "I'm just going to tell them about my resignation, and why I withdrew it, and how united we are now."

He did, too, but that was before the questions began. In answer to questions came a whole cascade of new facts and allegations:

He said the Munsinger affair was "worse than the Profumo case," the liaison of a British Minister of War with call girl Christine Keeler, which had almost upset the Macmillan Government three years before.

He said most of the stories published abut "Olga" Munsinger were substantially correct, including the incorrect version of her name and the false report then current that she was dead. (It was because she was dead, Cardin explained, that he saw no point in pursuing the matter further. When a reporter pointed out that, even if Munsinger were dead, the man or men involved with her were alive and perhaps running for public office, Cardin stared at him for about ten seconds before replying: "I will consider that point.")

He said "more than one" Conservative ex-minister had been involved in the case. He gave no indication which ones, but he did say he had learned of the Munsinger affair not as Minister of Justice but in "another department." The only other department Cardin had ever worked in was National Defense.

Moreover, "there certainly was a security risk," because "we know she was engaged in espionage before coming to Canada."

Cardin was so tired that, experienced lawyer and politician though he was, he did not seem to realize what a detonation he had just set off. When someone predicted that his statements would raise questions in the House that afternoon, his face fell. "Oh dear, do you think so?" he said. "Then I suppose I had better put off my holiday."

As things turned out, he had to postpone it indefinitely.

Parliament met at two-thirty that afternoon with the Opposition in a mood of controlled fury, the Government members bewildered and sheepish. The first man on his feet was the immensely respected Conservative ex-Minister of Defense, Douglas Harkness:

"I rise on a question of privilege, one which affects not only myself personally but a considerable number of other privy councilors both in the House and outside the House."

For procedural reasons it took Harkness some time to make his question of privilege quite clear, but he got it out at last:

"These statements, allegations and insinuations by the Minister of Justice . . . put every person who was a member of the

Conservative Cabinet under suspicion. . . . I wish to state very categorically that until the minister mentioned this matter on Friday last, I had never heard the name 'Munsinger.' I had never heard anything whatever in connection with that alleged case. . . .

"Now, I don't think we can have the—we'll say the undignified spectacle of every member who was a minister in that Cabinet rising, in order to clear his name, to make a statement along this line. . . . In order that an end may be put to the many rumors and speculations that have run around the country as a result of this, I move this motion:

"That the Minister of Justice be required forthwith to substantiate the charges . . . which have reflected unfortunately and improperly upon members of Her Majesty's Privy Council, or alternatively that he be asked to submit his resignation and to atone by the forfeiture of his seat."

Cardin rose to reply, pathetically conciliatory:

"I want everyone in the House to know, and I am quite sincere in saying this, that I feel very badly about the way things are turning out."

He went on to explain, as if this made everything both clear and innocent, that the only member he had intended to rebuke or impugn was John Diefenbaker. Since Diefenbaker was not in the House (he had gone to British Columbia on a fishing cum politicking visit) this did nothing to appease the angry Tories. NDP speakers supported them. The Prime Minister, also very conciliatory, asked "that I be permitted to consult with the mover of the motion to see how best the matter can be resolved immediately, so that justice can be done." But the Conservatives were in no mood for consultation.

Eventually Mr. Speaker ruled Harkness' motion out of order, and also rejected several motions to the simple effect that Cardin "do now resign," but there was no hope of bringing the House back to any other business. Most of Thursday and all day Friday were spent upon the Munsinger affair, with Cardin as the target of attack.

Liberals tried not so much to defend him as to deflect the

fire. The Prime Minister offered a judicial inquiry, which Conservatives rejected with scorn—Parliament itself should act in defense of its own honor. The argument continued into Friday afternoon, with the Liberals still trying to give the soft answer that turneth away wrath, when the next bombshell of the Munsinger case exploded.

Joe Greene, the new, young Minister of Agriculture, was laboring through his plea for a judicial inquiry when David Lewis of the NDP rose to ask:

"Mr. Speaker, would the minister permit a question? Has he been made aware that a Toronto newspaper now carries the story that the Munsinger woman, about whom we are talking, has been found alive in Germany and has offered to come back to Canada any time she is invited?"

The next entry in Hansard is:

"Some Hon. Members: Oh, oh."

This is the official record's device for recording that bedlam broke loose. When a semblance of order was restored, minutes later, Joe Greene went bravely on:

"Surely this is all the more reason for holding a judicial inquiry as quickly as possible, so that this good lady . . ."

Again "Some Hon. Members: Oh, oh." The roars of laughter had more than a touch of the ribald in them now. When Greene once more could make himself heard he continued:

"I use that term in the broadest possible sense, Mr. Speaker—so that this good lady may be permitted to give her evidence to enlighten the House."

But neither his argument nor the sensational news that Gerda Munsinger was still alive changed the tone of Conservative speeches. They continued to demand action by Parliament itself that would place the Minister of Justice in the dock and force him to prove his charges or resign. There was no motion before the House, but Mr. Speaker wisely let the talk run on until the adjournment hour, 6 p.m., when Parliament rose for the weekend.

During that weekend the impact of the scoop by Robert Reguly, the Toronto *Star*'s ace reporter, began to make itself felt.

Reguly and Ralph Allen, the *Star*'s managing editor, beat the whole world's press by using a simple journalistic virtue—hard-eyed skepticism. They did not believe Gerda Munsinger was dead. It was just too convenient, for too many people, that she should have faded from the scene with leukemia in Germany though she'd been perfectly healthy, so far as anyone knew, when she left Canada. Robert Mackenzie, the *Star*'s Montreal correspondent, began leafing through old telephone books, looking for the name "Munsinger." He found it, and by locating her Montreal address he found some Montreal friends who remembered her well. She had gone, they thought, to Munich, though they hadn't heard from her recently.

Within hours, Reguly was on a plane for Munich. Almost within minutes of his arrival he found Mrs. Munsinger.

"I suppose you want to ask about Sevigny," she said when he told her who he was.

Joseph Pierre Albert Sevigny came of a distinguished French-Canadian family. His father, Albert Sevigny, had been Speaker of the House of Commons after 1911, had joined the Borden Cabinet and stayed in it through the conscription crisis of 1917, had been rewarded by being made chief justice of the Superior Court of Quebec instead of facing inevitable defeat in the "conscription election." Pierre himself had lost a leg in World War II and came back a lieutenant colonel—a burly, jovial, thoroughly bilingual businessman with a handsome wife and three charming children. He worked for a while as the salaried director of the Conservative Party in Quebec. When he was elected in 1958, after two previous defeats, some Conservatives thought they had found in him "a Tory Ernest Lapointe," one who could give the party a foothold in Quebec it had not possessed for sixty-two years.

These hopes were not fulfilled. Pierre Sevigny turned out to be a more than doubtful asset to his party.

When he joined the Cabinet in 1959 as Associate Minister of Defense, he seemed to think federal ministers had the same kind of perquisites and personal authority that they had in the Duplessis regime in Quebec. Military advisers quickly disabused him of this notion, but the experience did not endear him either to them or to his senior colleague, the upright old soldier General George Pearkes, V.C. Nor were his relations particularly warm with Pearkes's successor in the defense portfolio, Douglas Harkness. When he was passed over for the second time after Harkness resigned over the nuclear issue, and Gordon Churchill became Defense Minister, Sevigny resigned—though not for that stated reason. He left the Diefenbaker Cabinet along with George Hees, and thus contributed his mite to the downfall of the Diefenbaker Government.

Now it turned out that there were other reasons why he was not promoted.

Sevigny denied everything. He went on national television with his wife and daughter by his side, to denounce this "Liberal plot," this attempt at character assassination. But the CBC had Gerda herself (at considerable expense) interviewed on the same program. A faded but still comely blonde of thirty-six, she made the ex-minister's denials sound curiously hollow.

In one of Robert Reguly's copyrighted stories over the weekend, Gerda Munsinger mentioned the name of another Conservative MP, the ex-Minister of Trade and Commerce, George Hees. She said very little about him—they'd had lunch once or twice, she remembered—but when Parliament met again on Monday Hees rose on a question of privilege.

"On several occasions in the last ten days I have publicly stated that I did not know a person by the name of Olga Munsinger. A person by that name is now reported to have said that she lunched with me twice, seven or eight years ago. She may well be right. Although I still do not recall knowing any person by that name, I have examined the pictures in the Saturday newspapers and I believe I recognize the woman pictured there. . . . I hasten to assure the House that at no time has my personal conduct jeopardized security. . . . Subject always to the nation's security and welfare, who my acquaintances are or may have been, or who the acquaintances of any honorable member of this House are or may have been, is not a public issue."

It was a brief statement, delivered with dignity. All parties applauded, and that, so far as the House of Commons was concerned, was the end of the Hees incident.

Meanwhile the Prime Minister had already risen to tell the House, in quiet tones, that the judicial inquiry was no longer merely an offer, it was a fact. An Order in Council had been passed appointing Mr. Justice Wishart Spence of the Supreme Court of Canada as a one-man Royal Commission to investigate the Munsinger affair and the conduct of all concerned therein.

Davie Fulton, the Conservative ex-Minister of Justice, was the next man up, to make what from one point of view was the finest speech of his political career. It was eloquent, dignified, comprehensive, closely reasoned. It also revealed a new fact—that a full week before Cardin's mention of the Munsinger case, Guy Favreau had called Fulton to his office to warn him that, if the Conservatives persisted in their demand for inquiry into the case of George Victor Spencer, the Liberals would dig up the Munsinger scandal.

Cries of "Shame" echoed through the chamber. Guy Favreau said something the Hansard reporter did not catch; when Fulton sat down he rose to make a brief, reproachful speech—he had no other motive, he said, than to appeal to Fulton's "sense of fairness and justice." It sounded unconvincing. The clear impression remained that he had called Fulton in for the purpose of threatening him, and suggesting he pass the threat on to Diefenbaker (which Fulton said he did not do).

But another passage in Fulton's speech, which at the time sounded crushingly effective, came back later to haunt him. Describing his recollection of the RCMP report which, as Minister of Justice, he had taken to Prime Minister Diefenbaker on December 12, 1960, Fulton said:

"[It] contained no suggestion that there had been any breach of security. It did not suggest that any security information had been sought by Mrs. Munsinger or conveyed to her. It did not allege or suggest that any offense had been committed in connection with security, or any other field within federal responsi-

bility. It did not allege or suggest any offense by any member of
the federal Government. It did not state that Mrs. Munsinger
was or had been engaged in espionage activities."

As a lawyer, Fulton had chosen his words with care. He said
there had been no *breach* of security, not that there had been no
security *risk*. No one had suggested any "offense" by any ex-
minister, in the technical sense of infraction of any law "within
federal responsibility." As for Mrs. Munsinger's "espionage activities," he said the report did not "state" that she had been so
engaged; he avoided, this time, the verb "to suggest" or "to allege."

In these narrowly limited meanings, everything Fulton said was
correct—but those were not the meanings he conveyed to the
House that Monday afternoon, or to the packed galleries. What
he seemed to be saying was that Cardin's whole accusation was
a tissue of lies, trumped up by partisan malice to stain the reputations of honorable men who had done no more and no less than
their duty. And under questioning in the House that evening,
with less assurance but equal vehemence, he repeated the gist of
what he had said:

"I am not going to go back on my statement, nor am I going
to retreat from it, that the investigation which gave rise to the
report I received was not initiated by any security checkup, in
the proper sense of the word security."

That speech made Davie Fulton the hero of the hour and put
the Conservatives in the position of aggrieved accusers rather
than defenders. Diefenbaker followed with a fighting oration in
which he said, "I unequivocally repeat that there never was a question of security in connection with this matter"; moreover "this
is a matter that cannot be shelved by the executive to the judicial,
to get rid of a matter that affects the rights, privileges and pre-
rogatives of Members of Parliament."

Cardin made a weak, defensive rejoinder; other Liberal speakers, of whom there were few, focused mainly upon niceties of
procedure. It seemed to be the Conservatives' day. Only Gilles

Grégoire, the fiery little Créditiste from Lapointe, Quebec, seized upon the obvious question that both major parties had ignored:

If there had been no security angle to the Munsinger case, what then was all the fuss about? Why had Davie Fulton felt it necessary, as soon as he got the RCMP report, to rush to the Prime Minister's office, brushing aside anyone with a previous appointment, to tell Diefenbaker what he had just heard? "Was it a security case? A theft? A murder? Indecent acts, or what? . . . What was the hurry, Mr. Speaker? A routine matter, we are told. Nothing urgent about it. No inquiry was necessary."

But Grégoire spoke so often, and always in a rasping French, that MPs had developed the habit of ignoring him. Not until a month later, when Mr. Justice Spence began his Royal Commission of inquiry, did the force of Grégoire's questions become fully manifest.

All but three brief sittings of the Spence inquiry were held in public. At one of the sessions *in camera* the RCMP gave a full account of its information about Gerda Munsinger, including the confidential sources thereof; later a synopsis of this testimony, with the security portions deleted, was made public with the consent of all counsel.

This and other evidence cast a curious light on the statement that "there never was a question of security in this matter." As summarized later in Mr. Justice Spence's report, it showed that Gerda Munsinger had indeed been Pierre Sevigny's mistress while he was Associate Minister of Defense. It showed also that she was "a self-admitted espionage agent" in Germany before coming to Canada; her espionage activities "had been of a minor character, but included contact over a considerable period with a major in the Russian Intelligence Service." Moreover, "she had a record of convictions as a common prostitute, a petty thief and a smuggler." For these reasons she was refused a visa when, in 1952, she sought entry into Canada under her maiden name. She was admitted in 1955 only because her immigration file did not reveal that Gerda Munsinger and Gerda Heseler were the same person. After her admission to Canada she had worked in various

Montreal night clubs "operated by well-known racketeers, and persons who had some association with various operators in the narcotics racket." All these things had been made known to Davie Fulton by the RCMP, and by him to Prime Minister Diefenbaker. The Prime Minister had thereupon summoned Pierre Sevigny to his office for a scathing verbal reprimand, and forbidden him to have any further association with the Munsinger woman, but had taken no other action. Sevigny remained in the Diefenbaker Cabinet as Associate Minister of Denfense, and Acting Minister in any absence of his senior colleague, for two more years thereafter.

Diefenbaker did not testify at the Spence inquiry, though at the outset he was represented by counsel (later withdrawn). Davie Fulton did testify. He continued to stress that there had been no *breach* of security in the Munsinger affair, but "a security risk, yes." It was a phrase that stuck in the memory of all who had heard his ringing speech to Parliament on March 14.

As for Pierre Sevigny, he was the star witness, the chief victim, and the tragic anti-hero of the investigation. His testimony began with denials and a certain amount of bluster, as had his confrontation with Diefenbaker five years before, but he was soon reduced to an admission: "I never denied during that interview that I had had a physical relationship with Mrs. Munsinger."

Mr. Justice Spence put it more severely:

"The Honorable Mr. Sevigny's association with Mrs. Munsinger during the whole of 1960 was much closer and more frequent than he desired the Right Honorable Mr. Diefenbaker to realize, and much closer than he desired this Commission to ascertain. . . . The Honorable Mr. Sevigny told his Prime Minister much less than the whole truth, and surely that fact alone should have driven him to tender his resignation. . . .

"Further investigation [by Diefenbaker] would have revealed that the liaison appeared to be within the knowledge of many other persons, some . . . of unsavory reputation. The danger of blackmail and improper pressure would have been revealed as startling."

But Pierre Sevigny by these strictures was hardly more damaged than he had been already. The major target of the Spence report was not Sevigny but Diefenbaker, for his failure to act upon the information he received:

"Doubt must always be resolved in favor of the 'national security.' . . . The Prime Minister determined he could resolve that doubt in favor of the Honorable Mr. Sevigny's retention in the Cabinet on the basis of his personal assessment of the man. . . . A more dangerous position than that of national defense, from the point of view of espionage by enemy agents or information-seeking by greedy racketeers, could hardly be imagined. Even if the decision could be made to retain the Honorable Mr. Sevigny in the Cabinet, surely enough doubt lingered to justify, indeed demand, that he be moved to a Cabinet post not so vital to national security. . . . The Honorable Mr. Sevigny's liaison with Mrs. Munsinger was of such a type as might expose him to blackmail or undue pressure, and nothing, even his outstanding war record or fine family background, could assure that he would not be subject to, and might yield to, such pressures. . . . Prudent conduct in the administration of government, as stressed in the Cabinet Directives, demanded that the doubt be resolved in favor of Canada and that his resignation be requested." The commissioner found it particularly "startling" that not even Douglas Harkness, the senior Defense Minister, was informed "of the security risk, for such I believe it was."

He also found it "regrettable" that Davie Fulton had not ordered the RCMP to make a more thorough investigation, but otherwise Fulton's conduct was deemed to have been proper. His Lordship did, however, note dryly that "the Honorable Mr. Fulton, in his testimony, made several corrections and explanations of his speech in the House of Commons on March 14." As for George Hees, his "lack of discretion was slight but regrettable," a sentiment with which Hees had already ruefully agreed.

All the Liberal ministers involved in the case were exonerated, as were the civil servants and the police. Lucien Cardin's statements at the press conference, in all important particulars, had been "confirmed." The Prime Minister's request for information on previous security cases had been "natural and proper." And "I can find no criticism whatsoever of the RCMP. The action of the Force was efficient, prompt and discreet."

When the Spence report came out in September it was news all over the world (it rated top headlines as far away as Beirut and Jerusalem) but it caused no surprise in Ottawa. The testimony of RCMP Commissioner George McClellan, and also that of Fulton and Sevigny, had left little doubt that the tenor of the Spence report, whatever its language, would be unfavorable to Diefenbaker and the other ex-ministers.

The Conservative counteroffensive was to impugn the inquiry itself. Much was made of the fact that Mr. Justice Spence had been named to the Supreme Court in June 1963, the first such appointee of the Pearson Government. In May, Diefenbaker and Fulton withdrew their counsel and announced, in angry public statements, that they would have nothing more to do with the Royal Commission's proceedings. (Mr. Justice Spence made no attempt to compel any witness to testify.) Thus before the hearings were even completed they had led to the unusual spectacle of a former Prime Minister and a former Minister of Justice personally attacking a judge of the Supreme Court of Canada.

What may be the final, net effect of Canada's two years of scandal, not even history will be able to tell for sure.

Among Conservatives, both orthodox and rebel, the conventional opinion is that the Munsinger affair was a boomerang that returned to smite the Liberals. Lucien Cardin's retirement from active politics in March 1967 might seem to confirm this view. Yet Cardin had long wanted to get out of public life, and friends said he regarded his outburst of 1966 as a kind of *kamikaze* operation, a willing sacrifice of his own career if he could end John Diefenbaker's at the same time.

Did he succeed? Again, the conventional opinion is that he

failed, that Diefenbaker was made stronger, not weaker, by the Munsinger episode. Dalton Camp, the national president of the Conservative Party who organized the campaign to unseat Diefenbaker from the party leadership, was careful to make his opening moves before the Spence report was published, the theory being that the report when it came out would rouse sympathy for the chief. But the report did come out before the meeting that voted for a leadership convention and started Diefenbaker toward retirement.

On the Liberal side, events were even more ambiguous. Guy Favreau fell ill in September 1966, and was in hospital for weeks. He came back to Parliament looking twenty years older. Many friends thought it was his ordeal of 1964–65 that caused the illness —but it was the illness, not the ordeal, that caused his retirement. (He died in Montreal on July 11, 1967, at the age of fifty.)

Maurice Lamontagne went to the Senate, that Valhalla of political warriors, at the same time as Favreau and Cardin left the Cabinet. Lamontagne had resigned from the Government a year and a half before, and spent the interim as a front-bench private MP along with his colleague René Tremblay. But by 1967 a consensus had developed that both these men had been harshly treated (and Tremblay, especially, with injustice). Lamontagne's "elevation" to the quiet security of the appointed Upper House (Canada's House of Lords, it was designed to be) appeared as a reward, not a dismissal.

The most curious footnote of all, and the most irrelevant, was the fate of Erik Nielsen, the accuser.

In June 1966, Nielsen made a presentation to the Conservative caucus, and then to the Yukon Council, of his view on the reorganization of northern administration. It was an excellent paper, well reasoned and full of thoughtful suggestions, but to Arthur Laing, the Minister of Northern Affairs, it sounded familiar. He looked up another document he had lately seen, a report on the same subject by one of his departmental officials, which had been circulated as "confidential" within the service. The two papers were identical. Apparently Nielsen, having got hold of the confidential report, had presented it as his own.

It was a trivial affair, but embarrassing for a man whose stock in trade was righteous indignation. Thereafter he appeared seldom in the House of Commons, and even more seldom spoke.

XXVII

Crises of Neighborhood:
The Other Identity Problem

WITHOUT AT LEAST a touch of anti-Americanism, Canada would have no reason to exist. Of all general definitions of the Canadians, this is the most nearly valid: twenty million people who, for anything up to twenty million reasons, prefer not to be Americans.

The choice was first made two centuries ago. The French in the 1770s rejected Benjamin Franklin's persuasion to join the American War of Independence. The English who began to arrive in strength a decade later were the defeated side in that war. (The experience of defeat was all they had in common with their new French-speaking compatriots.) Other nationalities, whose children now make up one quarter of Canadians, had their own variety of motives for settling north rather than south of the border —including, at some periods, the fact that they could not get into the United States. But for most of them most of the time, it was also by deliberate decision that they did not become Americans.

In every generation many Canadians have disagreed with this decision. They have thought it wiser to join the United States —and they have done so, in thousands that now run to millions. The undefended border, most cherished of continental clichés, has remained open both ways. For certain individuals there may have been obstacles—a police record, an unfashionable disease, or political eccentricity—but for healthy, heterosexual adults of conventional opinions, there has always been easy passage from either country to the other. Thus, unlike other non-American peoples of the world, the residual Canadians have been and still are non-American by choice.

Most of us do not know exactly why. This uncertainty, besides being irritating in itself, complicates our reactions to the gravitational pull of the United States. It is hard to agree on means of protection when there is no agreement on the nature of the threat, or even on the fact that it exists.

At least Canadians no longer think of Americans as a physical or military menace. The day when so wise a statesman as Sir John Macdonald could talk of inevitable war with "those wretched Yankees" is now a full century behind us, and its modes of thought absurdly quaint.

Today what Canadians fear is not invasion but absorption. Speaking, as we do, an American dialect, wearing American fashions, reading American magazines and news services, listening to American broadcasts, we have good reason to wonder what identity of our own is left to us, if any.

Yet from time to time something comes up to show there is such a thing as a Canadian self, different from the American. Exposed to the same media of information and opinion, we are still capable of reaching opposite conclusions. In the United States, for example, only a fringe of the left believes in trading with Communist China and Cuba. In Canada, only a fringe of the right has any objection to our doing so. In the United States most people seem to accept the national duty of "fighting Communism." In Canada this sounds to most people like a return to the wars of religion, which we thought came to an end in 1648. Americans in 1967 were still supporting the war in Vietnam, despite the increasing doubts of a minority. Canadians would argue among themselves about what *Americans* should do there, but unanimously took it for granted that Canada should do nothing at all.

Nothing except, perhaps, give Washington the benefit of our advice. In a national broadcast in 1965, a professor of political science at Canada's largest, most illustrious university suggested that the Canadian ambassador to Washington ought to call periodically upon the U. S. Secretary of State in order to rebuke him for pursuing the Vietnam war, and to remind him that Canadians disapprove of it.

Four months earlier, Prime Minister Pearson himself had journeyed to Philadelphia to accept the World Peace Award of Temple University. In the course of his address to this American audience he suggested "a measured and announced pause" in the bombing of North Vietnam: "A suspension of air strikes against North Vietnam *at the right time* [the words are underlined in Pearson's text] might provide the Hanoi authorities with an opportunity, if they wish it, to inject some flexibility into their policy without appearing to do so as a direct result of military pressure."

It was a tentative suggestion, embedded in a twelve-page manuscript that was mainly laudatory of American policies and peace efforts, but it infuriated Lyndon Johnson. He had invited Pearson to lunch the next day at the presidential retreat, Camp David, but when Pearson arrived he got a cool reception. Johnson spent most of the luncheon talking to other people on the telephone he had plugged in beside his plate. In the brief press conference that followed his private talks with the Canadians, he was pointedly short-tempered—so much so that the correspondents inferred, and reported, that the talks had been "angry."

Pearson denied these stories. On the plane going back to Ottawa he assured Canadian reporters that the meeting had been amicable enough, though he admitted the President was rather preoccupied. But apparently it was not until the reaction from Washington began to reach Ottawa that he realized just how deeply annoyed his host at Camp David had been.

This unawareness was all the stranger because, four years earlier, another American President had come to Ottawa and offered some friendly counsel to another Canadian Prime Minister, with the result that the Prime Minister was furious and the Canadian public, or anyway the Canadian editorial writers, seemed to share his choler.

President Kennedy's suggestion had been that Canada might

consider joining the Organization of American States, something
on which Canadian governments had been blowing hot and
cold for two generations. He was cautious enough to ask the Canadian ambassador to Washington whether these mild words
would be resented, and he was assured they would not. The advice, though sincere, was erroneous. Even this degree of "interference in Canadian affairs" by the Big Brother in Washington
was enough to wound Canadian sensibilities.

Soon there were graver causes of disagreement—the Canadian
reluctance to put the NORAD defense system on the alert in the
Cuba crisis of 1962; the Canadian refusal to accept nuclear warheads for the weapons, and the role, Canada had agreed to accept; Canadian opposition to the British attempt to enter the
European Common Market, which was then a major objective of
American as well as British foreign policy. But even those Canadians who disagreed with their own Government on these
issues (as many did, including the Liberal Opposition and its
leader, Lester Pearson) were resentful rather than grateful for
attacks upon it from abroad.

When the U. S. State Department issued a press release, in
February 1963, to contradict a statement the Prime Minister of
Canada had made, Pearson's Liberals as well as Diefenbaker's
Conservatives thought the intervention would help and not hurt
Diefenbaker with the electors. They had the same opinion about
an unflattering article about Diefenbaker in *Newsweek* magazine,
and the even less flattering photograph that appeared on the
cover. Similar rude remarks from Britain, although they too were
seized upon by Diefenbaker's friends rather than his enemies for
repetition at home, were deemed to have a less counterproductive
effect than criticism from the U.S.A. Every American knock was
assumed to be a political boost in Canada.

On this at least Canadians were agreed. On some other important aspects of Canadian-American relations they are not agreed
at all.

One is the cultural penetration which is perhaps the most
obvious of all the effects of neighborhood. Canadian newsstands

are hardly distinguishable, at a casual glance, from American. They offer dozens of American publications and, at most, two or three Canadian aside from local newspapers. And Canadian broadcasting, the most direct and influential of all media, is heavily laden with American programs.

To offset the electronic invasion the Canadian taxpayer spends, without serious complaint, more than $140 million a year. That is the cost, over and above its commercial earnings, of the Canadian Broadcasting Corporation, an agency of the Crown (but not of the Canadian government) which has been providing Canadian radio since 1932 and television since 1953.

The CBC is said to be "responsible to Parliament" rather than to the Government, and the distinction is vital. If it were a department of the Government the CBC would be subject to direct, explicit orders from the politicians who happen to be in office. As an independent "agency of the Crown" (which does *not* mean it takes orders from Queen Elizabeth II) it is subject to harassment by all politicians, in or out of office, but is not obliged to take orders from any. It is not, in fact, obliged to take orders from anyone at all, which creates another quite different problem for the Canadian democracy.

CBC expenditure is not as lavish nor as wasteful as it may sound. National broadcasting in Canada has to cope with six time zones, two languages, five major regions (plus a vast, still unsettled north which nevertheless cannot be ignored by the broadcasting agency), and great distances between the settled areas that must be bridged, at great expense, for live broadcasting.

In return for this outlay the CBC has brought Canada many cultural rewards. It has kept several Canadian orchestras alive, not only by paying substantial fees for performances but still more by providing a national audience, and the kind of national fame that makes local supporters proud and generous. It has given training and employment to Canadian actors, writers, musicians, intellectuals of all kinds. It has earned a gratifying number of international awards for excellence in broadcasting. And despite the chronic (and justified) grumbling about the inefficiencies and extravagances of CBC management, it has been accepted as an indispensable instrument of Canadian nationality. Hardly anyone (except such patently interested parties as the owners of private broadcasting stations) ever suggests that the CBC should be abolished.

Nevertheless it is an open question whether the CBC is succeeding in its principal functions, which are to help knit the country together and to help define and maintain a Canadian identity, distinguishable from the American colossus next door.

One reason why the CBC, unlike its British cousin the BBC, cannot dispense with commercial programs is that so many of the most popular are American, and can only be brought in by a commercial sponsor. If the CBC were to drop all these, like the Ed Sullivan show and Bonanza, it would simply lose its audience —about three quarters of Canadian listeners are within range of American stations, even if the Canadian private stations were not there to snap up the best American programs available. What the long-term effect of this daily exposure to the staple of American culture will be, few Canadians are brave enough to predict. (Lorne Greene was born in Ottawa and served his apprenticeship as an actor with the CBC, but that does not make the patriarch of Ponderosa any less American as a mythological figure.)

For the various media of print the situation is equally difficult, and has also prompted Government action that may or may not prove adequate.

In 1961 the near collapse of Canada's few remaining magazines led the Diefenbaker Government to appoint a Royal Commission headed by Grattan O'Leary, editor of the Ottawa *Journal* and dean of Canadian journalists. He recommended drastic action against a peculiar form of competition—the so-called "Canadian edition" of American publications which imported all or most of their editorial material (at no cost) but solicited Canadian advertising. The zero cost of editorial content made it easy to offer very attractive rates to Canadian advertisers. The O'Leary Commission recommended measures that would have put the "Canadian editions" out of business.

The two publications directly affected were *Time* magazine and the *Reader's Digest*. They had already been singled out for special taxation by the St. Laurent Government and had complained to the State Department and the White House, which in turn made strong protests to Ottawa, but the new Conservative Government had (for quite different reasons) repealed this legislation. Now that new and even more drastic action was planned, Washington renewed its protests even more strenuously.

As finally enacted (by the Pearson Government), the new law exempted the two American publications whose "Canadian editions" had been in being for many years. It did, however, effectively bar any future invasions of Canadian publishing by foreign owners from any country. Most Canadian newspapers opposed the new law (which diminished their potential value as commercial properties, by excluding foreign bidders) but the Government ignored this. Canada's communications industry, in all its forms and branches, was thus protected from take-overs from abroad.

Other Canadian industries have no such protection. Whether they should have, and if so what the protection ought to be, has become the great political controversy of the 1960s—an argument not between or among political parties, but within the Pearson Cabinet itself.

There is no disagreement about the cold facts. The Canadian economy is under direct American control to an alarming degree. U.S. parent companies control more than sixty per cent of Canadian manufacturing, about the same fraction of mining and smelting, and nearly three quarters of oil and natural gas. In the last-named case the effective control, in practice, is virtually a hundred per cent—there is not a single nation-wide, integrated oil company in Canada that is not controlled abroad (according to Walter Gordon in his book, *A Choice for Canada*). Morover U.S. control is increasing rapidly. So-called "direct" investment, the take-over of Canadian enterprises or the expansion of American-owned enterprises already established, ran to $660 million in 1966 compared to only $270 million in 1964 and $405 million in 1965.

One side effect of this American investment is a large, chronic deficit in Canada's current accounts with other nations. In 1965 this deficit ran just over, and in 1966 just under, one billion dollars—roughly forty per cent of Canada's entire reserve of gold and foreign exchange. In both years Canada had a surplus in merchandise trade, an excess of exports over imports. These surpluses were more than wiped out by colossal deficits in "non-merchandise transactions," mainly the payment of interest and dividends on American investments in Canada.

But the only way the deficit can be met, without drastic deflation of the Canadian dollar and a collapse of the Canadian standard of living, is by the continued flow of American capital —an inflow which has roughly balanced the current-account deficit over the years since World War II. This is the framework of Canada's economic dilemma.

Which is the more urgent danger? That American investors, if alarmed, will cut off the flow of capital to Canada and precipitate economic disaster? Or that American ownership of Canada, already far advanced, will become so nearly total that Canadian independence will cease to exist?

Each side finds a proof of its own point in the financial crisis, or near crisis, of July 1963. When President Kennedy announced the fifteen per cent "interest equalization tax" on export of U.S. capital, he threw Canadian stock exchanges into a worse panic than the crash of 1929. If Governor Louis Rasminsky of the Bank of Canada and his two colleagues had not managed to persuade the U. S. Treasury that this was against *American* interests, and that bankrupting Canada would mean more and not less depletion of American gold reserves, the Canadian economy would have been plunged into catastrophe.

To Walter Gordon, economic nationalist, former Minister of Finance and now chairman of a Cabinet committee studying U.S. ownership in Canada, the moral is clear: such dependence on American capital makes Canada hopelessly vulnerable, and Canadian independence a farce. The thing to do is reduce this dependence as rapidly as possible.

To Mitchell Sharp, Gordon's successor as Minister of Finance and leader of the opposing faction in the Liberal Party, the moral is equally clear but quite different: Canada is heavily dependent on American good will. If Rasminsky and his colleagues had not enjoyed instant entree to the very top in Washington, and if they had not got the immediate sympathetic hearing that they did get, the remedial action by Washington (exempting Canada from the fifteen per cent tax) would not have been taken in time. By the time the U.S. found out for itself that its action would be self-defeating, the Canadian economy would have been ruined.

A major confrontation between these two points of view concerns another episode that began in 1963, though it did not come to a head until early 1967. This was the attempt by the First National City Bank of New York to establish itself as a major factor in the Canadian banking system.

James Stillman Rockefeller, president of Citibank, and vice-president Robert McFadden came to Ottawa in June 1963 to discuss the possibility of buying the Mercantile Bank of Canada, a small institution owned by a Dutch firm but the only Canadian bank that was not Canadian-owned. After a first interview with Governor Louis Rasminsky at the Bank of Canada, they later saw Walter Gordon, then Minister of Finance.

Gordon told them not to buy the Mercantile Bank. The Canadian Bank Act was then about to go through its decennial revision, and he warned the Citibank executives that it would contain a clause forbidding any future expansion of Mercantile or any other bank under foreign ownership and control. He had no scruples about making such a law retroactive, because Citibank was not yet committed to the purchase of Mercantile and he was giving them fair warning.

Citibank went ahead and bought Mercantile anyway, ignoring Gordon's warning. Later, McFadden and Rockefeller both said they had not been warned in time, that by the time they saw Gordon they were in fact committed (in honor if not in law) to buy Mercantile, and that they were being victimized by retro-

active, discriminatory legislation. However, at a hearing of the
Commons committee on finance in February 1967, a memo was
produced from McFadden himself indicating that they were not
committed to the purchase when they saw Rasminsky, and that
they then engaged to "clear it with the Minister of Finance"
before the deal became final. Rasminsky's testimony confirmed
this, the Citibank version of the affair was discredited and Gordon's
vindicated.

Vindicated in Ottawa, that is. Not in Washington. The U. S.
State Department took up Citibank's side of the argument with
an energy that amounted to fury, and put extreme pressure on the
Canadian government to back down and let the Mercantile purchase stand unpenalized.

"We're not interested in who said what to whom," one State
Department man explained. "We're concerned with this combination of retroactivity and discrimination. We're concerned about
U.S. companies entering Canada under one set of laws, and then
having the rules changed after they get there."

Up to this point Mitchell Sharp had taken exactly the same
line as Walter Gordon. Whatever his personal views might be on
the stand Gordon took in the first place, he had spoken as Minister
of Finance and no succeeding Minister of Finance could back
down from his position. (He of course accepted Gordon's account
of the interview, already confirmed by two other Canadian witnesses, that the New York bankers had in fact been warned in time
to prevent any final commitment.)

Now that honor was satisfied, however, the fundamental difference of view began to emerge. Gordon had wanted, and still
intended, to keep the First National City Bank and any other
American company from invading the Canadian banking system.
Mercantile, a small bank owned by a small firm in the Netherlands,
had been no threat to the Canadian system under its previous
owners. As a foothold for Citibank it would be—especially as the
other big American banks would be sure to want in too, and
would complain of discrimination if they were kept out and Citibank allowed a special advantage.

To Sharp and the men who agreed with him, the problem was different. The problem was to restore the good relations with the American financial community which the Citibank affair had disturbed. And the compromise offered was to allow Citibank a five-year period of grace in which to expand its operations to a profitable size, before being obliged to sell off seventy-five per cent of its shares to Canadian buyers (as the new law stipulates). In other words they had no objection to American-owned banks as such, operating in Canada. Some argued that the new American competition would be a good thing for the rather conservative Canadian banking system.

The two schools of thought are irreconcilable. Compromises of various sorts have bridged the gap between them (Gordon at one point threatened to resign again from the Cabinet he had recently rejoined, but was persuaded to accept one of the compromises) but the issue will recur with every request from Mercantile to increase its authorized capital, with every request from another American bank to enter Canada under the same lenient conditions, with every interval of growth in American holdings among the major Canadian lending institutions.

Its essence is a question still unanswered, perhaps unanswerable:

Does a nation's independence reside in the ownership of property? Or can a sovereign government, equally sovereign over all proprietors domestic or foreign, maintain its integrity regardless of who owns its land and its factories?

There is also another question, related but not identical: Home-owned or not, can a small nation resist absorption into the culture, the folkways, the patterns of life in a neighbor ten times as big, twenty times as rich, a hundred times as strong? Will it always even want to resist?

XXVIII

The Once and Future Canadian

ONE OF THE FIRST acts of the new Pearson Government in the summer of 1963 was to set up a ten-man Royal Commission on Bilingualism and Biculturalism, to study the apparently widening breach between what it called, somewhat tactlessly, "the two founding races" of Canada. As an afterthought the Commission was also instructed to "take into account the contribution made by the other ethnic groups to the cultural enrichment of Canada," but the terms of reference made it clear that the focus of the inquiry would be on the relations of English and French, the classic "problem of Canadian unity."

The Commission was so alarmed by the state of disunity it discovered as to prepare, only eighteen months after beginning its researches, an interim report of 145 pages (plus 50-odd pages of appendices). Its keynote was sounded in a brief preamble:

"Canada, without being fully conscious of the fact, is passing through the greatest crisis in its history. . . . The state of affairs established in 1867, and never since seriously challenged, is now for the first time being rejected by the French Canadians of Quebec.

"Who is right and who is wrong? We do not even ask ourselves that question; we simply record the existence of a crisis which we believe to be very serious. If it should persist and gather momentum it could destroy Canada. On the other hand, if it is overcome, it will have contributed to the rebirth of a richer and more dynamic Canada."

It was painfully obvious that the last, optimistic sentence represented no more than a brave but futile attempt to keep a stiff upper lip. The burden not only of the preamble but of the interim report itself was that Canada is in a parlous condition. Drastic action was urgently suggested—"unless there are major changes the situation will worsen with time, and it could worsen much more quickly than many think"—but the precise nature of the changes was not specified.

Most English Canadians refused to take this warning seriously. It was alarmist, they said—like Chicken Little's report that the sky was falling, based on nothing more than a handful of nuts. So far, they appear to have been right. Neither view has yet been clearly proven by events, but in the two years that followed publication of the interim report, although nothing coherent was done to allay the cultural crisis, talk of separatism nevertheless ceased to be fashionable in either language. Daniel Johnson, the new Premier of Quebec, who in Opposition had often sounded like a French-Canadian separatist himself, in office became more worried about the falling off in Quebec's credit rating in Toronto and New York. He went about making speeches in his accented but impeccable English, emphasizing Quebec's sound and sober Canadianism. On both sides the strident mutual invective, which two years before had been amplified by every medium of broadcasting or print, dwindled down to the normal, low-pitched grumble.

Indeed, the whole cycle was not unfamiliar. Never in their history have Canadians demonstrated any warm affection for each other. Loyalties have always been parochial, mutual hostilities chronic.

No separatist of the 1960s spoke more bitterly than had Joseph Howe, the "Tribune of the People" whom Nova Scotia still regards as her greatest son, in his campaign of the 1860s against alliance with "three million frost-bound Canadians" in their alien fastness a thousand miles away. No French Canadian has used stronger languages against *les anglais* than was commonplace among western wheat farmers about the money barons of Bay Street and the tyrants of the CPR. (An old story, still current on the prairies, tells

of the farmer who woke one morning to find his ripe crop ruined
by blight. After a long silence he said to his wife: "Well, God
damn the CPR.")

Suspicion reigned not only among but within the regions. The
historian A. R. M. Lower quotes the prayer of a Presbyterian
minister in the nineteenth century, on Cape Breton Island, the
eastern tip of Nova Scotia:

"And most especially do we thank Thee, Lord, for the Gut of
Canso, Thine own body of water, which separateth us from the
sin and the wickedness on the other side thereof."

What held such people together was not love for each other, it
was love of the land itself, the vast empty land in which, for more
than three centuries, a certain type of man has found himself
uniquely at home.

It is commonplace to refer to Canada as one of the young
countries of the world. In fact it is one of the oldest. Few others
still look, as Canada does in about three quarters of its area, just
as they did two hundred and perhaps ten thousand years ago.

More than half of it is primordial granite, the great Pre-Cam-
brian shield rubbed clean of soil by the glacier of the latest Ice
Age. Since the glacier receded the land has recovered, at least in
the milder climatic belt that in the west runs as far north as the
Yukon and the Mackenzie Delta and in the east dips to south of
James Bay, enough shallow humus to support a coniferous bush.
Shallow lakes are everywhere upon its surface—Canada is thought
to contain about one third the fresh water of the entire world.

In the main this land is still empty. Westward from Lake Superior the old Voyageur Highway is intact as far as Rainy Lake—not
as busy now as it was when the freighter canoes carried the pelts
down and the trade goods back between Grand Portage and the
Athabaska region, but its portages still well marked, its lakes and
streams still clean.

Most Canadians, of course, have never seen this wilderness area
and never will. It is too far away. But it is typical, an extreme but
not misleading example, of something that is within the easy
reach of every Canadian, urban or rustic—an empty area of

forest or plain in which a man can still enjoy the illusion of solitude. This is the quality that makes Canada unique and gives root to Canadian patriotism.

It needs no excess of optimism to believe that the social problems of nationhood will solve themselves—to be succeeded, of course, by other problems, but not by national dissolution. Already the strains of biculturalism seem to be easing off, as English Canadians rush to learn French and English-speaking provinces move, still grudgingly but definitely, toward the establishment of schools in which French is the language of instruction. Regional prejudices ebb and flow, but each high tide is a little lower (if the printed word is true evidence) than the last one was.

Meanwhile "development" continues. Canada's standard of living, second highest in the world (by North American measurement), is in no danger of losing that proud position. Washing machines and television sets abound, as in no other nation save one. Superhighways devour uncounted acres of fertile land, and the second highest incidence of automobiles achieves, in the metropolitan areas, a second highest air pollution. Ugly little towns prosper, all calling themselves cities and all looking like faithful copies of Omaha, Nebraska.

This is not a Canada to call forth any man's love. But just north of it still lies a different kind of land—too barren ever to be thickly settled, too bleak to be popular like Blackpool or Miami. There is no reason to doubt that it will always be there, and so long as it is there Canada will not die.

Index

tax, 209–15; United States, 72–73, 307–11
Gouzenko, Anna, 44
Gouzenko, Igor, 34–35, 37, 43–44, 83
Graydon, Gordon, 21–22, 83
Great Britain, and Common Market, 174, 185; Commonwealth, 172–73, 186–87; Korea, 96, 98, 101; Suez, 152–57
Green, Howard, 22, 128–29, 133, 192–94
Greene, Joe, 290
Greene, Lorne, 166, 306
Grégoire, Gilles, 30, 294–95
Grey Cup, 267
Grosart, Allister, 182
Group of Seven, 111–12
Grove, Frederick Philip, 105
Guinness, Sir Alec, 109
Guthrie, Tyrone, 109

Hamilton, Alvin, 183–84, 196
Hansard, 10, 82, 290
Hanson, R. B., 10
Harkness, Douglas, 194–96, 266, 272, 285, 288–89, 292, 297
Harris, Walter, 125, 129, 164–65, 168, 238
Health insurance, 20
Heavy water, 50
Heeney, Arnold, 193
Hees, George, 186, 196, 292–93, 297
Hellyer, Paul, 219–21, 224–30
Henry, Alexander, 67
Herron, William Stewart, 56
"Hidden Report," 164, 177–80
Hitler, Adolf, 7, 32
Hollinger Mining Company, 68
Honest John Missile, 190, 192
Hong Kong, 102
Hospital insurance, 124
Houde, Camillien, 5–9
Howe, C. D., 41, 49, 94, 124, 131ff., 150–51, 168, 184; Minister of Munitions, 127–30; Minister of Reconstruction, 129–30, 136ff., 149; Minister of Trade and Commerce,

62–63, 140ff., 164–65
Howe, Joseph, 313
Hudson's Bay Company, 56
Hunter, Vernon, 55

Illinois, 71
Ilsley, J. L., 74–75, 213
Immigration, 113ff.
Imperial Oil Limited, 55
Imperial War Conference (1917), 77–78
Imports, 137
Income tax, 62, 175, 251
Indentured labor, 116–17
India, 53, 92
India, 53, 92
International Refugee Organization, 117–18
Iron mining, 67ff.
Isolationism, 76, 84, 95
Israel, 152, 156

Jackson, A. V., 111
James, F. Cyril, 42
John Inglis Company, 135
Johnson, Daniel, 202–3, 206–7, 313
Johnson, Lyndon B., 303
Joint Defense Board. *See* Permanent Joint Defense Board (U.S.-Canada)

Kapyong, Battle of, 100
Kennedy, John F., 193–95, 216, 303, 308
Kent, Tom, 250, 256–57
Kierans, Eric, 211, 274
Killam, I. C., 125
King, Mackenzie, 37, 63–64, 75, 95, 98, 213; Commonwealth, 92–93, 172; conscription, 11, 177; economics, 18, 63–64, 134; flag, 236–39; foreign relations, 6–7, 77–79, 92–93; Korea, 74–76; politics, 86–91, 123, 134
Knowles, Stanley, 29, 143, 180
Korea, 74–75, 95ff., 126–27
Krivitsky, Alexei, 34–35

ARCTIC
OCEAN

Date ?

ALASKA

Aklavik

MACKENZIE R.

DISTRICT OF FRANKL

YUKON R.

Dawson

GREAT BEAR
LAKE

YUKON
TERRITORY
1898

DISTRICT OF MACKENZIE
1920

DISTRICT O

1920

LIARD R.

GREAT SLAVE
LAKE

BRITISH
COLUMBIA
1871

PEACE R.

L. ATHABASKA

ALBERTA
1905

SASKAT-

MANITOBA
1912

FRASER R.

Edmonton

CHEWAN
1905

SASKAT-
CHEWAN R.

L. WINNIPEG

1912

1881

Calgary

N.S.

PACIFIC OCEAN

Vancouver

Saskatoon

1881

Victoria

S.S.

Regina

1870

LAKE
OF THE
WOD

Winnipeg

UNITED STATES
BOUNDARIES

———————— International

------------ Interprovincial

map by palacios